F

FINANCIAL MANAGEMENT FOR FARMERS

The basic techniques of 'money farming'

Martyn F. Warren, BSc, MSc

Principal Lecturer in Agricultural Business Management

Seale-Hayne Faculty of Agriculture, Food and Land Use

Polytechnic South West, Newton Abbot, Devon

THIRD EDITION

Stanley Thornes (Publishers) Ltd

Originally published in 1982 by Hutchinson Education
Reprinted, revised 1986
Reprinted 1987
Reprinted 1990

Third edition 1992 by
Stanley Thornes (Publishers) Ltd
Old Station Drive
Leckhampton
CHELTENHAM GL53 0DN

A catalogue entry for this book is available from the British Library.

ISBN 0–7487–1544–4

Typeset in 10pt Compugraphic Sabon by Action Typesetting Limited.
Printed and bound in Great Britain at the Bath Press, Avon.

Contents

in practice – Reconciling cash flow and profit – Further reading

Contents

Preface

The aim of this book is that you should learn how to use the basic skills of managing money, including budgeting, budgetary control, physical and financial recording. By the time you have read it, and completed the exercises, you should not only *understand* the ideas underlying the various techniques, but also be able to *do* the work involved. You should also be able to judge when and when not to use a particular technique.

The book is intended both for practising farmers, and for students on agriculture courses containing elements of farm management. It is suitable for courses from City and Guilds Phase IV, through Ordinary and Higher Diplomas to Degree level. Although inevitably geared to the UK, most of the principles and techniques described are universally applicable, and the previous editions have proved popular in a wide variety of countries.

Financial management can easily become regarded, by farmers and students alike, as a tedious, uninteresting pastime, obsessed with past history and epitomized by the chore of 'doing the books' on a wet weekend. This is little short of a tragedy, since financial management is not only vital to the well-being of farm businesses and their owners, but is a fascinating process in itself.

In this book I have tried to transmit my own enthusiasm for the topic, and to make it attractive. One way in which I have attempted to stimulate interest is by starting, after describing some initial concepts, with decisions about the future, rather than with records of the past. The reader learns first about potential problems and opportunities facing farm businesses, and realizes the need for careful planning. When studying the planning of a business, he comes to realize the need for control of the business's finances, and thus to appreciate that records and accounts play a vital role in the management process.

An essential component of the book is the *Home Farm Case Study*. This follows the progress of a young farmer through the planning and control of the various elements of his business, and is divided between the relevant chapters. For this edition the case study has been completely revised to update the figures and to eliminate unnecessary complication.

At the most basic level, use of such a case study can heighten the attractiveness of the subject by providing 'human interest'. More usefully, it emphasizes the continuity of the financial process and the interdependence of the techniques used. Most important of all, it provides a guide to help you in the practice of skills described in the main text. With a technique-orientated subject area such as financial management, it is impossible to learn effectively without *using* the techniques, and without learning from one's own successes and failures.

In writing this book I have confined myself to the practical problems of using basic farm financial management techniques. I have had to resist the temptation to write at length on topics which are peripheral to (or too advanced for) this main theme. Where this is the case, I have suggested further reading for those who wish to widen the area of their study. Two books deserve particular mention. *Farm Planning and Control* by C.S. Barnard and J.S. Nix (CUP, 1979), provides a detailed and scholarly exposition of the concepts underlying financial management techniques. *The Farmer as Manager* by A.K. Giles and J.M. Stansfield (2nd edition, Oxford, Commonwealth Agricultural Bureau, 1990) is a readable and comprehensive overview of the job of farm management, which puts all the component parts of that job (finance included) into perspective. *Financial Management for Farmers* is intended to complement these two books, and to form a link between the detailed theory of Barnard and Nix and the broader but more approachable advice of Giles and Stansfield.

I risk criticism from economists for not devoting a section of the main text to the principles of economic theory. In my experience, explicit discussion of such theory is off-putting to the newcomer, and often difficult to relate to practical issues. It is, I feel, easier and more palatable for the principles to evolve from the lessons learnt in practice, since the relevance of the theory is then immediately apparent. This implicit, evolved grasp of the principles may later be developed explicitly by reference to one of the many good textbooks on agricultural economics. In Appendix 1, I have explained briefly the economic concepts which I feel are most fundamental to financial management, including those of opportunity cost and diminishing returns.

Throughout the book I assume that the reader has access to a good farm management handbook. The most comprehensive is *The Farm Management Pocketbook* by J.S. Nix, published annually by Wye College, University of London, and referred to hereafter simply as 'Nix'. Alternatives are the *Agricultural Budgeting and Costing Book*, published half-yearly by Agro Business Consultants Ltd, and the *Farm Management Handbook* published annually by the Scottish Agricultural Colleges. Many of the references given in this book are from the journal *Farm Management*, published by the Centre for Management in Agriculture, the UK's leading farm management association. For anyone interested in farm management, a subscription to the Centre (including membership of a local branch and four copies of the journal per year) is an excellent investment. Details are available from CMA, Farm Management Unit, Reading University RG6 2AT.

The use of the masculine gender throughout the book is prompted by considerations of convenience, rather than sexism. For similar reasons the terms 'farmer' and 'manager' are treated as interchangeable. Inflation is ignored in most of the book, to allow concentration on the basics without unnecessary confusion. Some of the questions raised by the presence of inflation are discussed in a separate chapter at the end of the book.

A final point: before employing a management technique of any sort, from keeping feed records to using linear programming, you should always be sure that the potential costs (in terms of time, effort and money) are outweighed by the potential benefits (long-term and short-term; financial, physical and personal). The fact that a technique is described int his book does not mean that it should be used at every possible opportunity. Keep it simple.

MARTYN WARREN
1982

Preface to Third Edition

The original text of *Financial Management for Farmers* has been thoroughly revised for this new edition. The calculations have been reworked with more up-to-date figures, the references have been reconsidered and some procedures have been simplified. By popular demand, a discussion of the principles and methods of UK taxation is included for the first time, and the basic characteristics of partnerships and companies are described.

Although the emphasis remains firmly on manual calculation (in recognition of the fact that computer-owning farmers are still a small minority in the UK), the value of the personal computer is recognized throughout the book. In particular, an appendix gives layouts and formulae for a number of financial spreadsheets, allowing most of the example calculations in the text to be readily reproduced as working computer-based management tools.

I hope that the result is a tighter, even more practical book, attuned to the farm business needs of the 1990s, while not losing the qualities that have sustained its popularity over the 1980s.

MARTYN WARREN
1992

Acknowledgements

I remain ever grateful to the colleagues, students and farmers who have provided inspiration and dissuaded me from my more wayward flights of fancy.

My family deserve particular gratitude for having suffered, usually with good grace, my absences of body and mind during the writing of the original and subsequent editions. It is to them – Jenny, Cate, Tim and Abigail – that this book is dedicated.

PART ONE

Basic Issues

This part of the book deals with the basic principles of financial management. After discussing the need for financial skills in the running of a farm firm, it examines the three indicators of the financial health of a business – cash flow, profit and capital. It concludes with a chapter on the various methods of allowing for the depreciation of wasting assets.

Since each of the other parts draws on this material, Part One should be read in its entirety before moving on to the rest of the book.

1

Why bother?

Consider this story. For the last thirty years, Home Farm has been owned and farmed by Mr John Haynes, providing him with a modest profit to add to his other sources of income. It is a mixed farm of 58 hectares, on reasonable soils, somewhere in England. There are three enterprises: fattening bought-in weaner pigs; a dairy herd of about 80 cows with replacements bought in; and spring barley with grain and straw used in the dairy herd. The labour force consists of a farm foreman, due to retire this Michaelmas, and two full-time farm workers. Casual labour is hired at busy times.

With his 60th birthday approaching, Mr Haynes has decided that it is time to break away from his business interests and see the world. He has no desire to sell his farm though, and does not wish to let it to a stranger. He has found the solution to his problem in the shape of Adam Haynes, his nephew. Adam has been working for five years on a neighbouring estate as an assistant farm manager. By allowing Adam to rent the farm, Mr Haynes would be giving him a step on the farming ladder, while at the same time solving his own dilemma.

Adam has proved to be amenable to the idea, though understandably apprehensive, and has agreed in principle to take the farm over at the beginning of October 199X, at a rent of £6600. This will coincide with the retirement of the foreman, and Adam hopes that a combination of improved organization and hard work will avoid the need to replace him.

With his savings, an overdraft facility and a mortgage raised on his own house Adam should have sufficient funds to purchase the stocks and machinery already on the farm (see Figure 1.1 overleaf).

Adam has never before been solely responsible for the running of a whole business. In his previous work he had experienced the day-to-day problems of farming, but had little to do with longer-term issues. Since he is intending to invest all his life savings in the business, he will be seeking to reassure himself that he will have a good chance of success. Others are also affected. As the potential landlord and guarantor of Adam's overdraft, Mr Haynes will be anxious to ensure that Adam will generate enough cash to be able to pay the rent. The bank manager, before lending Adam money, will expect to be reasonably satisfied that he will not only be able to repay the money in due course, but also to pay the interest charges incurred.

In order to obtain both the tenancy and the necessary finance, therefore, and to assess the potential of the business from his own point of view, Adam will need to prepare plans in some detail. But *how* is he to prepare those plans, and where

(a) Crops   ha
Spring barley   12
Grass leys   42
Apples   4
                                                                              ───
                                                                               58

(b) Livestock   About 80 Friesian dairy cows, with replacements bought in. Buildings include a herringbone parlour with 8 stalls and 4 units, a cubicle house with accommodation for 70 cows, and dry cow housing for 10 cows. There is a milk quota of 500,000 litres. Average milk yield in the previous year was 4800 litres per cow, but has been showing signs of increasing.

About 1000 weaner pigs per year fattened to cutter weight and sold on contract.

(c) Labour force   Two full-time workmen, both in their fifties and long-standing employees, plus Adam and seasonal casual labour.

(d) Tenant's stocks on the farm at the end of September 199X	£
Livestock (77 dairy cows @ £650; 10 calves @ £80)	50,850
Barley: grain (42 tonnes)	3,780
straw (26 tonnes)	390
Pigs (550)	24,750
Orchard	10,000
Miscellaneous stores, cultivations, etc.	8,484

(e) Machinery and vehicles: written-down values	
Machinery and plant	39,000
Vehicles	10,000
(Note that land, buildings and milk quota remain the property of the landlord, and thus do not appear in the valuation of the business)	

(f) Liabilities	21,000
Overdraft	
Mortgage on house	34,000
Creditors (taken on with the business)	6,800

(g) Debtors (taken on with the business)	9,080

Figure 1.1   *Details of Home Farm*

should he start? How is he to use them in controlling the business? How is he to gather the information needed to use them effectively? How can he build into those plans an allowance for the considerable risks he is taking? It is questions such as these that this book is designed to answer.

It is easy, in examples such as that above, to see the logic in detailed financial planning and control of the business. On most farms, though, problems of this scale arise infrequently. The farmer's job is usually one of fine tuning: taking an established, well-tried system, and modifying it little by little in response to changes in the physical and/or economic climates. Why should he bother with the extra paperwork, when he could be out in the fields doing 'real farm work, or putting his feet up by the fire?

The answer is that he should not − provided, that is, he can afford the luxury, and does not resent paying for it. But he must be honest with himself, and recognize that it *is* a luxury and one which can cost dear.

There are large numbers of farmers in this enviable position, often with no mortgage, or paying low rents, lending money to the bank rather than vice versa, and content to make just enough income to provide a comfortable life.

At the same time, a great many farmers are under financial pressure, struggling to make a living in the face of inflation in costs, near-static product prices, and high interest rates. In order to get into farming, or to pay death duties, or to undertake much-needed improvements, they have often borrowed heavily. This in turn has reduced the margin for error, making their businesses more vulnerable to the considerable risks in farming.

These people may not be facing problems as dramatic as those of Adam Haynes. Careful money management is, none the less, as important to them as it is to Adam. In the 'fine tuning' of their businesses, they must be able to judge the relative effects of various possible changes on the farm finances. They must make reasoned forecasts of profits for the coming year, so that they can identify areas of inefficiency. They must be able to estimate the likely levels of borrowing in the future, so that they can persuade their bank managers, if necessary, to extend their overdraft facilities. They must be able to monitor closely the capital structure of their businesses so that, in the event of unexpected problems, changes can be made before too much damage is done.

In other words, the finances of a business must be managed as assiduously as any crop. A good farmer is thorough in his preparation for the crop, will monitor its growth and be ready to respond quickly to unexpected events such as epidemics of pests or diseases. Good money management is similar; indeed, it could be thought of as 'money farming'.

This book deals with the basic techniques of 'money farming'. A knowledge of financial techniques alone will not ensure good money management, any more than a knowledge of the principles of crop production will make a good arable farmer. What it can do, however, is to provide a sound foundation on which the individual may build, using his or her intelligence, ingenuity, and experience. This book, then, is one of the building blocks − the rest is up to you.

2

Building a framework

Before embarking on a discussion of financial management, it is important to have some sort of framework for that discussion; not so much a definition as a description in terms simple enough to remember throughout the book.

Anyone pressed to suggest one distinguishing feature of the job of management is quite likely to include the word 'decision'. All tasks, from digging a trench to the administration of a multi-national company, involve decisions of one sort or another, but there is little doubt that the former is physical, and the latter managerial work. In the administration of a company, the greater part of the work is concerned with taking decisions, while decision-making is a very minor aspect of digging holes in the ground.

The process by which a manager makes a decision might be broken down like this:

1 Determines what he wants to achieve, i.e. sets himself targets or 'objectives'.
2 Makes as informed a guess as possible about future events, i.e. makes forecasts.
3 Examines all possible ways of achieving his objectives.
4 Selects, in the light of his forecasts, the action that seems most likely to lead to his objectives being achieved.
5 Takes that action.

This process could be described as *planning*. When an immediate decision is called for, it will be made in the manager's mind, and may take only a second or two. When the decision concerns a major change in the running of a business, or in the personal life of the farmer, it may take many months before action is taken.

But, surely, management means more than just planning? A manager is not likely to achieve his objectives merely by formulating plans at the beginning of a period of time and sticking to them rigidly, irrespective of events during that period. His planning includes guesses about the future: it is important that he recognizes that these guesses may well turn out to be wrong, and be ready to act accordingly. If his plans are based on the assumption of a warm, dry spring, and it turns out to be cold and wet, he must be prepared to revise his plans to make the best of the new situation.

Our description of management must include, therefore, the regular monitoring of the progress of the plans: comparison of *actual* results against the *expected* results built into the plans, followed by action to alleviate any problems (or to capitalize on any opportunities) shown up by the comparison. This process of *control* of a business has been likened to the control of a car: it is not enough to point the vehicle towards your destination; you must be continually checking for unforeseen hazards and be ready to modify your route accordingly.

Finally, it would be wise to acknowledge the dependence of the farmer on accurate information at all stages of the planning process. The less use he makes of information available from *outside* the business (from weather forecasts to reports of price trends and new crop varieties) the less chance he has of his own forecasts being accurate. Without information on what is happening *within* the business, he is in no position to monitor its progress.

We can thus describe management as 'planning and control of all or part of a business in an effort to meet the objectives of that business; a process which is heavily dependent on reliable information from both within and outside the business' (see Figure 2.1).

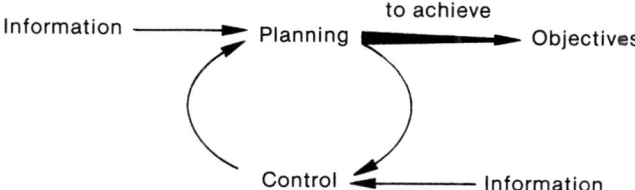

Figure 2.1 *Illustration of the management process*

This description provides a useful framework for the study of any aspect of management. Since this book is concerned essentially with the management of money, Chapters 3 – 14 use the framework solely in the context of the finances of the business. This involves an assumption that the only objectives of the business are financial ones, and that the managerial work of the farmer is primarily the planning and control of money. This is, of course, a narrow and unrealistic view, but it does help us to take a clear initial look at the techniques of financial management without too many complications.

By the time you reach Part Five of the book you should have a clear enough understanding of the basic ideas and techniques to be able to take a wider look at management, and to cope with some of the more common complications that arise in the financial management of a business.

Before going on to discuss the techniques of financial planning and control, it would be sensible to decide just what we mean by 'financial'. The first thing that comes to mind is cash; it is obvious that a healthy *cash flow*, ensuring a steady bank balance, is vital to businesses and individuals alike. Cash flow is not a reliable guide to the operational performance of a business, however, and a special measure, *profit*, has to be used for this purpose. Neither cash flow nor profit give information about forms of wealth other than cash and trading stocks, so this is provided by a third measure, net *capital*.

For the purposes of study, all aspects of financial management can be classified in terms of cash flow, profit, and capital. Using an example relating to Home Farm, Adam Haynes's financial objectives for the first year might be expressed thus:

1   Sufficient cash flow to avoid an overdraft of more than £30,000 while
     providing at least £10,000 for Adam's private expenses.
2   A net profit of at least £10,000.
3   A stable or growing net capital.

The remaining chapters in Part One take a closer look at these three measures,
which are so central to the whole financial management process.

Further reading

This chapter sought to establish a framework for the discussion of management,
rather than to arrive at a unique definition. There are as many different viewpoints
as to the nature of management as there are writers on the subject, and it is worth
investigating a selection of those ideas. The following are likely to prove
particularly rewarding:

Barnard, C. S. and Nix, J. S., *Farm Planning and Control*, 2nd edition
    (Cambridge, Cambridge University Press, 1979), chapter 1.
Carsberg, B., *The Economics of Business Decisions* (Harmondsworth, Penguin
    1975), chapter 1.
Castle, E. N., Becker, M. H. and Smith, F. J., *Farm Business Management*, 2nd
    edition (London, Collier-Macmillan, 1972), chapter 1.
Dexter, K. and Barber, D., *Farming for Profits*, 2nd edition (London, Iliffe,
    1967), chapter 1.
Dillon, J. L., 'The definition of farm management', *Journal of Agricultural
    Economics*, vol. 31, pp. 257–8.
Giles, A. K. and Renborg, U., 'Farm management: what is all about?', *Farm
    Management*, vol. 7, no. 8, Winter 1990/91.
Giles, A. K. and Stansfield, J. M., *The Farmer as Manager*, 2nd edition (Oxford,
    CAB International, 1990), chapter 2.
Harwood Long, W., 'The definition of farm management', *Journal of Agricultural
    Economics*, vol. 32, pp. 225–7.
Nix, J. S., 'Farm management: the state of the art (or science)', *Journal of
    Agricultural Economics*, vol. 30, pp. 227–91.

$$\boxed{3}$$

Cash flow versus profit

Cash flow

The term 'cash flow' means exactly what it says: the movement of cash through the business during a given period. It is rather akin to housekeeping; just as a family must keep a regular check on cash receipts and payments and their effect on the bank balance, so must the manager ensure that cash is available when required for the purchase of essential requisites and services. If the business runs so short of cash that it cannot pay the wages, buy the cattle feed, or pay the rent, it is doomed to failure.

The *annual net cash flow* of a business is calculated by taking the total of cash payments during the year from the total cash receipts. 'Cash' refers to money either in hand or in a bank current account; hence transactions by cheque or standing order are counted as cash transactions, although they do not fit the everyday use of the term. *Anything* which affects the cash balance must be included, even such items as money taken out to pay for the owner's holiday, income tax payments, or the receipt of a loan from a kindly aunt. Conversely, no item should be counted as part of the net cash flow until the money concerned has actually entered or left the business.

Given the amount of cash available at the beginning of the year (the *opening cash balance)*, the *closing cash balance* is found by adding the annual net cash flow to the opening balance. As an example, take a business which starts the year with £1000 in the bank. During the year, cash receipts total £10,000 and cash payment total £6000. The annual cash net flow is thus £4000 which, added to the opening balance, gives a closing cash balance of £5000. If the cash payment had been £16,000 instead of £6000, the result would have been an annual net cash flow of −£6000, and thus a negative closing balance, i.e. a bank overdraft, of £5000.

It is unlikely that any businessman will be content with an annual review of cash flow. He will probably wish to keep at least a monthly check; in some trades weekly or even daily. Whatever time period is concerned, the principles are the same: opening balance plus net cash flow for the period gives the closing balance at the end of the period.

As a means of trouble-spotting, the measurement of cash flow is invaluable. Forecasts of cash flow can identify periods where cash is likely to be short, and give clues to the alleviation of such shortages. Records of actual cash flow can be combined with forecasts to monitor progress throughout the year.

As a guide to the economic performance of the business, however, it has many limitations. Take, for instance, two businesses, *A* and *B*, each with an annual net cash flow of £5000 in 199X. On this basis their performances appear to be identical.

Now consider various possibilities:

1   *A* has sold all the goods it has produced during the year, while *B* still has goods worth £1000 in store.
2   *A* has been paid cash for all the goods it has sold during the year; *B*, on the other hand, is owed £2000 for goods that it sold just before the end of the year.
3   *A* made no investments in buildings or machinery during the year, while *B* spent £10,000 on equipment.
4   The owner of *A* drew £3000 in cash for his living expenses for the year; the owner of *B* drew double that amount.
5   The owner of *A* consumed none of the produce of the business, while the owner of *B* took home £500 worth of goods for the consumption of himself and his family.

So *B* finishes the year with £1000 worth of goods in store, £2000 due to be paid in the near future, and up-to-date equipment. Its owner has spent £6000 on himself and his family, and has consumed, without cash payment, produce of the business worth £500. The situation of *A* and its owner is but a shadow of this, and yet its annual net cash flow is identical to that of *B*.

What is needed is a measure of the operational performance of a business which takes these factors into account. Such a measure is net profit.

Net profit

Revenue and expense

Like cash flow, *net profit* is measured by the difference between the output and input of value during a given period. Whereas cash flow is concerned exclusively with *cash* values, however, profit is concerned with the revenues and expenses, cash or otherwise, arising from the productive activity of the business during that period.

Revenue is calculated by taking cash receipts arising during the period, excluding any capital receipts, e.g. grants, sale of machinery, injections of cash by the owner, and including changes in valuation of stock of output items, benefits in kind, and adjustments for opening and closing debtors.

Expense is calculated by taking cash payments, excluding any capital payments, personal drawings, or tax payments, and including changes in the valuation of stocks of purchased inputs, benefits in kind, adjustments for opening and closing creditors, and depreciation of 'wasting' possessions such as buildings and machinery.

The following sections examine the elements of revenue and expense in more detail.

Change in valuation of stocks

Stocks can be defined loosely as possessions of the business (other than cash) that are likely to be consumed within one production cycle. They are conventionally classifed as:

Raw materials
Work in progress
Finished goods
Goods purchased for resale

As an example, the stocks of a potter's shop may include clay, paint, and other materials; unglazed pots; completed pots; and various items bought in from other potters in an attempt to broaden the shop's range of goods.

The stocks of a farm typically include purchased stores: growing crops and tillages; breeding livestock; and crops in store. Goods purchased for resale rarely appear. Note also that although breeding livestock do not strictly conform to the one-production-cycle definition, they are conventionally included in the valuation. (The 'herd basis' method of valuation is an exception. This is primarily an adjustment for tax purposes.)

If, inflation aside, a business ends the year with a greater value of stocks than it possessed at the beginning of the year, it has sold fewer goods than it has produced, and/or it has purchased more materials than it used in production. If these effects are ignored, profit will not be a fair reflection of the 'productive activity' of the business; the production of the business will be undervalued, and its costs will be overstated. Any increase of valuations, whether of raw materials, work in progress, or of finished goods, must therefore be added to net cash flow in calculating profit.

The reverse is true if the valuation of stocks declines. Output will be overstated, since some of the sales will have arisen from depletion of stocks; costs will be understated due to the failure to replace stocks of materials used in production. A decline in stock valuation is thus *deducted* from net cash flow in calculating profit. (Stock valuation is extensively discussed in Chapter 11.)

Debtors and creditors

A large proportion of the transactions of a typical business are credit transactions. The seller sends goods to the purchaser, together with an invoice, or bill. The purchaser is given a certain time to pay this invoice (say 28 days) and is not likely to do so until towards the end of this time.

It is very likely, then, that at any point in time a business will be owed a certain amount of money by its customers, and will owe money to its suppliers. These amounts are known as *trade debtors* and *trade creditors*, respectively. Those outstanding at the beginning of the year are opening debtors and creditors, and those at the end of the year as closing debtors and creditors.

In the example earlier in this chapter, business *B* was owed £2000 at the end of the year. This represents goods that, although produced and sold, have not been paid for (and are thus excluded from the net cash flow). Clearly the £2000 has arisen from the productive activity of the year; to exclude it from profit would be to understate the value of goods produced by the business during that time. This 'closing debtor' must therefore be added into the cash receipts of the year in calculating profit.

Similarly, closing creditors must be added to the cash payments of the year. If this is not done, the costs of the business will be understated. A consignment of dairy feed could, within a 28-day credit period, have been turned into milk. Although no cash has changed hands, the purchase has definitely contributed to the productive activity of the business. If it has not been consumed, the feed will appear in the valuation change and, if not balanced by the closing creditor, will be double-counted.

The closing debtors and creditors of one year are, inevitably, the opening debtors and creditors of the next. Shortly after the beginning of this next year these debtors and creditors will be paid. The cash receipts of the second year will thus include items arising from the productive activity of the first. To avoid double-counting opening debtors of a given year are *deducted* from the cash receipts and payments of that year in the calculation of profit.

Prepayments and accruals

Certain services are paid for at infrequent intervals, either in advance or arrears. Insurance premiums, for instance, are typically payable yearly in advance; farm rents half-yearly in arrears. At the end of the financial year, it is quite likely that the services represented by these payments will not have been fully consumed. The last half-yearly payment of rates, for instance, may have been made two months before the end of the financial year of the business. The local authority thus owes the business four months' worth of services; this is a special form of debtor called a *prepayment*.

Similarly, the business may have made its last half-yearly payment of rent, in arrears, three months before the end of the financial year. It has consumed a service (the use of the land) without payment for three months. This unpaid rent is a form of creditor known as an *accrual*.

The same arguments apply to receipts in advance (*deferred revenue* – a form of creditor) and in arrears (*accrued revenue* – a type of debtor). In calculating profit, these items are used to adjust payments and receipts in exactly the same way as 'ordinary' trade debtors and creditors.

Benefits in kind

The owner(s) and employees of a business often consume produce or goods and services bought by the business, without any cash payment. In a farm business these benefits may include produce such as milk, potatoes, meat, fruit and firewood; and such inputs as housing, private use of car and telephone, electricity and heating fuel.

If profit is to be a reliable assessment of the performance of the business, the value of produce consumed as benefits in kind must be included in revenue. The fact that they have not been paid for in cash does not alter the fact that they arise from the productive activity of the business. Inputs consumed as benefits in kind must be deducted from payments: although they have been paid for by the business, they have not contributed to its productive activity. Since both of these adjustments increase profit, and involve relatively small amounts, they are frequently combined as a single item under 'revenue' (see, for instance, Figure 2.1).

Depreciation

Included in the annual net cash flow of a business will often be items relating to the purchase or sale of assets such as machinery and equipment, buildings and improvements to property. Such assets can be expected to last longer than just one production cycle, and therefore relate to the productive activity of more than one financial year. It would be illogical to include the whole of the payment or receipt in the profit of the year of purchase or sale.

On the other hand, such items do represent a continuing cost to the business. They will not last for ever; they will wear out, or rot, or become obsolete, or all three. They are *wasting assets*. If their purchase or sale is removed from profit without making a corresponding allowance for this continuing cost, an exaggerated impression of profit will result. A new item is therefore included as an expense – that of *depreciation* of wasting assets. The calculation of depreciation is discussed in greater detail in Chapter 5.

Exclusion of capital, personal and tax transactions

Certain transactions appear in the cash flow which do not directly arise from or contribute to the productive activity of the business. One example has been considered in the previous section, the purchase and sale of wasting assets. These are converted into an annual depreciation charge, and are otherwise excluded from the profit calculation.

The business may make other capital payments (such as the purchase of land or investments and the repayment of borrowed money) and receive capital sums (such as the proceeds of the sale of land, capital grants, loans, gifts, and injections of cash by the owner). None of these are included in profit, since (for a farm business at least) they lie outside the productive activity of the business.

The same arguments apply to drawings of cash by the owner(s) of the business, and the payment of income and capital taxes. These items concern the *deployment* of income rather than its generation. They reflect the behaviour of the owner(s) rather than the productive activity of the business. They are therefore excluded from the profit calculation.

Profit statements

Net, gross and operating profits

The calculation of profit is shown in a profit statement, which should be clear, comprehensive, and consistent in form from year to year. The simplest form of profit statement is the *trading and profit and loss account (or budget).** Payments (adjusted for creditors), depreciation and the opening valuation of stocks are weighed against receipts (adjusted for debtors), benefits in kind and the closing valuation of stock. The balance is *net profit*. (See Figure 3.1.)

	£		£
Opening valuation		Closing valuation	
of stocks	50,000	of stocks	52,000
Payments		Receipts	
Livestock	2,000	Milk	60,000
Materials	37,000	Livestock	20,000
Labour	6,000	Cereals	1,000
Machinery expenses	6,000	Sundry receipts	1,500
Rent	9,000		
Farm services	5,000	Benefits in kind	500
Administration	2,000		
Finance	2,000		
Depreciation	6,000		
	125,000		
NET PROFIT	10,000		
	135,000		135,000

Figure 3.1 *Trading and profit and loss account – simplified example*

Note the process of 'finding the balance', which is used in a variety of financial statements. The two sides of the statement are totalled, the difference found and added into the smaller side to appear, in this case, as net profit. If expenses had exceeded revenues, adjusted for valuations, this balance would have appeared on the right-hand side as a loss.

As an alternative to this 'horizontal' form of statement, it is possible to use a 'vertical' or 'columnar' form, as summarized on Figure 3.2.

A slightly more complex form of profit statement results from the separate calculation of gross profit and net profit. Gross profit is calculated by taking sales and revenue, adjusted for changes in stock valuation, and deducting only the 'cost of sales' – those expenses which are incurred directly in the generation of sales. The latter usually comprise materials and that labour which can be related directly

---

*A profit statement is known as an *account* if it is compiled from historic information, and as a *budget* if derived from information forecast for the future.

		£
Receipts and benefits in kind		83,000
Change in valuation of stocks:		
Closing valuation	52,000	
Opening valuation	− 50,000	+ 2,000
Less: Payments and depreciation:		
Payments	− 69,000	
Depreciation	− 6,000	− 75,000
NET PROFIT		10,000

Figure 3.2 *Columnar form of trading and profit and loss account − simplified example*

to production (on a farm this implies all wages except the salaries of managers and secretaries). This statement of gross profit is known as the *trading account*. (See Figure 3.3.)

To arrive at a net profit, the remaining expenses are deducted from gross profit, and any non-sales revenue added in. This statement is known as the *profit and loss account*.

	£		£
Opening valuation stocks	50,000	Closing valuation of stocks	52,000
Cost of sales:		Sales:	
Livestock	2,000	Milk	60,000
Materials	37,000	Livestock	20,000
Labour	6,000	Cereals	1,000
	95,000		
GROSS PROFIT carried forward	38,000		
	133,000		133,000

Figure 3.3 *Trading account − simplified example*

The two-stage calculation of net profit shown in Figure 3.4 (overleaf) is suitable particularly for manufacturing and trading organizations, but is less popular in farming (probably due to the tendency of farming businesses to be more concerned with production performance than with selling performance). The most commonly found form of farm profit statement is the combined trading and profit and loss account. It is referred to variously as the trading account, or the profit and loss account, but rarely by its full title.

A third variant, which can be used in conjunction with either of the other two, is the calculation of *operating profit* (or loss). This attempts to measure more fairly the efficiency of the business by excluding payments of interest, and revenues and expenses which have no bearing on the main productive activity of the business,

	£		£
Other costs		Gross profit brought	
Machinery expenses	6,000	forward	38,000
Rent	9,000		
Farm services	5,000	Sundry receipts	
Administration	2,000	Training grant	400
Finance	2,000	Rent received	1,000
		Interest on	100
Depreciation	6,000	trade investment	
	30,000	Benefits in kind	500
NET PROFIT	10,000		
	40,000		40,000

Figure 3.4   *Profit and loss account – simplified example*

such as the receipt of dividends or interest from investments outside the business. (See Figure 3.5.)

In addition to measures of profit in general use, certain measures have been devised for specific use in farm businesses. Two of these, net farm income and management and investment income, are described in Chapter 14. A third is a development from operating profit; this is *rent – interest – profit* (RIP). **RIP** is profit before deducting any land expenses (including rent) and interest charges. It can be used in comparisons between farms or between years, where it has the advantage over other agricultural measures (see Chapter 14) of not requiring estimates of the rental value of owned land or the value of family labour. It is particularly useful when determining the amount of rent or finance charges one can afford to pay.

	£		£
Opening valuation of		Closing valuation of	
stocks	50,000	stocks	52,000
Payments	67,000	Sales	81,000
Depreciation	6,000	Benefits in kind	500
	123,000		133,500
OPERATING PROFIT			
carried down	10,500		
	133,500		133,500
Interest charges	2,000	Operating profit brought	
		down	10,500
		Sundry external receipts	1,500
	2,000		
NET PROFIT	10,000		
	12,000		12,000

Figure 3.5   *Calculation of operating profit*

The likely level of RIP is estimated by means of a budget, and allowances are made for the likely level of private drawings and new investments. This gives an indication of the maximum burden of rent and/or interest that the business can stand.

'Management' profit versus 'financial' profit

A businessman has a legal obligation to keep accounts, of which, together with the balance sheet (see Chapter 4), the profit statement is a central feature. This obligation exists largely to enable the Inland Revenue to verify the income of the owner(s) of the business and thus assess income tax (or corporation tax) liability.

It is usually advisable to have these *financial accounts* prepared by a chartered accountant in order that the Inland Revenue may have a reasonable degree of faith in the figures shown. This has the added advantage that an accountant can often use his expertise to help the farmer exploit legitimate opportunities for reducing his tax liability.

Problems can arise when trying to use financial accounts as a guide to decision-making, however. The accountant works within various assumptions and conventions which are appropriate for the task which he has been asked to do, but may not be appropriate for the task of management. Items most likely to be affected are valuation changes (especially of breeding livestock), depreciation, and benefits in kind, all of which are likely to be understated.

One way of dealing with these problems is to make the necessary adjustments to the 'financial' profit in order to arrive at a figure that is more useful in decision-making – a 'management' profit. It is generally more satisfactory, however, to establish a separate system of *management accounts,* with the object of arriving directly at a management profit.

Since this book is concerned largely with the latter approach, the term 'net profit', unless otherwise stated, refers here to 'management', rather than 'financial' profit.

The financial period

Profit is concerned with revenues and expenses arising during a given period of time. The period used for the measurement of profit is usually a year, although it may be six months or even less. Generally, the quicker the turnover and the more variable the business environment of a particular firm, the more frequent will be the need for profit statements. Large corporate businesses, where the owners (shareholders) of the firm have little say in the week-by-week decisions, may need to publish frequent profit statements in order to keep the shareholders informed.

Agriculture is characterized by small, non-corporate businesses, with production cycles measured in months rather than days. The year is thus adequate as a financial period for most agricultural purposes.

The financial year used by a business may start on any day of the calendar year. It is usually determined by the date at which the business was taken over by the present owners. Thus it is common in farming to find businesses with financial years starting at Michaelmas (29 September) or Lady Day (25 March), since these are traditional dates for the commencement of farming tenancies or the sale of farm land. The owner(s) of a business may choose (only once) to change the financial year used for income tax assessment, for the sake of convenience or to make the most of tax concessions.

Since both financial and management accounts are based on the same raw information, it is convenient to be able to use the same period for both, if possible. Where the financial year is very different from the farming year, the management accounts and budgets should be based on the farming or 'crop' year (see Chapter 11).

Further reading

Berry, A. and Jarvis, R., *Accounting in a Business Context* (London, Chapman & Hall, 1991), chapter 2.

Bull, R. J., *Accounting in Business*, 6th edition (London, Butterworths, 1990), chapters 3 and 4.

4

Capital

Introduction

Of the three vital financial indicators – cash flow, profit and capital – only capital remains to be discussed. Unlike the other two, it is not concerned with flows of money during a financial period, but with the wealth owned by a business *at one particular point in time*. A hackneyed but useful analogy is that of a photograph; the picture shown is a representation of the state of affairs at the moment the shutter clicked, and at that moment only.

You will know from your own experience that wealth imparts financial security. The more possessions a person owns, the less likely he is to be bankrupted by some unexpected event such as an unwise gamble or the loss of his job. Money in the bank can be used as a substitute for income, and non-cash possessions can be sold or used as collateral for borrowing money. The same applies to a business.

Wealth also imparts freedom of action. The businessman with little wealth is able to take few risks where his income is concerned and has little chance of getting out of this position by expanding or diversifying his business. The wealthy person, on the other hand, is able to take more risks (since he has wealth to fall back on even if his income fails) and can more easily raise money to finance new ventures.

To summarize, then, capital provides stability in times of change, whether this change is a response to problems, or a response to opportunities. The business with a sure capital foundation can afford to adapt to change in its environment without risking its own downfall.

What is capital?

Capital is not exclusively concerned with possessions. Take the examples of businesses *A* and *B*. *A* has possessions worth £50,000 on 31 December; *B* owns £100,000. Looking at possessions alone, it appears that *B* has more capital. But suppose we find that *A* has debts of £1,000, whereas *B* owes £60,000 to various people. Common sense tells us that in fact *A* is the more wealthy, since it could pay off its debts and still retain £49,000, while *B* would have only £40,000 after settling its debts.

Wealth must therefore be considered in terms of *net capital*, which is calculated by

| NET CAPITAL | *equals* | ASSETS | *minus* | LIABILITIES |

Figure 4.1

deducting debts, or *liabilities*, from possessions, or *assets* (see Figure 4.1). Note that net capital is also known as *net worth* or *owner equity*. If the business is a partnership or a limited liability company, it will be shared between two or more people. The effects on the balance sheet and other accounts are considered in Appendix 4. Here a sole proprietorship is assumed.

The assets of a farm business may include some or all of the following:

Cash in hand
Cash in bank
Trade debtors and prepayments
Stocks
Machinery and equipment
Buildings and improvements
Purchased production quotas
Land
Other investments
Goodwill

The liabilities of a farm business may include:

Bank overdraft
Trade creditors and accruals
Bank and other medium-term loans
Mortgages and other long-term loans

Classification of assets and liabilities

Not all wealth is equally useful in a given situation. The man losing his job, for instance, will be in a better position if most of his wealth of (say) £5000 is in the bank, or is due to arrive any day in the form of a redundancy cheque, than if it is in the form of long-term investments which are difficult to cash in a hurry. On the other hand, in more happy circumstances, the long-term investment would be more beneficial to him (since it generates income) than money lying idle in the bank current account.

The same arguments apply to businesses, and it is useful to make some distinction between long-term and short-term assets and liabilities. In a farm business, cash, debtors, and all stocks other than breeding livestock are regarded as short-term, or *current assets*; the remainder (including breeding livestock) as long-term or *fixed assets*. It is often useful to take the distinction further and examine the very short-term assets (cash and debtors) separately; these are termed *liquid assets*.

Liabilities are divided typically into short-term, or *current liabilities*, including bank overdraft and creditors; and *long-term* liabilities, which include all medium- and long-term loans.

Capital statements

The 'horizontal' balance sheet

The derivation of the net capital of a business is shown in a statement known as a *balance sheet*. A balance sheet may be drawn up to show the capital position at any time, but the most useful balance sheets are those drawn up at the beginning and end of the financial year (the *opening* and *closing* balance sheets respectively). Changes in capital between the beginning and end of the year may then be related to profit and cash flow generated during the same period. The closing balance sheet for one year is, of course, the opening balance sheet for the next.

The traditional form of balance sheet is the *horizontal balance sheet*, where assets and liabilities are set out on either side of the page, net capital being the balance between the two sides. An example of this type of format is shown in Figure 4.2 (overleaf).

Note that opening and closing balance sheets may be combined by use of extra columns; this saves space and eases comparisons between opening and closing figures. Note also that the assets and liabilities are shown in order of liquidity, i.e. shortest-term progressing to longest-term, or vice versa. A great many variations of this format are used. Some put the assets on the left, some on the right. Some start with current liabilities and assets at the top (as in Figure 4.2), others with long-term assets and liabilities. The most important thing is to ensure that the format adopted is clear, and consistent from year to year.

The capital account

Associated with the balance sheet is the *capital account*, a calculation which shows how the net capital has been increased or depleted over the year.

There are only three ways by which net capital can be increased over the year; by injections of capital from the owner(s); by grants or gifts from organizations or individuals outside the business; or by reinvesting profits made by the business. Other sources of capital involve entries on both sides of the balance sheet, and thus leave net capital unaltered. (A loan of £1000, for instance, will increase the cash in bank by £1000, but will also incur a liability of the same amount.)

The only ways in which capital can be depleted are by the withdrawal of cash for the personal use of the owner(s) or to pay tax due; by the business making a loss; or by the consumption of benefits in kind by the owner(s) and/or employees.

Therefore the capital account takes the net capital at the beginning of the year (from the opening balance sheet) and adjusts for the various items mentioned

Balance sheet at 28 September, 199Y

Liabilities

	28/9/9X			28/9/9X	
	£	£		£	£
Bank overdraft	25,000	40,000			
Trade creditors	7,000	10,000			
Mortgage	65,000	60,000			
Total liabilities	97,000	110,000			
NET CAPITAL	141,000	134,000			
	238,000	244,000			

Assets

	28/9/9X			£	£
Cash in hand	30				50
Cash in bank					0
Trade debtors	1,970				7,950
Valuation of stocks:					
Crops in store		5,000			
Crops in ground		2,000			
Dairy herd		30,000			
Other cattle		12,000			
Misc. stores	50,000	3,000			52,000
Machinery	26,000				25,500
Buildings	10,000				8,500
Land (at cost 198S)	150,000				150,000
	238,000				244,000

Figure 4.2   *Horizontal balance sheet – simplified example (related to the profit statement examples used in Chapter 3)*

	£
Opening net capital	141,000
plus	
Net profit	10,000
	151,000
less	
Private drawings	10,500
Tax paid	6,000
Benefits in kind	500
Closing net capital	134,000

Figure 4.3 *Capital account – example*

above, in order to arrive at the closing net capital – see Figure 4.3 Not only does this show how the owner's capital has been deployed, but it acts as a valuable check on the accuracy of the profit and loss account, cash flow statement and balance sheet. If any of these has been miscalculated, the capital account will not give the same result for net capital as that given by the closing balance sheet.

The vertical balance sheet

The *vertical* or *narrative* form of balance sheet has rapidly gained popularity owing to its economy of space and ease of setting-out. As with the horizontal balance sheet, there are many variations on the theme. One version is shown in Figure 4.4 (overleaf), incorporating a classification of assets and liabilities.

Management versus financial accounts

A profit and loss account intended as a basis for tax assessment must be used with great care, and the accompanying balance sheet checked thoroughly for possible distortions. This applies particularly to the values of stocks, wasting assets and land, which in a time of inflation are often likely to be understated to a very large degree. In the balance sheet shown in Figures 4.2 and 4.4, for instance, the value used for the land is the price of purchase several years ago – the 'historic cost'. Depending on the way land prices have moved in the interim, the current market value could be double – or half – the historic cost.

The historic cost convention also means that assets acquired without a transaction between the business and another party do not have a value and are not shown. While such events are rare in most industries, dairy farmers in the UK were allocated milk production quotas in the early 1980s that have rapidly acquired considerable market value. Unless the business has subsequently bought quota (which, having been paid for, has a historic cost), milk quota will not be included in the financial accounts.

29/9/9X	Balance sheet at 28 September 199Y		
£		£	£
	Fixed assets:		
150,000	Land (at cost 198S)	150,000	
10,000	Buildings	8,500	
26,000	Machinery	25,500	
30,000	Dairy herd	30,000	
216,000	Fixed assets		214,000
	Current assets:		
20,000	Stocks (other than breeding livestock)	22,000	
1,970	Trade debtors	7,950	
30	Cash in hand	50	
22,000	Current assets	30,000	
	Current liabilities (due within one year):		
7,000	Trade creditors	10,000	
25,000	Bank overdraft	40,000	
32,000	Current liabilities	50,000	
10,000	Net current liabilities		20,000
206,000	Total assets less current liabilities		194,000
	Creditors due after one year:		
65,000	Mortgage		60,000
141,000	*Net capital (owner's equity):*		134,000
206,000			194,000

Figure 4.4 *Vertical balance sheet*

The use of historic cost is fundamental to the preparation of financial accounts. It does, however, limit the value of the 'financial' balance sheet as an aid to decision-making: for instance, none of the measures described in the next section will make any sense if historic cost is markedly different from current value.

As with the profit and loss account, it is usually worth adjusting the financial accounts to produce a 'management' balance sheet using current market values. Caution is needed, however. The values used should be 'forced sale' values – i.e. the price you would be likely to receive, net of transport, legal and other presale costs, if you had to sell in a hurry. Be careful in revaluing quota: the value could disappear as quickly as it arrived. Particular care should be taken to check whether machinery is leased before revaluing. Finance leasing (see Chapter 19) is a popular way of borrowing money for machinery and other medium-term assets. However, since it is technically a lease neither the outstanding lease payments nor the value of the leased asset need appear on a sole trader's balance sheet. There is a temptation, on seeing the resulting low value for machinery, to substitute a current value. This ignores the fact that the assets do not belong to the business, and that there is a contractual obligation to make payments for the rest of the duration of the lease.

Before making a major decision on the strength of your revised balance sheet it is wise to check with your accountant in case you have made an expensive mistake. He or she will be able to advise you on other hidden items which will only become due when you sell an asset, such as tax liabilities.

Interpreting the balance sheet

The net capital figure tells us little on its own, and further analysis is required to reveal the implications of the balance sheet. In particular we can gain an impression of the stability of the business, and the way in which it has changed over the years.

Overall stability

Some indication of stability may be gained by examination of net capital, but only by relating it to other aspects of the balance sheet. Take two businesses, C and D. Their respective balance sheets on 31 December look like this:

	C	D
Assets	60,000	250,000
Liabilities	10,000	200,000
Net capital	50,000	50,000

Their net capital figures are identical, yet it is obvious that D is far less stable than C. A proportionately small increase in liabilities would bring D to the point where the assets were outweighed by liabilities; in other words, where D would be 'insolvent'.

The quickest and simplest guide to the overall stability of a business is the *percentage owned* or *percentage equity*. This is a measure of the owner's stake in the business, expressed as a percentage of the total assets, i.e.

$$\frac{\text{net capital}}{\text{total assets}} \times 100$$

Thus the percentage equity of C is 83 per cent, and that of D is 20 per cent. Suggesting an appropriate target percentage is difficult, as it will vary with the type of business, the level of profitability and the general risk level. In an industry with relatively low profitability and significant seasonal fluctuations, such as agriculture, a percentage owned of less than 66 per cent should give rise to some concern. Further investigation can make use of the *gearing ratio*, which in its most common form relates loan capital to net capital, i.e.

$$\frac{\text{loan capital}}{\text{net capital}} \times 100$$

Loan capital is specified because it gives rise to a constant drain on the finances of the business in the form of interest charges and the repayment of principal, thus adding to the risk level. Short-term liabilities can also act as a drain on the business, but they are usually balanced to some extent by short-term assets. As an example, let us return to businesses C and D, and assume that C has long-term liabilities of £1000, and D has long-term liabilities of £40,000. Their gearing ratios are, respectively, £1000/£50,000 or 20 per cent, and £40,000/£50,000 or 80 per cent.

Business D has increased its capital considerably by borrowing, while C employs little more than its owner's own capital. As long as D is obtaining a higher rate of return on capital than the interest rate payable on the borrowed money, its profits are likely to be higher than those of C. In a bad year, however, the return on capital could be below the rate of interest, and could indeed be negative. Since payments of interest and capital have to be made in good years and bad, the profit and loss position of business D in a poor year could easily be worse than that of business C (see Figure 4.5). Thus a high gearing implies a high level of risk.

The maximum 'safe' gearing ratio again depends on the type of business, and in particular on its profitability in relation to the capital employed. In most farming businesses, a ratio of 40 per cent is probably the highest that can be tolerated, and then only if the business is specializing in high-profit enterprises. Ratios of double

	Business C	Business D
	£	£
Owner equity	50,000	50,000
Long-term loans	1,000	40,000
Gearing	2%	80%
Good year		
Net profit before interest, say	12,150	36,000
Interest on long-term loans at, say, 15%	− 150	− 6,000
Profit after interest	12,000	30,000
Poor year		
Net profit before interest, say	2,550	6,000
Interest on long-term loans at, say 15%	− 150	− 6,000
Profit after interest	2,400	0

Note: The example does not account for the repayment of loan capital, which would exacerbate the effect.

Figure 4.5 *Effect of gearing on risk levels*

that level can be sustained in some other industries, such as electronics, but these are characterized by high turnover and high return on capital.

Other measures of overall stability include the *solvency ratio* (total assets as a percentage of total liabilities) and the *debt/equity ratio* (total liabilities as a percentage of net capital). Since these are alternative (though less easily understood) ways of expressing the percentage owned, the equivalent 'rule of thumb' guidelines are, respectively, more than 300 per cent and less than 50 per cent.

Short-term stability

It is not enough to look at the overall stability of the business. Even if the gearing ratio is healthy, shortage of cash for purchase of essential materials and services can force a business out of operation. The best guide to the availability of this cash, or 'working capital', is a cash-flow budget (see Chapter 7). If only a balance sheet is available, an alternative is to calculate a short-term safety margin, the *acid test* or *liquidity ratio*. This is the liquid assets as a percentage of current liabilities, and is a test of the ability of the business to survive should all the short-term (or current) liabilities be called in.

The 'textbook' definition of *liquid assets* is cash and debtors, but may include any crops or livestock which could readily be sold without detriment to future profits. This includes sale crops in store and ready-for-sale trading livestock, but excludes items such as breeding livestock, and half-grown bullocks which would otherwise be reared to slaughter weight.

The 'textbook' definition of *current liabilities* is overdraft and creditors. Where the farmer has a particularly good relationship with his bank manager, it is possible to think of the overdraft as a medium-term liability, and thus exclude it from the liquidity calculation. The farmer must be very sure of his ground before doing this, however, since any overdraft is still technically at short call.

In theory the liquidity ratio should be at least 100 per cent, indicating that the business could meet short-term demands on its funds without resorting to the sale of assets and thus possibly reducing potential profitability. Analysis of balance sheets of Farm Business Survey co-operators in south-west England (as shown in the Exeter University Farm Management Handbook) shows that during the 1980s liquidity ratios of farms were averaging under 50 per cent, with some (particularly livestock farms) falling as low as 20 per cent (Shepherd 1991). While the 100 per cent ratio remains a useful target, especially at a time when the business environment is very uncertain, it now seems that there is no great cause for alarm until liquidity reaches 50 per cent.

A further short-term ratio may also be used; the *current ratio*, which is current assets (i.e. cash, debtors and stocks) as a percentage of current liabilities. A target figure often quoted is a minimum of 200 per cent, but this is highly dependent on the type of business, and particularly on the type and level of stocks carried. In south-west England, current ratios have fallen from an average of around 180 per cent in 1979/80 to about 145 per cent in 1989/90 (Warren and Pierpoint 1991).

As with the liquidity ratio, the 200 per cent level remains a useful conservative target for a business which is anxious to avoid undue risk in an uncertain environment, but the 'acceptable' guideline can be revised to 150 per cent.

Flexibility

A business needs not only to be stable in the present, but also to be capable of adapting to future changes in the business environment. An important determinant of adaptability or flexibility is the proportion of assets that are fixed: by definition, such assets are difficult to realize quickly, and thus a business with a high proportion will find speedy adaptation more difficult than one with all its wealth in current assets. It is useful to calculate the *fixed asset ratio*, i.e.

$$\frac{\text{fixed assets}}{\text{total assets}} \times 100$$

The ratio is not very useful as an absolute measure − it is strongly influenced by the degree to which the farmer is a tenant or an owner-occupier, amongst other things − but is best used in comparisons. Moreover, a high fixed asset ratio is not in itself a bad thing: the fixed assets may be those that generate the highest return when capital growth is taken into account. Nevertheless, comparisons between years will indicate whether the business is becoming more or less dominated by fixed assets over time, and in some regions it is possible to compare a farm's fixed asset ratio with other similar businesses through the results of the Farm Business Survey (see Chapter 14).

When assessing business flexibility it can be helpful to consider the degree of specialization of fixed assets. A business which has a lot of its capital tied up in highly specialized buildings, or where the land is only suitable for a narrow range of farming activities, will find it more difficult to adapt to changing economic circumstances.

Efficiency of capital use

A measure that links both profit and loss account and balance sheet is return on capital. A business may be very stable, but yet yield very low profits compared with the capital invested (indeed, most farm owner-occupiers are permanently in this position). Return on capital is discussed in more detail in Chapter 19: in the meantime, a useful general measure is *return on owner equity*, calculated by:

$$\frac{\text{net profit}}{\text{net capital}} \times 100$$

The resulting percentage can be compared with the interest rate the business is paying on borrowed capital, if any, and the return which could be obtained if the capital were realized and invested elsewhere (remembering that interest on capital invested in government stocks or a building society is virtually risk-free − as well as work-free).

Changes over time

Providing that balance sheets are available for both the beginning and the end of a particular year, it is possible to examine the way in which the capital structure has changed over time. This is at least as important as the ratio analysis of a single balance sheet: a satisfactory set of ratios relating to one point in time may well conceal a significant decline in the stability of the business.

Changes can be investigated at three levels. The first is a 'common-sense' look at movements in certain key items. Foremost among these is net capital; others include the bank balance, levels of debtors and creditors, and loans. It can also be useful to examine changes in stock values, especially in times of inflation. Any significant increase in fixed assets should be accompanied by an increase in liquid assets, in order to avoid 'overtrading', the use of all available funds to finance expansion and running short of working capital as a result.

The second level of investigation is the comparison of stability ratios for the beginning and end of the year, in order to detect any signs of deterioration in the levels of those ratios.

The third level of analysis uses a more systematic approach. This is the technique known as *flow of funds analysis* or *source and allocation of funds analysis*. This technique works by tracing the flow of cash through the business during the year, and in the process monitoring changes in the various assets and liabilities. It comprises two lists: one of sources of cash, and the other of uses of cash. Sources of cash can be grouped into four categories: the trading activities of the business; external sources; increase in liabilities; and reduction in assets. Similarly the uses of cash may be classified as losses; external uses, reduction in liabilities; and increase in assets.

These main categories may be further subdivided to give a list such as that in Figure 4.6 (overleaf). (There are various ways of presenting a flow of funds statement, but they all include the same components.) Here cash from trading is separated from other sources: note here that because we are concerned with the flow of cash, it is necessary to adjust the profit or loss in order to remove the effects of depreciation, changes in debtors, creditors and stock valuations, and benefits in kind. Similarly, in accumulating the various uses of cash, commitments such as private drawings, tax payments and loan repayments are identified separately. This latter distinction is more useful in using the flow of funds as a budgeting aid (where it is important to know what is left to spend after basic financial obligations have been met) than in analysis of a historic balance sheet.

The total uses of cash should exactly match the total cash available. If it does not, the analysis should be checked for mistakes.

The aim of the technique is to show the effect of decisions on long-term uses of cash, and to ensure that there is a sufficient supply of liquid funds available when required. It is useful both as a historical analysis, and as a budgeting device to test the likely effect of an expansion (or a foreseen difficulty) on the overdraft. It can act only as a summary budget, however, and a cash-flow budget should be used for detailed analysis (see Chapter 7).

FLOW OF FUNDS ANALYSIS	£
SOURCES: NET PROFIT (LOSS)	
Depreciation (+)	
Change in debtors (increase −, decrease +)	
Change in creditors (increase +, decrease −)	
Valuations (increase −, decrease +)	
Benefits in kind (−)	
CASH FROM TRADING	
ADD: Capital introduced	
Sale of land, property, investments	
Increase in overdraft	
Increase in loans	
Reduction in cash balances	
CASH FROM OTHER SOURCES	
TOTAL CASH AVAILABLE	
USES: COMMITMENTS	
Private drawings	
Tax payments	
Reduction in loans	
TOTAL COMMITMENTS	
ADD: Purchase of land, property, investments	
Net purchase of buildings	
Purchase of machinery	
Less sale of machinery	
Repayment of overdraft	
Increase in cash balances	
TOTAL CASH USED	

Figure 4.6 *Flow of funds worksheet*

A particular benefit of funds flow analysis is its ability to link the sources of cash with the manner of its use. Among the points to watch for are significant increases in liabilities (especially in conjunction with slow-growing profits), growth in fixed assets at the expense of current assets, growth in fixed assets financed largely by short-term liabilities, and private drawings which seem excessive relative to the other calls on cash.

Illustration of balance sheet analysis techniques

The following example relates to the balance sheet shown in Figure 4.4. It is assumed in the first instance that the valuations of all assets are accurate.

Stability (see Figure 4.7)

The business appears to be unstable, both overall and in the short-term. This judgement could be faulty on either of two counts: the assumption that asset values are accurate (land prices, for instance, could have risen considerably since the land was valued in 198X), and the assumption that the overdraft is a very short-term liability (in many businesses this can be regarded as a medium-term loan).

		Closing balance sheet	Opening balance sheet
(a) Overall stability		%	%
Percentage equity	134,000/244,000	55	59
Gearing ratio	60,000/134,000	45	46
(b) Short-term stability			
Acid test ratio	8,000/50,000	16	6
Current ratio	30,000/50,000	60	69
(c) Adaptability			
Fixed asset ratio	214,000/244,000	88	91
(d) Efficiency of capital use			
Return on owner equity	10,000/134,000	8	not available

Figure 4.7 *Results of balance sheet ratio analysis*

Adaptability

The high fixed asset ratio reflects the importance of land in the balance sheet, this being an owner-occupier rather than a tenant of the land. There has been some movement downwards over the year, but not sufficient to allow firm conclusions to be drawn.

Efficiency of capital use

At the time of writing the return of 7.5 per cent on net capital is lower than the return available from safe and effort-free investments outside the business. On the face of it, the owner would be better off selling the business, but it would be unwise to make a judgement on the results of just one year. Moreover, the long-term gains from capital growth may outweigh the lack of profits in the short term. The non-financial benefits of living and working on the farm are also likely to be a significant factor in the farmer's decision-making.

Changes during the year

Net capital is down by £7000 (5 per cent), with the overdraft rising by £15,000 (60 per cent) and creditors by £3000 (43 per cent). The mortgage has declined, presumably due to normal repayment of the principle. Debtors are up by £6000 (400 per cent) but there is little change in the other assets. The capital account (Figure 4.3) shows a high level of private arrears, the implication is that 199X was a better year than 199Y, and that part of the problem lies in poor profitability. There is no major change in any of the ratios, but they give the impression of a decline in stability.

For a flow of funds analysis, we need to refer to the calculation of depreciation shown in Figure 4.8. The flow of funds analysis itself is shown in Figure 4.9. It shows that the major sources of funds were short-term borrowing together with trading. The funds were used partly to replace machinery and make loan repayments, but mainly to allow substantial private drawings and tax payments. The latter point is particularly worrying, as the money is leaving the business altogether.

Summary

The business appears to be in a weak, and declining, position. The first action must be to verify the valuations of assets and to check on the nature of the overdraft. Next the reason for the high level of private drawings should be ascertained, in order to check the likelihood of it recurring next year. An investigation of profitability should also be carried out, in an attempt to raise the level of cash generated by the trading activity of the business (see Chapter 14). The nature of the debtors should be determined, in case there is a possibility of reducing the burden of unpaid bills on the business. Very tight control should be exercised over cash flow (see Chapters 7, 11 and 13).

The above remarks assume that the balance sheet in question is a historical statement. If it were a budgeted balance sheet, there would be the further option of amending the current year's plans in order to alleviate the situation.

Further reading

Atkinson, J. M., Hastings, M. R. and Warren, M. F., *Using your Accounts* (Agricultural Training Board/Seale Hayne College/Manpower Services Commission (The Family Farm Series), 1986, revised 1990).

Barnard, C. S. and Nix, J. S., *Farm Planning and Control*, 2nd edition (London, Cambridge University Press, 1979), pp. 542–51.

Berry, A. and Jarvis, R., *Accounting in a Business Context* (London, Chapman & Hall, 1991), chapter 3.

Bull, R. J., *Accounting in Business*, 6th edition (London, Butterworths, 1990), chapter 2.

Machinery	£	Buildings	£
Opening value	26,000	Opening value	10,000
Add Purchases	6,000	*Less* Depreciation	1,500
Less Sales	2,000	Closing value	8,500
	30,000		
Less Depreciation	4,500		
Closing value	25,500		

Figure 4.8 *Depreciation calculations for 199Y*

FLOW OF FUNDS ANALYSIS		£
SOURCES:	NET PROFIT (LOSS)	10,000
	Depreciation (+)	6,000
	Change in debtors (increase −, decrease +)	−5,980
	Change in creditors (increase +, decrease −)	3,000
	Valuations (increase −, decrease +)	−2,000
	Benefits in kind (−)	−500
CASH FROM TRADING		10,520
ADD:	Capital introduced	0
	Sale of land, property, investments	0
	Increase in overdraft	15,000
	Increase in loans	0
	Reduction in cash balances	0
CASH FROM OTHER SOURCES		15,000
TOTAL CASH AVAILABLE		25,520
USES:	COMMITMENTS	
	Private drawings	10,500
	Tax payments	6,000
	Reduction in loans	5,000
TOTAL COMMITMENTS		21,500
ADD:	Purchase of land, property, investments	0
	Net purchase of buildings	0
	Purchase of machinery 6,000	
	Less sale of machinery −2,000	4,000
	Repayment of overdraft	0
	Increase in cash balances	20
		4,020
TOTAL CASH USED		25,520

Figure 4.9 *Flow of funds analysis – worked example*

Griffis, D., 'Classifying businesses according to their financial health', *Farm Management*, vol. 6, no. 12. A valuable, and now widely-used 'short-hand' analysis of the vulnerability of a farm business.

Shepherd, C. G., *An analysis of performance by size, type and form of ownership of farms*, unpublished Diploma in Farm Management project report, Seale-Hayne Faculty, Polytechnic South West, 1991.

Warren, M. F. and Pierpoint, P. R., 'Vulnerability of farm businesses in the far South West of England', *Farm Management*, vol. 7, no. 12.

5

Depreciation

The concept of depreciation *

The expense of depreciation arises from the tendency of certain types of fixed assets, e.g. machinery and buildings, to 'waste' due to wear and tear, decomposition, and/or obsolescence. It may be thought of in two ways. Firstly, it may be considered as a way of 'saving' money within the business (though not necessarily in cash form) to provide for the eventual replacement of the assets. Alternatively, it may be considered as a means of spreading the initial cost of the assets 'fairly' between the years of their possession by the business. This is a slightly easier concept to understand, and at the time of writing is the convention used in the preparation of farm financial accounts. It is therefore used as the basis for the following discussion.

In a time of stable currency, the two conventions will give identical results. In times of inflation, however, the results will diverge, since the former is aimed at the *cost of replacing* assets at their future (inflated) price, while the latter is concerned with allocating the *historic* cost of assets between years (see Chapter 21).

In order to allocate the initial cost of an asset over the years of its life it is necessary:

1   To calculate the net initial cost of the asset.
2   To estimate its likely useful life in the business.
3   To estimate its likely resale value at the end of that life.
4   To calculate the depreciation charge for each year of the asset's life.

The net initial cost of an asset is the actual cash paid for it, after deducting grants and discounts received, but ignoring money allowed on part-exchange (this is part of the depreciation of the asset being sold, and not of that being bought).

Estimating the likely life of the asset is largely a matter of experience and judgement (if short of either, use someone else's – take advice). It is possible to obtain guides to the likely useful lives of particular types of machine, see, for instance, J. S. Nix, *Farm Management Pocketbook*, Section III. Such guides can only indicate the effects of wear and tear and corrosion, however, leaving the reader to judge the likely impact of obsolescence.

---

*It is important to distinguish between depreciation and *capital allowances*. The latter, though calculated in a similar fashion to depreciation, are used solely in the assessment of income and corporation tax (see Appendix 3).

Estimating eventual resale values is again a matter of judgement. An indication can often be obtained from current second-hand prices of similar assets.

Calculating annual depreciation charges

Choice of method

There are various ways of calculating the depreciation of wasting assets, each with its own advantages and disadvantages. No method can provide an exactly accurate measurement of depreciation, since the calculation depends on forecasts of asset life and future resale value. The aim must therefore be to find a method which most nearly represents the likely pattern of depreciation. Three methods are in common use:

1   The straight-line method;
2   The sum-of-the-digits method;
3   The diminishing-balance (or reducing-balance) method.

It is essential to be consistent in the methods used: once a method of calculation has been chosen for a type of asset, it should be used thereafter.

The straight-line method

By this method, the difference between initial cost and eventual resale value is divided by the estimated life in the business (in years). The result is the annual depreciation charge. As an example (see Figure 5.1), an asset costs £10,000 to buy, net of grants, etc. Its estimated useful life in the business is four years, after which its resale value is likely to be £2000. The annual charge will then be (£10,000 − £2000)/4 = £2000. This charge may be used to find the *written-down value* or *book value* at the beginning of the year by deducting the charge from

Year	WDV at beginning of year	Annual depreciation	WDV at end of year
	£	£	£
1	10,000	2,000	8,000
2	8,000	2,000	6,000
3	6,000	2,000	4,000
4	4,000	2,000	2,000
Accumulated depreciation		8,000	
Plus WDV at end year 4		2,000	
Initial cost of asset		10,000	

Figure 5.1   *Calculation of straight-line depreciation and written-down values*

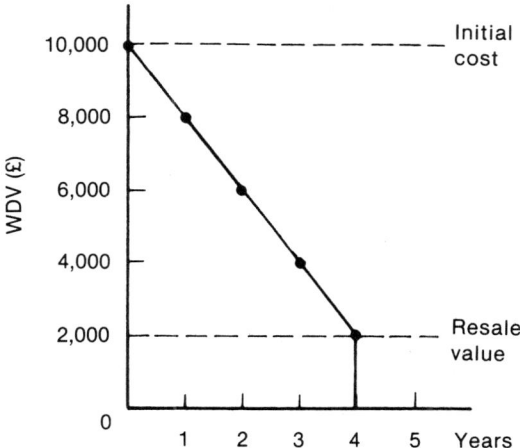

Figure 5.2 *Straight-line depreciation – graphical representation*

the written-down value (WDV) at the beginning of the year. This is the value that is used in the closing balance sheet for the year concerned.

Note that since the depreciation charge is constant throughout the life of the asset, the WDV declines at a constant or 'straight-line' rate (see Figure 5.2).

This method is easy to use, and is especially popular for budgets, where one calculation provides the depreciation charges for all the years of an asset's life. It is appropriate particularly for buildings and improvements, where the services provided are likely to be relatively constant over the asset's life.

Where machinery and equipment are concerned, however, it is reasonable to suppose that the business benefits more from the services of the asset in the early years of its life than later. This is partly a matter of wear and tear, partly a matter of the likelihood of the asset being superseded by newer, better machines.

The remaining two depreciation methods make allowance for this by allocating a greater proportion of the total depreciation to the early years than to the later years of the asset's life.

Sum-of-the-digits method

This method begins with the summing of the digits representing the years of the asset's life and dividing the result into the difference between initial cost and resale value. Using the example above, the sum of the years' digits is 1 + 2 + 3 + 4 = 10. Dividing the result into £10,000 – 2000 gives £800.

The next step is to reverse the numbering of the years, and to multiply each of the

Year	Reverse numbering	Depreciation	WDV at beginning of year	WDV at end of year*
		£	£	£
1	4 × 800 =	3,200	10,000	6,800
2	3 × 800 =	2,400	6,800	4,400
3	2 × 800 =	1,600	4,400	2,800
4	1 × 800 =	800	2,800	2,000
Accumulated depreciation		8,000		
WDV at end year 4		2,000		
Initial cost of asset		10,000		

*WDV at beginning of year minus depreciation

Figure 5.3 *Sum-of-the-digits depreciation*

new numbers by the result of the first calculation to obtain the depreciation charge for each year (see Figure 5.3).

The WDV of the asset declines sharply in the first year, levelling off in later years (see Figure 5.4).

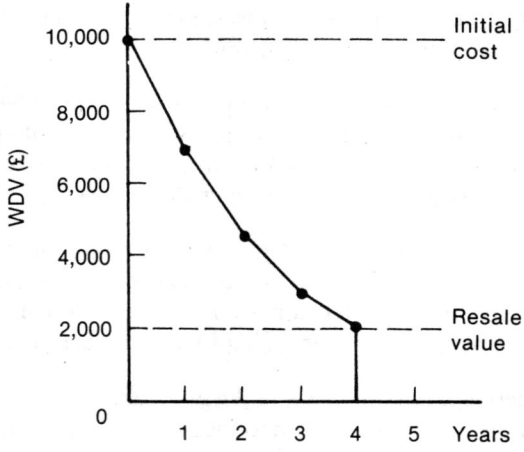

Figure 5.4 *Sum-of-the-digits depreciation – graphical representation*

The diminishing-balance or reducing-balance method

In this method, a percentage depreciation rate is applied to the WDV of the asset as at the end of the previous year. Using the same example as above, and depreciating at the rate of 20 per cent per year, the annual charge would be as shown in Figure 5.5.

A major problem with this method is the selection of a depreciation rate which will result in a WDV at the end of the asset's life in the business which is identical to the

Year	WDV at beginning of year	Depreciation at 20% of WDV	WDV at end of year
	£	£	£
1	10,000	2,000	8,000
2	8,000	1,600	6,400
3	6,400	1,280	5,120
4	5,120	1,024	4,096
Accumulated depreciation		5,904	
WDV at end of year 4		4,096	
Initial cost of asset		10,000	

Figure 5.5 *Diminishing-balance depreciation – example*

anticipated sale value of the asset; in the example above the rate used has resulted in a WDV in year 4 which is £2096 higher than the resale value assumed.

One way of dealing with this problem is to try a variety of rates until a suitable resale value is found. A useful starting point is to take a rate which is double the appropriate straight-line rate. (In the example above, the straight-line depreciation charge is £2000 per year, or 20 per cent; the initial trade diminishing-balance rate is thus 40 per cent.) A quicker method, for the mathematically minded, is to use the formula:

$$r = [1 - \sqrt[n]{(R/C)}] \times 100$$

where r is the percentage rate of depreciation, R the resale value, C the initial cost and n the years of life of the asset in the business. Then, using the previous example, the appropriate rate is:

$$(1 - \sqrt[4]{[2000/10,000]}) \times 100$$
$$r = 33 \text{ per cent}$$

This results in a pattern of depreciation as shown in Figure 5.6.

Year	WDV at beginning of year	Depreciation at 33% of WDV	WDV at end of year
	£	£	£
1	10,000	3,300	6,700
2	6,700	2,211	4,489
3	4,489	1,481	3,008
4	3,008	1,008	2,000
Accumulated depreciation		8,000	
WDV at end of year 4		2,000	
Initial cost of asset		10,000	
Note that a small adjustment (£11) has to be made to the final year's depreciation to allow for rounding errors.			

Figure 5.6 *Diminishing-balance depreciation – example of use of formula*

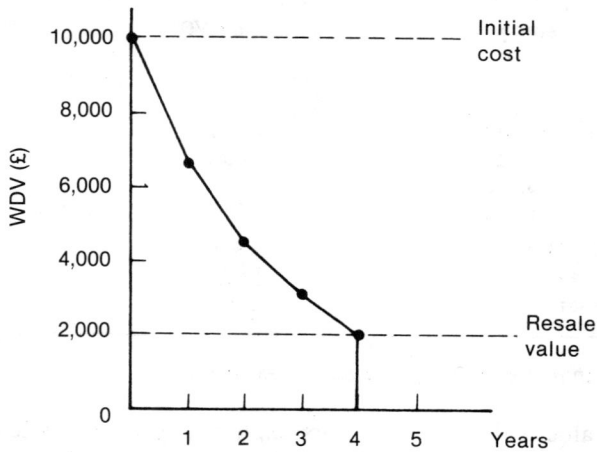

Figure 5.7   *Diminishing-balance depreciation*

Note that the diminishing-balance method shown in Figure 5.7 gives rise to a greater decline in WDV in the earlier years than does the sum-of-the-digits method. Diminishing-balance is popular in the UK, probably because it is the method used for calculating capital allowances for machinery for tax-assessment purposes. Its biggest drawback, which is not shared by sum-of-the-digits, is the necessity of fixing a percentage rate of depreciation. The impact of this drawback is reduced by the widespread use of 'pooling' in diminishing-balance calculations.

Pool calculations

In a farm business of typical size, depreciation calculations of the form described earlier would have to be repeated many times in order to find the appropriate annual charge for each asset. This implies, in turn, making assumptions for each asset concerning its useful life and resale value. *Pooling* assets for diminishing-balance depreciation entails grouping similar types of assets together, e.g. tractors, cultivation equipment and motor vehicles, and treating each group as a block with a single depreciation rate. Additions and sales of assets can be incorporated in the calculations without separate treatment.

The rate at which the group is depreciated is found in the first place by taking an average of the appropriate rates for the individual assets in the group. These rates can be determined either by using the formula or by trial and error. Once the average rate has been calculated, it can be used thereafter; an adjustment of the rate will be needed only if the make-up of the group changes dramatically.

The mechanism of the pool calculation is shown in the following example. Suppose that a farmer starts the financial year with his tractor 'pool' having a WDV of £30,000. During the year he buys a new tractor for £15,000, selling an

	£
WDV of tractors at beginning of year	30,000
Plus Purchases	15,000
Less Sales	2,000
	43,000
Less Depreciation charge at 20%	8,600
WDV of tractors at end of year	34,400

Figure 5.8 *Pool calculations – example*

old one in part-exchange for £2000. Using an annual depreciation rate of 20 per cent, the annual charge for this year is calculated as shown in Figure 5.8.

It may seem that the use of pooling detracts from the accuracy of the depreciation calculation. It must be remembered, however, that in most farm businesses the expense of depreciation is a relatively small component of the total expenses. It needs a large error in the depreciation calculation to affect total expense by a significant proportion. The use of pooling thus costs little in accuracy while gaining much in convenience.

Profit or loss on sale

Because depreciation calculations are based on guesses about future values, it is unlikely that the *actual* resale value will be exactly the same as the written-down value at the time of sale. The resale value is likely to be more or less than the WDV, giving rise to a *profit on sale* or a *loss on sale*, respectively.

A profit on sale implies that too much allowance has been made for depreciation in earlier years. The profits of those earlier years have thus been underestimated. The ideal remedy would be to apportion the profit on sale between those years. In practice, this creates much effort for little extra benefit, and the usual solution is to attribute profit on sale as a revenue to the year in which it arises. A loss on sale is treated similarly, being shown in the profit and loss account as an expense.

Fractional depreciation

The calculations shown above assume implicitly that assets are bought at the beginning of the financial year. In practice this is not often the case; indeed a large proportion of purchases are made towards the end of the financial year, to take full advantage of capital allowances against income tax.

It is possible to make allowances to remove this distortion. Depreciation can be calculated on a monthly or quarterly basis and allocated between financial years accordingly. This is known as *fractional depreciation*. It can be a complex and tedious exercise, especially as similar adjustments must be made when the asset is eventually sold.

An alternative is to ignore fractional depreciation and hope that the effect of acquisitions made part-way through the year is balanced by similarly timed disposals. This is particularly appropriate when dealing with groups of assets, and is the approach used in this book.

A full discussion of fractional depreciation is given in Garbutt's *Accounting Foundations*, pp. 278 – 80.

Appreciation of assets

It is possible for an asset to appreciate in value, as a consequence of inflation and/or relative scarcity. This increase in value does not arise from the productive activity of the business, and as such should not be included in the calculation of profit. If the asset is revalued in the balance sheet, the capital account should be credited with a 'holding gain' of an equal amount, to allow reconciliation (see Chapter 21).

Further reading

Berry, A. and Jarvis, R., *Accounting in a Business Context* (London, Chapman & Hall), chapter 8.
Bull, R. J., *Accounting in Business*, 6th edition (London, Butterworths), chapter 6.
Garbutt, D., *Accounting Foundations*, 3rd edition (London, Butterworths, 1980), pp. 272 – 85.
Rockley, L. E., *Finance for the Non-accountant*, 3rd edition (London, Business Books, 1979), pp. 23 – 40.

PART TWO

Basic Budgeting

We left Adam Haynes, at the end of Chapter 1, facing the task of making major decisions about the future of the business. Ideally, he should undertake a systematic and comprehensive review and replanning of the whole business. This ideal is difficult to achieve in Adam's case, since he lacks experience of managing Home Farm, and has only a small knowledge of the options open to him and of the constraints on the business. Moreover, he has little time for consideration, as decisions must be made very soon concerning the crops for the coming year.

It would be quite sensible, therefore, for Adam to continue operation of the existing system, leaving major replanning until the end of his first year, when he will have got the 'feel' of the farm. One advantage of this approach is that Adam would be looking at the financial consequences of just one course of action, rather than wrestling with several alternatives. It would enable him (and us) to become accustomed to the techniques of budgeting, before becoming enmeshed in the complexities of a major replanning.

For the moment, then, we follow this course, leaving discussion of a complete 're-think' to Part Five. The first requirement is the preparation of budgets to show the effect on profit, cash and capital of continuation of the existing system. The obvious starting point in this process is to build up a picture of the operational aspects of the business. This involves the compilation of a profit and loss budget, showing the anticipated profit over the first year of operation and, just as important, how that profit is to be achieved.

6

A profit budget for the whole farm

Introduction

Adam is faced with the task of preparing a *whole-farm profit and loss budget*,* referred to hereafter as a *profit budget*. This will involve two processes: first, forecasting the physical and financial performance of the farm during the coming year; and second, assembling this information in such a way as to give an estimate of net profit for that year.

Forecasting prices and quantities

Forecasting for a farm business can be extremely difficult. To the uncertainty of the physical environment (e.g. climate and disease) is added the considerable uncertainty of the economic environment. And yet, as indicated in Chapter 1, the greater the uncertainty, the greater the need to plan carefully. How, then, can Adam, a novice in farm management, ensure that his guesses about the future are the best possible?

First, he could use history; look at past performance and use it as a base for decisions about the future. History can be particularly valuable for forecasting physical performance. The fact that a certain patch of land has consistently yielded only 4 tonnes per hectare of wheat in the past provides a useful guide for next year's budget.

Past events are not always a reliable guide to the future, however. In estimating *prices* of most agricultural inputs and outputs, for instance, it is unwise to forecast purely on the basis of historical trends. Even within the protective barriers of the EEC, prices can be unexpectedly and dramatically affected by natural, political and economic events on the other side of the world.

A second way of improving the quality of forecasting is to use the expertise of others. Academic, commercial and government researchers are employed to make forecasts in various areas, such as the rate of inflation over the next five years; the world production of wheat during the coming year; or the weather in the next four weeks. These forecasts are published in various media, and regular study of trade journals, radio programmes, etc. can pay dividends. At a more local level, Adam

*Often referred to, ambiguously, as a *complete budget*.

45

can learn a great deal from discussions with neighbouring farmers and local advisers, and from telephone calls to merchants and dealers.

Adam has still no guarantee that he will make the right decisions. On the other hand, by blending historical evidence with the expert predictions of others, and adding a measure of his own intelligent reasoning, he is likely to reduce the uncertainty surrounding his forecasts.

Variations on the profit theme

The conventional format

Let us assume that Adam has made his best possible forecasts of the inputs and outputs of Home Farm for the coming year. He has to arrange this information in such a way that, (a) it results in the calculation of anticipated net profit, and (b) it provides sufficient information for precise control throughout the year.

The simplest and quickest method of calculating profit would be to compile a budget on the lines of a conventional profit and loss account, as described in

	£	£		£	£
Opening valuation			*Closing valuation*		
Cattle	60,000		Cattle	60,000	
Produce	20,000		Produce	22,000	
Valuations	8,000	88,000	Cultivations	8,000	90,000
Purchases and expenses			*Sales and receipts*		
Wages	15,000		Milk	45,000	
Casual labour	2,000		Stock	29,000	
Feed	20,000		Cereals	18,000	
Fertilizers	8,000		Potatoes	20,000	
Seeds	4,500		Others	3,000	115,000
Sprays	2,500				
Rents	10,000				
Rates and insurance	1,000				
Fuels	5,000				
Vet	2,000				
Building repairs	2,500				
Machinery repairs	5,000				
Other expenses	5,500	83,000			
Depreciation					
Drainage	6,500				
Machinery	8,500	15,000			
Interest	—	—			
BALANCE: NET PROFIT		19,000			
		205,000			205,000

Figure 6.1 *Simplified profit and loss budget in 'conventional' form, Farm X*

Chapter 3. This can be valuable as an initial test of farm profitability, but it omits so much detail that it is virtually useless for precise control.

The biggest fault of the 'conventional' approach is that it treats the business as a single, homogeneous unit, whereas most farm businesses are more logically thought of as combinations of enterprises. An *enterprise* is a division of the business, usually identified by the type of product. Thus Home Farm comprises five enterprises: winter wheat, spring barley, sugar beet, main-crop potatoes and a dairy herd.

In controlling the business, it is vital to be able to monitor each of these enterprises individually. If one of the enterprises does not appear to be pulling its weight, steps can be taken to improve its performance or to replace it in part or in whole by another enterprise. To use a conventional format in making such decisions is risking confusion, at the least; the information is too highly summarized to show enterprise performance.

It is difficult to check the budget in Figure 6.1, for instance, since there is so little information presented. By lumping outputs together (dairy heifers and beef; wheat and barley; main-crop and early potatoes, etc.) and inputs together (fertilizers, seeds, feeds, etc.) it enables omissions and errors of judgement to be easily overlooked. Moreover, it is impossible to relate the output of a particular enterprise to the costs directly incurred in its production.

Enterprise budgets in full costing form

For his profit budget to be truly useful, Adam thus needs to formulate it in such a way that the anticipated performance of each enterprise is shown clearly.

At first sight, the simplest way of achieving this is to complete a profit and loss budget for each enterprise, or *profit centre* individually. The profits, or *net margins*, of the enterprises are accumulated to give the net profit of the whole farm. The result is a budget in the form of a *full-costing* (more precisely, a *full absorption costing*): see Figure 6.2.

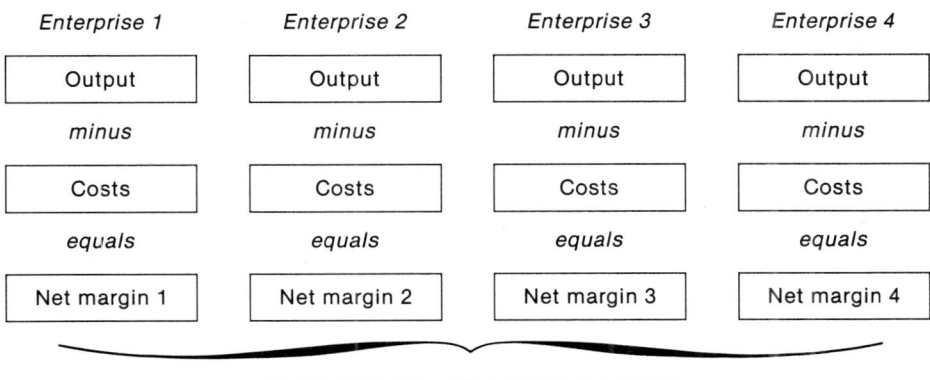

Figure 6.2 *Full absorption costing*

Despite the apparent simplicity, however, the full costing approach is fraught with difficulties. Awkward, and usually arbitrary, decisions have to be made concerning the allocation of 'general overhead' expenses (i.e. those incurred by the whole business such as office expenses and the use of the farm Land-Rover) between enterprises. Labour and machinery costs must be estimated in great detail and allocated carefully.

These problems may be overcome in *planning*, with the expense of a little time and effort. The major difficulties arise, however, in *recording* control information in sufficient detail to enable the use of this extra sophistication in the budget. On a typical mixed farm, this implies the careful recording of the amount of labour and machinery used in each enterprise. Elaborate timesheets must be kept by all employees, since the man who fed the cattle and counted the sheep before coffee-break may well have top-dressed wheat, barley and grass before lunch, and spent the afternoon drilling sugar beet – and all with the same tractor.

Leaving aside the arguments about the likely accuracy of timesheets, the collation of this information will add considerably to the farmer's paperwork burden. On most farms, the benefit gained does not justify the huge effort involved. The exceptions are those where either the task is relatively easy (such as self-contained enterprises in intensive livestock, horticulture or very large-scale arable production), or where the potential benefits are particularly large (where, for instance, the information is to be used in education or research, or for price-fixing on contracts).

A further, more serious criticism of the full-costing approach in planning is that there is a danger of the farmer treating all costs as equally variable. Suppose a farmer were to use full-cost budgets in order to test the pros and cons of scrapping a potato enterprise in favour of winter wheat (Figure 6.3).

	Main-crop potatoes (£/ha)	Winter wheat (£/ha)
Output	2,000	600
Costs		
Fertilizer	250	100
Seed	500	40
Sprays	200	70
Harvesting, casual labour, transport, etc.	300	5
Regular labour	170	20
Machinery, running cost	150	40
Machinery, depreciation	210	55
Miscellaneous overhead costs	200	200
	1,980	530
NET MARGIN	20	70

Figure 6.3   *Budgets in full-cost form for potato and wheat enterprises*

If he is unwary, he may well deduce that the proposed change would increase the profits of his business by £50/ha (70 – 20). But many of the costs associated with potato production will still be there, whether or not potatoes are grown on the farm.

To take a single example, the change may give rise to no savings in the cost of regular labour. Unless the farm is heavily overstaffed, the replacement of a small area of potatoes by wheat is not likely to enable the business to dispense with the labour of one man for the whole year. The wages will have to be paid, whether or not potatoes are produced. If this cost is eliminated from the calculation a rather different picture emerges (see Figure 6.4).*

Therefore, the effect of dropping potatoes in favour of wheat is to *reduce* profit by £100/ha (190 – 90).

	Main-crop potatoes (£/ha)	Winter wheat (£/ha)
Output	2,000	600
Costs		
Fertilizer	250	100
Seed	500	40
Sprays	200	70
Harvesting, etc.	300	5
Machinery, running costs	150	40
Machinery, depreciation	210	55
Miscellaneous overhead costs	200	200
	1,810	510

Figure 6.4 *Revised enterprise budgets, excluding regular labour*

Enterprise budgets in gross margin form

Adam thus requires a method of budgeting for profit which provides enterprise detail, but bypasses the difficulties of allocating overhead costs. It must also avoid confusion between those costs which vary as the result of a change in the enterprise, and those which do not. One such method is the preparation of budgets in *gross margin form*: a pragmatic adaptation of what an accountant would term 'marginal costing'.

With this method, only certain costs are allocated to individual enterprises. These are known as *variable costs*. A variable cost is one that satisfies *both* of the following criteria:

1   It tends to vary directly with *small* changes in enterprise size.
2   It is relatively easy to allocate to a specific enterprise.

*This is obviously a simplistic example. See Chapter 9 for discussion of planning for partial changes

Any cost which does not satisfy *both* of these criteria is termed a *fixed cost*. No attempt is made to divide such a cost between the various enterprises.

As an example, the cost of wheat seed is easy to allocate to the wheat enterprise, and will vary with small changes in enterprise size; it is therefore a variable cost. The cost of diesel fuel used in drilling the wheat will vary with enterprise size, but will be difficult to allocate without very detailed timesheets. It is thus classified as a fixed cost. The cost of depreciation of the grain store is not likely to vary with small changes in the cereal hectarage, nor, if there is more than one cereal enterprise, will the cost be very easy to allocate. It is therefore a fixed cost.

A list of assorted costs and expenses is shown in Figure 6.5.

Variable costs	Fixed costs
Feedstuffs (including forage)	Regular labour
Veterinary, medical and AI fees	Power and machinery running costs
Fertilizers	(except contract hire)
Seeds	Machinery and building depreciation
Sprays	Rent and/or landowning expenses
Casual labour	Rates
Contract hire of machinery	Interest charges
Miscellaneous, e.g. baler twine,	Miscellaneous overheads, e.g.
recording services, transport	office expenses, accountant's fees,
	fencing costs, property insurance

Figure 6.5   *Examples of variable and fixed costs*

A profit budget in gross margin form is built up as follows. For each enterprise, variable costs are deducted from enterprise output to give the *enterprise gross margin*. The gross margins of the various enterprises are added together to give a *total gross margin*. From this are deducted the *total fixed costs* of the whole business, to give the net profit (see Figure 6.6).

Note that all three formats (conventional, full costing and gross margin) will give identical net profits, providing that identical figures are used in the computation. The differences between the methods are merely those of calculation and layout.

A further development of the gross margin approach is suggested by Giles (1986), involving the allocation of those 'fixed costs' which can be reasonably identified with particular enterprises. For reasons of simplicity and consistency with other publications, *Financial Management for Farmers* adheres to the gross margin system, but the 'Giles approach' has many attractions, particularly in comparison of profitability between enterprises on the same farm. The method is also described in Giles and Stansfield (1990), Chapter 9.

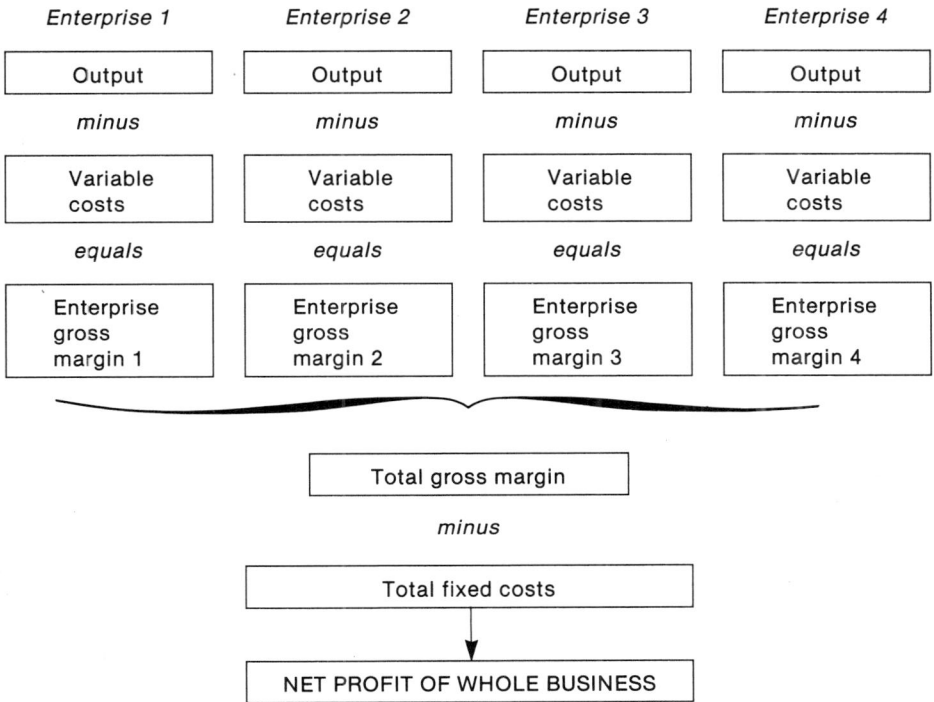

Figure 6.6 *Profit budget in gross margin form – outline*

Compiling a profit budget in gross margin form

How much detail?

The division of the budget into enterprise sections enables it to spread over several pages, and thus allows space to be used for extra detail. The degree of detail provided can make the difference between a useless budget and an invaluable one. At the same time, the provision of *too much* detail can confuse rather than enlighten, and incur unwanted extra work.

The first problem is how far to take the division into enterprises. Of the barley grown on a farm, for instance, some may be winter barley and some spring barley. Of the winter barley, some may be destined for seed, some for animal feed. The feed barley area may be drilled with three different varieties. Should all the barley be treated as one enterprise; should each separate variety be treated as an enterprise; or does the answer lie somewhere between the two extremes?

As a rule, a division should be made where there are likely to be significant differences in output and/or variable costs. In the above example, therefore, the barley should be treated as at least three enterprises: spring barley, winter barley (seed) and winter barley (feed). Each has a specific product and a specific management regime. Therefore, each needs to be budgeted separately if the farmer is to make sensible decisions about both the management of each crop and their relative proportions.

On some farms, it may even be worth budgeting the different varieties separately, especially where large areas are involved and there are distinct differences in performance between varieties. In most cases, however, the benefits gained would not justify the time and effort involved (remember that every such division increases not only the effort involved in budgeting, but also the burden of recording of control information).

The second question of detail is that of how much to present within each enterprise gross margin budget. Consider a possible budget for the output of the Home Farm spring barley enterprise shown in Figure 6.7.

Enterprise output	£
Grain sales	19,800
Straw sales	2,800
	22,600

Figure 6.7   *Aggregated output calculation*

This budget is adequate if the only purpose of it is to estimate the likely profit of the whole business. If, however, the intention is to *use* the budget constructively in financial control of the business, this format is virtually useless. When the time comes to compare actual and budgeted results, Adam will want to know what assumptions he made in the budget concerning yields and prices. Only then can he draw conclusions about his management of the enterprise. The budget shown in Figure 6.8 gives much more detail about the components of the output, at the expense of little extra effort.

Enterprise output (40 hectares)	Yield per hectare (tonnes)	Total yield (tonnes)	Price per tonne	Total output (£)	Output per hectare (£)
Grain sales	4.5	180	110	19,800	495
Straw sales	2.0	80	35	2,800	70
				22,600	565

Figure 6.8   *More detailed output calculation*

The farmer has estimated the likely yield of his crop at the next harvest, and has multiplied this by the price he hopes to receive. Variable costs would be treated in the same way, working from the rate of application and the anticipated prices per unit. This approach has the great virtue of simplicity, and is particularly useful for rapidly testing a number of alternative options.

A full budget

As an accurate reflection of the performance of the enterprise and its contribution to the business, however, this simple approach can leave much to be desired. It takes no account, for instance, of the possibility of variation of stocks between the beginning and the end of the year. Figure 6.9 includes opening and closing valuations of grain, reflecting a situation where the farmer's estimates of sales ignore the fact that he has an unusually high stock of grain left unsold from the previous harvest, which will be disposed of during the year. The use of some of the grain and straw for feeding livestock in other enterprises on the same farm is also acknowledged. The final gross margin is the same, but the budget is more explicit, and thus easier to relate to the realities of the business.

Winter wheat	GROSS MARGIN				
Hectares: 40	Total yield (tonnes)	Yield per hectare (tonnes)	Price per tonne (£)	£ total	£ per hectare
Grain					
Sales	100	2.5	104.4	10,435	261
Transferred to livestock	95	2.4	115.0	10,925	273
Closing valuation	45	1.1	112.0	5,040	126
Less opening valuation	−60	−1.5	110.0	−6,600	−165
Straw					
Transferred to livestock	85	2.1	35.0	2,975	74
Closing valuation	22	0.6	40.0	880	22
Less opening valuation	−35	−0.9	30.0	−1,050	−26
OUTPUT				22,605	565
Variable costs	Total input (tonnes)	Input per hectare (tonnes)	Price per tonne (£)	£ total	£ per hectare
Seedbed fertilizer	12	0.3	180.00	2,160	54
High-nitrogen fertilizer	8	0.2	150.00	1,200	30
Seed	8	0.2	200.00	1,600	40
Sprays				1,500	38
Casual labour				300	8
VARIABLE COST				6,760	169
GROSS MARGIN				15,845	396

Figure 6.9 *Example gross margin calculation*

It is when trying to estimate the true profit of the farm that such adjustments become essential, rather than just making the budget easier to follow. Net profit, for reasons discussed in Chapter 3, must incorporate changes in valuation of stocks, changes in debtors and creditors, benefits in kind and depreciation. A profit budget in gross margin form, rather than a back-of-the-envelope test of alternative possibilities, must therefore incorporate all these. Furthermore, it should incorporate any transfers between enterprises (such as barley used for feeding dairy cattle). To be 'fair' to each enterprise, these must be shown as non-cash 'sales' and 'purchases' at the market values prevailing at the time of transfer.*

In a full crop gross margin, the components would be calculated as follows:

Enterprise output
Sales (adjusted for debtors) and subsidies
plus Transfers to other enterprises (at market value)
plus Increase (or less decrease) in valuation of stocks of products
plus Benefits in kind (products consumed by families of farmer and farmworkers)

Variable costs
Purchases (adjusted for creditors)
plus Transfers from other enterprises (at market value)
less Increase (or plus decrease) in valuation of stocks of inputs
less Benefits in kind (inputs consumed by families of farmer and farmworkers).

Note that an increase in valuation of stocks of produce is *added* to output, whereas an increase in the valuation of stocks of inputs is *deducted* from variable costs. In the former case, sales and transfers alone do not show the full value of all that has been produced, and any increase in the level of stocks must be added in order to give a true reflection of enterprise performance. In the latter, an increase in stock levels implies that (inflation apart) more inputs have been purchased than were actually used in producing the output. To obtain a fair picture of the relationship between inputs and outputs, therefore, the increase must be deducted from the purchases.

A similar argument applies to benefits in kind. These arise where the business has produced goods which do not appear in sales or transfers and/or (less likely) has purchased goods which, having been diverted outside the business for no cash payment, have made no contribution to the performance of the enterprise.

It is generally accepted that, in calculating livestock enterprise gross margins, the cost of purchasing or transferring in livestock is shown not as one of the variable costs but as a deduction from the enterprise output. This convention appears to be largely the result of historical accident and now has little conceptual or practical justification. However, the convention is so firmly entrenched in the farming world that there is no alternative but to adopt it.

The output of a livestock enterprise will thus be calculated as follows:

Sales (adjusted for debtors) and subsidies
plus Transfers to other enterprises
plus Increase (or less decrease) in valuation of stocks of outputs
plus Benefits in kind
less Purchases or transfers in of livestock (adjusted for creditors).

*If they were transferred at cost of production, the 'selling' enterprise would look unduly poor and the 'buying' enterprise unrealistically good.

It is often the case that some minor items of output and variable costs do not fit exactly into the enterprise classification. An increase in the value of miscellaneous stores, for instance, may be so small that the effort of allocating it accurately between enterprises is not justified; the same may apply to casual labour hired for harvest work. Such items may be either divided arbitrarily between the relevant enterprises (on the grounds that they are too small for any consequent distortions to have a significant effect on the enterprise gross margins), or deducted from the *total* gross margin without any attempt to allocate them. The latter is the approach adopted here (see Figure 6.10).

The fixed costs of the enterprise must now be estimated. These will include all or some of:

Regular labour costs
Running costs and depreciation of machinery, buildings and improvements
Rent and/or costs of maintaining property
Miscellaneous overhead costs
Interest and other finance charges.

Any relevant benefits in kind (e.g. private use of car, telephone or fuel) should be deducted from fixed costs.

Total fixed costs may now be deducted from total gross margin to give net profit.

	£
Sum of enterprise gross margins	70,000
Plus unallocated output items	2,000
Less unallocated variable cost items	−1,500
TOTAL GROSS MARGIN	70,500
Less total fixed costs	55,500
NET PROFIT	15,000

Figure 6.10 *Financial summary*

A gross margin worksheet

To allow for all these adjustments and still be able to understand the results (and to have confidence in your calculation) takes a certain amount of discipline. It helps greatly to use a worksheet such as the one shown in Figure 6.11 (computer spreadsheet formulae for this worksheet are given in Appendix 5). Everyone has their own needs and preferences in setting out gross margin calculations, and you may prefer to design your own.

The worksheet is in two parts, the lower part showing the familiar gross margin calculation. The upper part, which is where the raw material of the gross margin

Enterprise: Dairy   Ha or head? 80   Year 199x/9y
                                                       Version 2

Products:	Milk Qty	Milk £	Calves Qty	Calves £	Culls Qty	Culls £
Cash received	400,500	76,095	74	7,400	20	11,000
Closing debtors	11,000	1,980	7	700		
−Opening debtors	−12,000	−2,280		−500		
Sales	399,500	75,795	81	7,600	20	11,000
Transfers out						
Benefits in kind	700	133				
Closing valuation			10	800		
−Opening valuation			−10	−800		
OUTPUT	400,200	75,928	81	7,600	20	11,000

Inputs:	Purch. livestock Qty	£	Conc. feed Qty	£	Straw Qty	£	Vet/med Qty	£	Forage £	Other £
Cash paid	25	17,500	86	12,900			1	2,500	5,755	3,000
Closing creditors			20	3,000						
−Opening creditors			−25	−4,000						
Purchases	25	17,500	81	11,900			1	2,500	5,755	3,000
Transfers in			42	3,780	26	390				
−Benefits in kind										
Opening valuation			20	2,800						
−Closing valuation			−20	−2,800						
VARIABLE COST	25	17,500	123	15,680	26	390	1	2,500	5,755	3,000

MISCELLANEOUS VALUATION CHANGES

	Breeding livestock no.	£	Crops in gd. £	Total £
Closing valuation	82	53,300		53,300
−Opening valuation	−77	−50,050		−50,050
Valuation change	5	3,250		3,250

Dairy			GROSS MARGIN		
Ha or head 80	Total Quantity	Qty/ha or /head	£ per unit quantity	£ Total	£/ha or /head
Milk	400,200	5,002	0.1897	75,928	949
Calves	81	1.0	93.83	7,600	95
Culls	20	0.2	550.00	11,000	137
Misc. valn. changes	xxxxxxxx	xxxxxxxx	xxxxxxxx	3,250	41
OUTPUT				97,778	1,222
VARIABLE COSTS	Total Quantity	Qty/ha or /head	£ per unit quantity	£ Total	£/ha or /head
Purch. livestock	25	0.3	0.3	17,500	219
Conc. feed	123	1.5	1.5	15,680	196
Straw	26	0.3	0.3	390	5
Vet/med	1	0.0		2,500	31
Forage				5,755	72
Other				3,000	37
VARIABLE COST				44,825	560
GROSS MARGIN				52,953	662

Figure 6.11 *Gross margin worksheet used for Home Farm dairy enterprise*

is gathered, is in three sections: output calculation, variable cost calculation and miscellaneous valuation changes. In the output section, the various products of the enterprise are identified, and, working from the cash to be received, the adjustments are made to arrive at an output for each product. This output is calculated in both physical (total quantity) and financial terms, thus giving two figures that can be transferred down to the relevant columns (shaded) in the gross margin calculation below. From that point it is a simple matter to divide each by the number of head to arrive at quantity produced per head and financial output per head (third and sixth columns in the gross margin).

The variable cost section works in the same way, although in some categories it is not appropriate to include quantities (in this case 'forage', brought forward from another worksheet, and 'other'). The 'miscellaneous valuation changes' section allows the inclusion of valuation changes which are not easy to relate to specific products or cost categories; particularly breeding livestock number and value, and values of crops in ground.

There are good arguments for alternative ways of setting out the worksheet. In budgeting, for instance, it is often more convenient to *start* with output, calculating either cash sales or closing stock valuations as a residual figure. The format shown in Figure 6.11 (pages 56 – 7) provides a good compromise between the needs of budgeting future performance and recording that of the past, however, and leaves plenty of scope for you to experiment with variations on the theme.

To make budget preparation even more organized, the use of a gross margin assumptions sheet is recommended (Figure 6.12). This allows you to set out clearly the basis of all your estimates for each product and variable cost. Not only does this make completing the gross margin worksheet much easier, but it gives you a clear record of what you assumed in your budget – and why. This could save you precious time and avoid needless frustration when, in the future, you come back to the gross margin to adjust it, or to use it in control (see Chapter 14).

If you are used to a more casual use of gross margin budgets, the above might seem to be bureaucratic overkill. It cannot be stressed too highly, however, that an organized approach at the outset is the key to efficient use of time and accurate calculation. Other benefits will become clear when budgeting for cash flow and capital: you will find that your gross margin worksheet is an excellent starting point for both, with many of the assumptions and calculations already made.

A number of difficulties may be encountered in applying the theory of profit budgeting to actual problems. The following points may be of some assistance.

1   The easiest way to start a profit budget is to work out a plan in physical quantities, i.e. numbers of hectares and/or head per enterprise, followed by the levels of input and output expected per hectare/head. Forecast prices may then be applied to the physical data to enable calculation of the gross margins. This leaves only the fixed costs to estimate in order to arrive at a net profit. (Chapter 18 gives some guidance on the estimation of labour and machinery costs.)

2   It is not enough to budget for only one year at a time. This is especially true

GROSS MARGIN ASSUMPTIONS

Budget title:
Year:
Version no:

Enterprise	Item	Amount Bought/sold	Price per unit (£)	Total Rec'd/paid	Notes
Example: dairy	Milk sales	399,500 litres	0.19/litre	76095	Last year's yield + 2%: price forecast by MMB

Figure 6.12 *Gross margin assumptions worksheet*

where the budget is for a plan which will take some time to become established, but ideally should apply whatever the circumstances. In most cases it will be sufficient to prepare plans for the second and subsequent years in outline only. These outline budgets may then be updated, and the detail filled in, before the end of the previous budgeting year. The result is a 'rolling plan': as the business moves through time, the budget are extended progressively so that there is always a minimum period of time covered. Life doesn't stand still at the end of one year while you sort yourself out ready for the next 12 months.

3   When budgeting for the coming year, it is important to forecast prices and quantities as accurately as possible for that year, using the best outlook information available. When preparing outline budgets for subsequent years, use the first year's values, except where you have strong feelings about likely price movements in particular commodities. You will have the opportunity to revise these values as the first year passes and it becomes easier to make specific forecasts for later years. (Chapter 21 includes discussion of the problems of budgeting in times of inflation.)

4   Be careful to retain a sense of proportion when preparing the budget. Avoid spending hours calculating items which will have an insignificant effect on profit. This commonly applies to benefits in kind and valuations of miscellaneous items.

5   When more than one grazing livestock enterprise is present on the farm, it is necessary to make some attempt to allocate the variable costs of grass and other forage crops between them. In order to avoid undue complications at an early stage, this topic is treated in full in Chapter 17.

6   Forecasts, and thus budgets, are based on guesses about the future. Techniques such as sensitivity analysis and break-even budgets are useful in showing the likely effects of those guesses being wrong (see Chapter 20).

7   Interest charges on overdraft and loans must be deducted in calculating net profit; they are part of the fixed costs of the business. It is advisable at this stage to first calculate profit before interest, leaving the calculation of net profit until a cash-flow budget has been compiled. This will show the likely levels of overdraft and allow calculation of interest on that overdraft (see Chapters 7 and 19).

8   You *will* make mistakes in calculations. Therefore always use pencil for initial drafts, and have an eraser ready. Remember that it is far easier to trace errors by systematic checking at each stage of compiling the budget, than to start looking for them when the budget is complete.

9   As a final test, calculate profit by the conventional method and check against the result obtained by the gross margin method. If the two figures do not tally, check and check again until they *do*.

Normalized budgets

The most common use of the whole-farm profit budget is in examining the likely effects of a specific year's trading, e.g. 199X – 199Y for Home Farm.

Where a farm plan incorporates changes which will take some time to establish, e.g. one that involves a programme of investment in stock, machinery and buildings over many years, a *normalized* budget may be used. This depicts the make-up of profit or loss of the business after all the changes have been completed and the new system is running smoothly. The assumption is that economic and physical conditions will be those of a 'typical' year. This allows the exclusion of valuation changes from the calculation, since fluctuations between years are averaged out. For the same reason, a normalized budget can be calculated on a 'crop year'* basis irrespective of the dates of the financial year. All depreciation must be calculated by the straight-line method, since the other methods are designed to provide specific depreciation charges for particular years.

Although the actual farm system is unlikely to resemble exactly that in the plan (since most businesses are continually evolving, rather than stabilizing at a particular point), the normalized budget is valuable in giving an impression of the eventual worthwhileness of a long-term reorganization. It may also be used in the 'short-list and budget' method of choosing between alternative farm systems (Chapter 16), where the problem is too complex for partial budgets (Chapter 9) and limited time precludes the calculation of several fully detailed whole-business budgets. The exclusion of valuation changes and crop/financial year adjustments is particularly helpful in this respect.

Home Farm profit budget

Adam Haynes has completed his gross margin budget for the first year, using the procedures described above. You have already seen one of his budgeted gross margins (Figure 6.11): the rest follow, together with calculations of forage variable cost and depreciation on a 'pool' basis. The remaining fixed costs have been estimated on the basis of previous years' figures adjusted for expected increases. Note that the opening values of stocks, machinery and bank balance have been brought forward from Figure 1.1. If Adam's assumptions are correct, he

	Machinery and plant	Vehicles
	£	£
Opening value:	39,000	10,000
plus purchases	15,000	7,000
less sales	5,000	4,000
Sub-total	49,000	13,000
less depreciation @ 20%	9,800	2,600
Closing ('written-down') value	39,200	10,400

Figure 6.13   *'Pool' depreciation, diminishing balance method*

*That is, enterprise budgets/accounts based on time periods identical to the product on cycles of those enterprises (see Chapter 11).

Enterprise: *Spring barley* Ha or head? *12* Year *199x/9y*
Version *2*

Products:	Grain		Straw					
	Qty	£	Qty	£	Qty	£	Qty	£
Cash received								
Closing debtors								
−Opening debtors								
Sales								
Transfers out	42	3,780	26	390				
Benefits in kind								
Closing valuation	48	4,560	24	360				
−Opening valuation	−42	−3,780	−26	−390				
OUTPUT	48	4,560	24	360				

Inputs: *20.10.10*	Seed		Sprays		Casual lab		Other					
	Qty	£	Qty	£	Qty	£	Qty	£	£		£	£
Cash paid	5	575	1.5	400	1	360	1	100	120			
Closing creditors												
−Opening creditors												
Purchases	5	575	1.5	400	1	360	1	100	120			
Transfers in												
−Benefits in kind												
Opening valuation												
−Closing valuation												
VARIABLE COST	5	575	1.5	400	1	360	1	100	120			

MISCELLANEOUS VALUATION CHANGES	Breeding livestock		Crops in gd.	Total
	no.	£	£	£
Closing valuation				
−Opening valuation				
Valuation change				

Spring barley			GROSS MARGIN		
Ha or head 12	Total Quantity	Qty/ha or /head	£ per unit quantity	£ Total	£/ha or /head
Grain	48.0	4.00	95	4,560	380.00
Straw	24.0	2.00	15	360	30.00
Misc. valn. changes	xxxxxxx	xxxxxxxx	xxxxxxxx		
OUTPUT				4,920	410.00
VARIABLE COSTS	Total Quantity	Qty/ha or /head	£ per unit quantity	£ Total	£/ha or /head
20.10.10	5.0	0.42	115	575	47.92
Seed	1.5	0.12	267	400	33.33
Sprays	1.0	0.08	360	360	30.00
Casual lab	1.0	0.08	100	100	8.33
Other				120	10.00
VARIABLE COST				1,555	129.58
GROSS MARGIN				3,365	280.42

Figure 6.14 *Home Farm barley gross margin*

Enterprise: *Fattening pigs*   Ha or head? 1000   Year 199x/9y   Version 2

Products:	Bacon pigs					
	Qty	£	Qty	£	Qty	£
Cash received	1,060	66,780				
Closing debtors	90	5,670				
−Opening debtors	−100	−6,300				
Sales	1,050	66,150				
Transfers out						
Benefits in kind						
Closing valuation	500	22,500				
−Opening valuation	−550	−24,750				
OUTPUT	1,000	63,900				

Inputs:	Bought weaners		Conc. feed		Transport		Other		Vet/med, etc.		
	Qty	£	Qty	£	Qty	£	Qty	£	£	£	£
Cash paid	1,100	27,500	210	29,400	1		650		600	1,200	
Closing creditors			18	2,520							
−Opening creditors			−20	−2,800							
Purchases	1,100	27,500	208	29,120	1		650		600	1,200	
Transfers in											
−Benefits in kind											
Opening valuation											
−Closing valuation											
VARIABLE COST	1,100	27,500	208	29,120	1		650		600	1,200	

MISCELLANEOUS VALUATION CHANGES	Breeding livestock		Crops in gd.	Total
	no.	£	£	£
Closing valuation				
−Opening valuation				
Valuation change				

Fattening pigs			GROSS MARGIN		
Ha or head 1000	Total Quantity	Qty/ha or /head	£ per unit quantity	£ Total	£/ha or /head
Bacon pigs	1,000	1.00	64	63,900	63.90
Misc. valn. changes	xxxxxxxx	xxxxxxxx	xxxxxxxx		
OUTPUT				63,900	63.90

VARIABLE COSTS	Total Quantity	Qty/ha or /head	£ per unit quantity	£ Total	£/ha or /head
Bought weaners	1,100.0	1.10	25	27,500	27.50
Conc. feed	208.0	0.21	140	29,120	29.12
Transport	1.0	0.00	650	650	0.65
Other	1.0	0.00	600	600	0.60
Vet/med, etc.				1,200	1.20
VARIABLE COST				59,070	59.07
GROSS MARGIN				4,830	4.83

Figure 6.15 *Home Farm pig enterprise gross margin*

Enterprise: Culinary apples   *Ha or head?* 4   *Year* 199x/9y   *Version* 2

Products:	Apples					
	Qty	£	Qty	£	Qty	£
Cash received	100	23,000				
Closing debtors						
–Opening debtors						
Sales	100	23,000				
Transfers out						
Benefits in kind						
Closing valuation						
–Opening valuation						
OUTPUT	100	23,000				

Inputs:	Fertilizer		Sprays		Cas. lab.		Packaging/trans.				
	Qty	£	Qty	£	Qty	£	Qty	£	£	£	£
Cash paid	3	360	1	1,150	1	2,400	1	2,800			
Closing creditors											
–Opening creditors											
Purchases	3	360	1	1,150	1	2,400	1	2,800			
Transfers in											
–Benefits in kind											
Opening valuation											
–Closing valuation											
VARIABLE COST	3	360	1	1,150	1	2,400	1	2,800			

MISCELLANEOUS VALUATION CHANGES	Breeding livestock		Crops in gd.	Total
	no.	£	£	£
Closing valuation				
–Opening valuation				
Valuation change				

Culinary apples		GROSS MARGIN				
Ha or head	Total Quantity	Qty/ha or /head	£ per unit quantity	£ Total	£/ha or /head
4					
Apples	100.0	25.00	230	23,000	5749.99
Misc. valn. changes	xxxxxxxx	xxxxxxxx	xxxxxxxx		
OUTPUT				23,000	5,749.99

VARIABLE COSTS	Total Quantity	Qty/ha or /head	£ per unit quantity	£ Total	£/ha or /head
Fertilizer	3.0	0.75	120	360	90.00
Sprays	1.0	0.25	1,150	1,150	287.50
Cas. lab.	1.0	0.25	2,400	2,400	600.00
Packaging/trans.	1.0	0.25	2,800	2,800	700.00
VARIABLE COST				6,710	1,677.50
GROSS MARGIN				16,290	4,072.49

Figure 6.16 *Home Farm apple enterprise gross margin*

Enterprise: Forage　　　　　*Ha or head? 42*　　　　　*Year 199x/9y*
Version 2

Products:	Qty	£	Qty	£	Qty	£
Cash received						
Closing debtors						
−Opening debtors						
Sales						
Transfers out						
Benefits in kind						
Closing valuation						
−Opening valuation						
OUTPUT						

Inputs:	Ferts: 17:17:17		Ferts: 35% N		Ferts: 20:10:10		Seed		Sprays					
	Qty	£	Qty	£	Qty	£	Qty	£	Qty	£	Qty	£	Qty	£
Cash paid	21	2,835	13	1,495	7	805	0.4	200		420				
Closing creditors														
−Opening creditors														
Purchases	21	2,835	13	1,495	7	805	0.4	200		420				
Transfers in														
−Benefits in kind														
Opening valuation														
−Closing valuation														
VARIABLE COST	21	2,835	13	1,495	7	805	0.4	200		420				

MISCELLANEOUS VALUATION CHANGES	Breeding livestock		Crops in gd.	Total	
	no.	£	£	£	
Closing valuation					
−Opening valuation					
Valuation change					

Forage						
				GROSS MARGIN		
Ha or head 42	Total Quantity	Qty/ha or /head	£ per unit quantity	£ Total	£/ha or /head	
						There is no output in this case: the worksheet is used for calculation for variable costs only.
Misc. valn. changes	xxxxxxx	xxxxxxxx	xxxxxxxx			
OUTPUT						
VARIABLE COSTS	Total Quantity	Qty/ha or /head	£ per unit quantity	£ Total	£/ha or /head	
Ferts: 17:17:17	21.0	0.50	135	2,835	67.50	
Ferts: 35% N	13.0	0.31	115	1,495	35.60	
Ferts: 20:10:10	7.0	0.17	115	805	19.17	
Seed	0.4	0.01	500	200	4.76	
Sprays				420	10.00	
		Transferred to the dairy enterprise as a variable cost				
VARIABLE COST				5,755	137.02	
GROSS MARGIN				-5,755	-137.02	

Figure 6.17 *Home Farm forage variable costs*

	Per head or ha	Total	Total
Gross margins	£	£	£
Pigs	5	4,830	
Dairy	662	52,953	
Barley	280	3,365	
Apples	4,073	16,290	
			77,438
Unallocated revenue items			
Misc. trading receipts			2,650
Unallocated variable costs			
Contract muck-carting			848
TOTAL GROSS MARGIN			80,936
Fixed costs			
Regular labour			20,700
Machinery and vehicle running costs			15,400
Buildings and property repairs			200
Rent and rates			6,600
Misc. fixed costs:			8,600
LESS benefits in kind, input items			−4,650
TOTAL FIXED COSTS			46,850
NET PROFIT before depreciation and finance			34,086
Depreciation: machinery		9,800	
vehicles		2,600	
orchard		880	
NET PROFIT before finance costs			20,806
Finance costs: overdraft interest*		5,963	
loan interest		1,100	
leasing charges		2,100	
NET PROFIT after finance costs			11,643

*Calculated via the cash flow budget (Chapter 7)

Figure 6.18 *Home farm profit budget: financial summary* seems likely to achieve his profit objective of £10,000 per year: t remains to be seen whether his other goals are realistic.

Once you are sure you understand how the budget works, try producing your own gross margin budget for a farm you know or, failing that, a fictitious farm (perhaps one that you would like to own in the future!). Don't be too adventurous at first, though – stick to a simple system with a few straightforward enterprises.

Further reading

General

Berry, A. and Jarvis, R., *Accounting in a Business Context* (London, Chapman & Hall, 1991), chapter 17.

Bull, R.J., *Accounting in Business*, 6th edition (London, Butterworths, 1990), chapter 14.

Lucey, T., *Management Accounting* (Eastleigh, Hampshire, DP Publications, 1983). A cheap and very thorough text on all aspects of management accounting, including costing.

Rockley, L. E., *Finance for the Non-accountant*, 3rd edition (London, Business Books, 1979), pp. 23–40.

Agricultural

Atkinson, J. M., Hastings, M. R. and Warren, M. F., *Improving Farm Profits* (Agricultural Training Board/Seale Hayne College/Manpower Services Commission (The Family Farm Series), 1986, revised 1990).

Barnard, C. S. and Nix, J. S., *Farm Planning and Control*, 2nd edition (London, Cambridge University Press), pp. 45–7 (gross margins), 317–27 (complete budgets), 537–9 (full costings).

Giles, A. K., 'Net margins', *Farm Management*, vol. 6, no. 6, 1987.

Kerr, H. W. T., 'Management accounting and the marginal concept', *Farm Management*, vol. 6, no. 10, 1988.

Ministry of Agriculture, Fisheries and Food, *Definition of Terms Used in Agricultural Business Management*, Section 4 (Margin Terms) (1977).

$$\boxed{7}$$

A cash-flow budget for
the whole farm

Basic principles

It is not enough for Adam to prepare a budget to show the likely profits of his
business. In his situation as the new tenant of a busy mixed farm, and with little
spare cash, it is vital that he should estimate the likely effect of his plans on the flow
of cash into and out of the business. This he may do by means of a *cash-flow
budget*.

In compiling a cash-flow budget for a given year, Adam must estimate all the likely
cash receipts for that period (including capital and personal items) and deduct
from them all the cash payments. This will give him an estimate of the *net cash
flow* of the period or, in other words, it will show him how the bank balance of the
business is likely to be affected during the year. You will remember from Chapter
3 that if the bank balance at the beginning of the year is known, or can be
estimated, the bank balance at the end of the year can be calculated by adding the
net cash flow to the opening balance.

It is normal to break up the year for the purpose of budgeting, so as to give a net
cash flow and closing bank balance for each of the coming twelve months. Possible
alternatives are bi-monthly or quarterly divisions, but the use of these longer
intervals results in loss of precision and could lead for example to the overlooking
of a severe fluctuation in the bank balance within a particular quarter. The
monthly division has the further advantage that banks normally send statements to
their customers at monthly intervals. The significance of this in the monitoring of
cash flow is discussed in Chapter 10.

As well as a budget for each of the twelve months ahead, there should ideally be
outline budgets for the following two or three years; quarterly budgets will usually
suffice for this purpose. As with the profit budget, the cash-flow budget should be
'rolling' (see Figure 7.1). In the example of the 'basic' twelve-monthly budget, as
each half year passes, the equivalent half of the succeeding year should be
budgeted. By this means, the farmer always has at least six months' worth of
budget to guide him. Where cash control is particularly important, quarterly rebudgeting may be necessary.

72

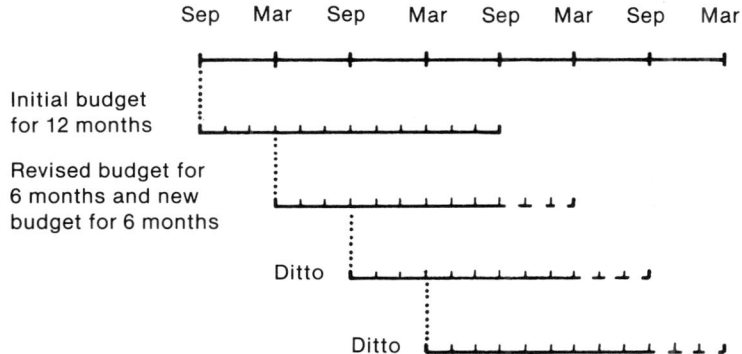

Figure 7.1 *'Rolling' cash-flow budget − graphical representation*

A simplified example of a twelve-monthly cash-flow budget is shown in Figure 7.2 (page 74) The net cash flow for each month is added to the opening bank balance for that month to give the closing bank balance. This is then carried to the next column as the opening bank balance for the succeeding month.

An important feature is the 'total' column. This performs two functions; first it provides a summary of the whole year's cash flow, and secondly it enables checking of the arithmetic. The latter works through calculation of the annual net cash flow. This may be found both from the total column (taking total payments from total receipts) and by deducting the opening bank balance for the year from the closing bank balance (since any change in the bank balance can be attributed to the net flow of cash into or out of the business). If, when the annual cash flow is calculated in both ways, the two figures are identical, the arithmetic is likely to be correct. If they are not, a mistake has been made somewhere, and must be found. The value of this check may not be obvious with respect to such a simple example, but will be readily appreciated on first contact with a full-blown farm budget.

The 'total' column in this example appears as the first of the columns. This ensures that the annual summary is adjacent to the category headings, and helps when reconciling with other budgest and interpreting the implications of the cash flow. Many prefer the 'total' column to be the last on the sheet: the choice is yours.

VAT and overdraft interest

The calculation of monthly net cash flows and bank balances is really very simple: the only possible difficulties are connected with Value Added Tax (VAT) and interest on overdraft, since calculation of each of these depends on the figures you put into the rest of the cash flow.

VAT is explained in more detail in Chapter 10. Briefly, certain types of product are taxed at a 'standard' rate of tax (17.5 per cent at the time of writing) and others at

CASH FLOW BUDGET	Year: 199x/9y		Version: 1									
% interest rate: 15	TOTAL	October	November	December	January	February	March	April	May	June	July	August	September

Receipts:	TOTAL	October	November	December	January	February	March	April	May	June	July	August	September
Milk	89,195	8,910	8,894	8,823	8,751	8,680	8,609	8,446	7,705	6,530	6,417	7,430	8,608
Cottage let	2,500							300	400	600	600	600	300
Machinery sales	5,000											5,000	
TOTAL	96,695	8,910	8,894	8,823	8,751	8,680	8,609	8,746	8,105	7,130	7,017	13,030	8,908

Payments:	TOTAL	October	November	December	January	February	March	April	May	June	July	August	September
Feed: cows	9,200	3,000		2,500		1,000		700				2,000	
Vet. and med.	4,800	500	700	600	600	400	300	200	500	300	300	400	500
Wages - permanent	36,000	4,000	3,000	3,000	3,000	3,000	4,000	3,000	3,000	3,000	3,000	4,000	4,000
Machinery purchase	51,000				30,000				1,000			20,000	
TOTAL	101,000	7,500	3,700	6,100	33,600	4,400	4,300	3,900	4,500	3,300	3,300	26,400	4,500
Net cash flow	-4,305	1,410	5,194	2,723	-24,849	4,280	4,309	4,846	3,605	3,830	3,717	-13,370	4,408
Opening balance	-8,000	-8,000	-6,590	-1,396	1,327	-23,522	-19,242	-14,933	-10,087	-6,482	-2,652	1,065	-13,370
Closing balance	-12,305	-6,590	-1,396	1,327	-23,522	-19,242	-14,933	-10,087	-6,482	-2,652	1,065	-12,305	-7,897

Figure 7.2 *Cash flow budget – outline example 1*

'zero rate' (meaning what it says − 0 per cent). Others are 'exempt', or outside the scope of VAT. If a business buys standard-rated inputs to produce standard- or zero-rated outputs, it is allowed to set the VAT it has paid on the inputs against the VAT it has collected on its outputs: the balance is forwarded to the Customs and Excise. Since most food products are zero-rated, the UK farmer tends to pay out more VAT on inputs than he collects on outputs, and therefore periodically claims a refund of the balance *from* the Customs and Excise.

Under this system the farmer is essentially a collector of tax: VAT has no net effect on the cash flow of the business. In most cases, therefore, it is sensible to ignore VAT in cash-flow budgeting, in the interests of simplicity. On the other hand, there is an inevitable delay between the payment of tax on inputs, and the refunding of that tax by the Customs and Excise. If the amounts are large and/or the delay long (if the farmer is only claiming refunds quarterly, for instance) this lag can seriously affect the bank balance.

In such cases, VAT can be incorporated by adding two further lines to the budget: in receipts, 'VAT charged on outputs' and 'VAT refunds'; and in payments, 'VAT paid on inputs' and 'VAT paid to Customs and Excise' (see Figure 7.3 overleaf). Outputs and inputs are entered into the budget in the normal way, net of VAT. Taking the column for the first month, add up the value of all the outputs on which VAT will be charged (starred in Figure 7.4) multiply by the percentage tax rate and enter the result under 'VAT charged'. Do the same for the standard-rate input items, entering the result under 'VAT paid on inputs'.

If the VAT charged is more than the VAT paid, the difference between the two will be the amount payable for that month to the Customs and Excise. If, as is more likely in farming, the VAT charged is *less* than that paid, the difference represents the refund due from the Customs and Excise. Where the farmer is claiming refunds monthly, this refund should be shown under 'VAT refunds' in the next month's column. Where a farmer is claiming quarterly, the balance has to be accumulated for the three months before the business's usual VAT assessment date, and then shown in the next month's column under 'VAT refunds'. This is the method used in Figure 7.3. All other examples in this book, however, leave VAT out of the budgets.

One of the important functions of a cash-flow budget is to give an estimate of likely overdraft interest payments − indeed in calculating profit as well as cash flow. This must be done after all the other figures have been included in the budget. The first step is to estimate an interest rate for the year, based on forecasts in the business pages of the 'quality' press, phone calls to your accountant and other sources. This can be converted to a monthly rate by dividing by 12 (a crude estimate, since it ignores compound interest, but erring on the cautious side). Thus if you feel you are likely to be paying 15 per cent interest per annum, the approximate monthly rate will be 1.25 per cent.

If the opening bank balance is negative (as in Figure 7.3), multiply it by the monthly rate (e.g. 1.25 per cent) and enter the result under 'overdraft interest' in the first month's column. Most banks charge interest monthly, one month in

CASH FLOW BUDGET	Year: 199x/9y			Version: 2								
% interest rate: 15	**TOTAL**	**October**	**November**	**December**	**January**	**February**	**March**	**April**	**May**	**June**	**July**	**August**	**September**

Receipts:	TOTAL	October	November	December	January	February	March	April	May	June	July	August	September
Milk	97,803	8,910	8,894	8,823	8,751	8,680	8,609	8,446	7,705	6,530	6,417	7,430	8608
Cottage let*	2,800							300	400	600	600	600	300
Machinery sales*	5,000											5,000	
VAT charged on outputs	1,365							53	70	105	105	980	53
VAT refunds from C.&E.	6,100		325			5,583			105			88	
TOTAL	113,068	8,910	9,219	8,823	8,751	14,263	8,609	8,799	8,280	7,235	7,122	14,098	8961

Payments:	TOTAL	October	November	December	January	February	March	April	May	June	July	August	September
Feed: cows	9,200	3,000		2,500		1,000		700				2,000	
Vet. and med.*	5,300	500	700	600	600	400	300	200	500	300	300	400	500
Wages - permanent	40,000	4,000	3,000	3,000	3,000	3,000	4,000	3,000	3,000	3,000	3,000	4,000	4,000
Overdraft interest	1,487	100	85	18		363	246	195	137	95	47	1	199
Machinery purchase*	51,000				30,000				1,000			20,000	
VAT paid on inputs	9,853	88	123	105	5,355	70	53	35	263	53	53	3,570	88
VAT paid to C.&E.													
TOTAL	116,839	7,688	3,907	6,223	38,955	4,833	4,598	4,130	4,900	3,447	3,400	29,971	4787
Net cash flow	-3,771	1,223	5,312	2,600	-30,204	9,429	4,011	4,668	3,380	3,788	3,722	-15,873	4174
Opening balance	-8,000	-8,000	-6,778	-1,466	1,134	-29,070	-19,641	-15,630	-10,962	-7,581	-3,794	-72	-15,945
Closing balance	-11,771	-6,778	-1,466	1,134	-29,070	-19,641	-15,630	-10,962	-7,581	-3,794	-72	-15,945	-11,771

Figure 7.3 *Cash flow budget – outline example 2*

CASH FLOW BUDGET		YEAR 99x/9y		VERSION	1 (1st try)									
% interest rate: 15		TOTAL	Oct	Nov	Dec	Jan	Feb	Mar	Apr	May	Jun	Jul	Aug	Sep
Receipts:														
Milk	1	72770	2280	3800	8550	10450	10070	8550	6650	6080	5700	5510	5130	3325
Calves	2	7400	500	3500	2000	1000	400							
Cull cows	3	11000										6600	4400	
	4													
Sheep	5													
	6													
Pigs	7	63000	6300	6300	3150	6300	6300	6300	6300	6300	3150	6300	6300	3780
	8													
Poultry	9													
	10													
Wheat	11													
Wheat straw	12													
Oats	13													
Apples	14	23000			10000	5000	5000	3000						
Potatoes	15													
	16													
	17													
Sundries	18	420				220				200				
VAT charged	19													
VAT refunds	20													
Capital: grants	21													
machinery sales	22	9000		4000		5000								
	£0													
Personal receipts	24	3200										3200		
TOTAL		189790	9080	17600	23700	27970	21770	17850	12950	12580	8850	21610	15830	9335

Figure 7.4 *Continued*

		TOTAL	Oct	Nov	Dec	Jan	Feb	Mar	Apr	May	Jun	Jul	Aug	Sep
	Payments:													
25	Feed: cows	12900	3750		3000	3750		1350				1050		
26	young stock													
27	pigs	29400	2800	14000					12600					
28														
29	Vet and med.: cows	2292	212	208	208	208	208	208	208	208	208	208	208	208
30	pigs	1100	100	100	100	100	100	100	100	100	100	100	100	100
31	L/stock purch.: cows	17500										10500	7000	
32	pigs	25000	2500	2500	1750	2500	2500	2500	1750	2500	2250	1750	2500	2500
33	Misc. dairy costs	2750	250	250	250	250	250	250	250	250	250	250	250	250
34	Misc. pig costs	1146	104	104	104	104	104	104	104	104	104	106	104	104
35	Seed	600						600						
36	Fertilizer	6070		6070										
37	Spray	1930								1930				
38	Misc. crop costs	2870	650	75	750	450	350	200	150	75	20		150	50
39	Wages: permanent	17875	1625	1625	1625	1625	1625	1625	1625	1625	1625	1625	1625	1625
40	casual	3700	1000	800	400	400	400	400	50	50	50	50	100	
41	Power: fuel	6360	540	540	540	740	540	540	550	540	740	550	540	540
42	repairs	6875	625	625	625	625	625	625	625	625	625	625	625	625
43	contract hire	600	300			300							300	400

	line	TOTAL												
Rent and rates	44	3300						3300						3300
Property repairs	45	200	200											
Overdraft interest	46	4320	1201					1565			1554		1554	1643
Loan interest	47	550	550					550						550
Hire purchase	48													
Leasing charges	49	2100	525	525			525			525			525	525
Overhead sundries	50	7975	1725	625	625	625	625	625	625	625	625	625	625	625
	51													
Capital: orchard	52	12000			6000			4000		2000				
machinery	53	22000	7000	15000										
capital repayment	54	8200	4100	4100		4100						4100		
Personal: drawings	56	11600	960	980	980	980	960	980	960	980	960	960	960	960
tax	57	3000		1500	1500							1500		
VAT paid	58													
TOTAL		214213	15741	37327	16238	35157	12812	17522	19597	10137	9111	23999	15612	13480
Net cash flow	59	-24423	-6661	-19727	7462	-7187	8958	328	-6647	2443	-261	-2389	218	-4145
Opening balance	60	-21000	-21000	-27661	-47388	-39926	-47113	-38155	-37827	-44474	-42031	-42292	-44681	-44463
Closing balance	61	-45423	-27661	-47388	-39926	-47113	-38155	-37827	-44474	-42031	-42292	-44681	-44463	-48608
Monthly interest		263	346	592	499	589	477	473	556	525	529	559	556	608

Figure 7.4 Cash flow budget (first try) for Home Farm

arrears, and this represents the interest due on the last month of the previous year. Now repeat the process using the closing balance of each month in turn: at the end of the year you will be left with the interest on the final month: this is a 'closing creditor' and will be paid in the first month of the following year.

Some bank accounts will have interest charged in the traditional manner: three months in arrears in September, December, March and June. In this case the monthly interest must be accumulated for a quarter before entering in each of these 'charging months'. This process is illustrated in the full budgets of Home Farm (e.g. Figure 7.4).

Cash-flow budgets in practice

A typical cash-flow budget (the one prepared by Adam Haynes for Home Farm) is shown in Figure 7.4. The most obvious difference between this and Figures 7.2 and 7.3 is the increase in detail and volume of figures: nevertheless, the calculation is exactly the same. To make things simpler, capital and personal receipts and payments have been separated from the trading items at the bottom of each of the relevant sections. This makes it easier to link the cash-flow budget with those for profit and capital: the trading items have all appeared already within the profit budget.

The choice of headings needs care. Compiling the budget, and checking it subsequently, are made very much easier if the headings used in the trading section of the cash-flow budget correspond to the categories used in the profit budget. This applies particularly to costs. Every effort should be made to ensure that variable costs and fixed costs are classified separately. Similarly the task of compiling a budgeted balance sheet and capital account is simplified by careful classification, so as to distinguish machine purchase from loan repayment, private drawings from tax payments, and so on.

An extra column headed 'actual' is often added for each month. This allows the budget to be used in 'control' of the business, by entry of the actual cash transactions for the month, and their comparison with the expected (i.e. budgeted) results (see Chapter 13).

There is no 'right' way to complete a cash-flow budget form, but the following may help:

1   A sensible starting point is a profit budget in gross margin form such as that described in the previous chapter. You can then go through each gross margin calculation in turn, and then the fixed costs, deciding when the various items of cost and output are likely to arise. Better still, a cash-flow assumption form can be drawn up, such as the example in Figure 7.5: as well as helping to organize your budgeting process, it gives you a valuable source of reference when you come to use the budget throughout the year. Best of all, it reduces the inevitable frustration when you are trying to locate errors by cross-checking between gross margins and cash flow, since all the assumptions are spelt out in detail rather than left in your head.

CASH FLOW ASSUMPTIONS

budget title: *Home farm – example entries*

year: *199x/9y*

version no: *1*

Item	Amount bought/sold	Price per unit (£)	Total rec'd/paid	Notes (including timings)
milk	400500 l.	0.19	76095	yields peaking Nov – Jan, v. low Aug–Oct. 1 month delay
calves	74	100	7400	5 Sep, 35 Oct, 20 Nov, 10 Jan, 4 Feb. 1 month delay
cull cows	20	550	11000	12 July, 8 Aug – paid same month
pigs	1050	63.6	66780	50 Nov, April and May – rest 100/month. 1 month delay
apples	100	230	23000	40 Nov, 20 Dec, Jan & Feb. 1 month's delay
machinery			9000	4000 Nov, 5000 Dec, 1 month delay. MF tractor, plough

Figure 7.5 *Cash flow assumption sheet*

2   Deciding the timing of trading items is helped considerably by a sound knowledge of agricultural husbandry. The pattern of milk sales from a dairy herd, for instance, cannot be projected without an understanding of lactation curves (whether that understanding derives from experience or from books). Similar considerations apply to items such as fertilizer purchases, lamb sales, and overtime payments. Chapters 17, 18 and 19, together with the milkflow spreadsheet in Appendix 5, may help in this respect.

3   When deciding on the allocation of receipts and payments between months, it is important to remember that many of the transactions are likely to be made on a credit basis, i.e. the bill will not be paid until two, three or more weeks after the goods or services have changed hands. Since we are concerned with the effect of transactions on the bank balance of the business, an item which is bought or sold on credit should be entered in the month following that in which the goods are expected to be delivered, or the services provided. For instance, the cost of a 10-tonne load of feed delivered in January, bought on normal trade credit terms, should be entered in the February column of the budget.

Occasionally a farmer may be able to obtain longer periods of credit (particularly for purchases of fertilizer) or be forced to give more than a month's credit himself. If this is anticipated, it should of course be allowed for in the budget.

4   Items bought or sold on credit in the last month of the financial year will not be paid for until the first month of the following year: these are the closing creditors and debtors referred to in Chapters 3 and 6. It helps to ensure consistency between the various budgets if these are noted in the right-hand margin of the cash-flow budget form.

Similarly, most businesses will have, at the beginning of the year, unpaid bills outstanding (i.e. opening creditors and debtors) which are likely to be settled in the first month of the year. Allowance must be made for this in the first column of the budget.

5   Although it is inevitable that in practice a farmer will use a combination of cheques and cash-in-hand when buying and selling, it is not worth making the distinction between the two when budgeting; assume that all cash changes hands via the bank. The alternative is to have a separate budget for petty cash (see Chapter 11) which adds much work and potential confusion for little benefit.

6   When calculating overdraft interest, remember to charge interest only on negative closing balances. Positive balances do not automatically attract interest, but if cash is siphoned off to a deposit account, it may be worth incorporating an 'interest received' heading in the 'receipts' section of the budget. The contents should be calculated in the same way as overdraft interest, but on positive closing balances and at a different (lower) monthly interest rate.

Interest on loans outstanding should be incorporated in the 'payments' section of the budget.

7   Do not calculate to the nearest penny — use your judgement as to how far to

round up or down. The larger the assumptions on which a figure is based, the more it should be rounded.

8   The cash-flow budget contains so many figures and involves so many additions and subtractions that it is almost inevitable that you will make errors or omissions in its construction. It is essential to use pencil throughout the budget, and to keep an eraser handy. It is no less important to check the budget at each stage, as described in the previous section, so that any slips may be spotted and remedied.

Reconciling cash flow and profit

Reference has been made in both this and the preceding chapter to the need for checks *within* the profit and cash-flow budgets. These checks can only verify the accuracy of calculation, however, and will not detect items that have been omitted, or wrongly included, in one or other of the budgets. One way of checking for such errors is to perform a *reconciliation* of cash flow with profit (see Figure 7.6 overleaf).

The aim of the reconciliation is to take the budgeted annual net cash flow and use it to arrive at a budgeted profit or loss. Reference to Chapter 3 will provide a reminder that profit differs from cash flow in including certain non-cash revenues and expenses, and excluding capital and personal receipts and payments. The reconciliation process may thus be summarized as:

Take annual net cash flow
Include non-cash revenue and expenses:
    Add increase (or deduct decrease) in the value of stocks
    Deduct depreciation
    Add closing debtors and opening creditors
    Add benefits in kind

Exclude capital, tax and personal items:
    Add back capital, tax and personal payments
    Deduct capital, tax and personal receipts

Gives budgeted net profit

The result will be a budgeted net profit or loss which *should* be identical to that given by the profit budget. If it is not, the two budgets must be checked, checked and checked again until the errors are found. It is important to approach this task methodically; perhaps the best way is to take the profit budget and work through it checking that each relevant item is included in the cash-flow budget, and ticking it off if the entry is correct.

This can be a dispiriting process, but it is essential if you (and the bank manager) are to have any confidence in your budgets. Some small consolation can be derived from the knowledge that it is rare for even the most accomplished practitioner to get his budgets to reconcile first time round.

		£
Take:	Annual net cash flow	−27,608
Add: (from cash flow budget)	Capital payments (such as machinery, loan repayments) Personal (such as drawings and tax)	42,200 14,600
and: (from profit budget)	Benefits in kind Closing valuation of stock Closing debtors Opening creditors	4,783 81,568 8,350 6,800
Sub-total		130,693
Then deduct: (from cash flow budget)	Capital injections Capital receipts (such as machinery sales receipt of loan)	−9,000 −3,200
And: (from profit budget)	Opening valuation of stock Opening debtors Closing creditors Depreciation (on machinery, buildings, etc.)	−78,970 −9,080 −5,520 −13,280
Gives:	Net profit after finance costs	11,643 √

Net Profit before finance costs (from profit budget)		20,806
Finance costs:	overdraft interest (from Figure 7.8) loan interest leasing charges	5,963 1,100 2,100
Net profit after finance costs		11,643 √

Figure 7.6 *Reconciliation of cash flow and profit, Home Farm*

It would be a mistake, having completed the calculations and checked for accuracy, to breathe a sigh of relief, put it away and get on with other jobs. The budget is a means to an end – a way of assessing cash needs over the next year and planning accordingly. It is something to be manipulated to test various possible actions and their effects on bank balances and interest payments: thus Adam Haynes's budget in Figure 7.5 has to be regarded as a 'first try' rather than a finished article.

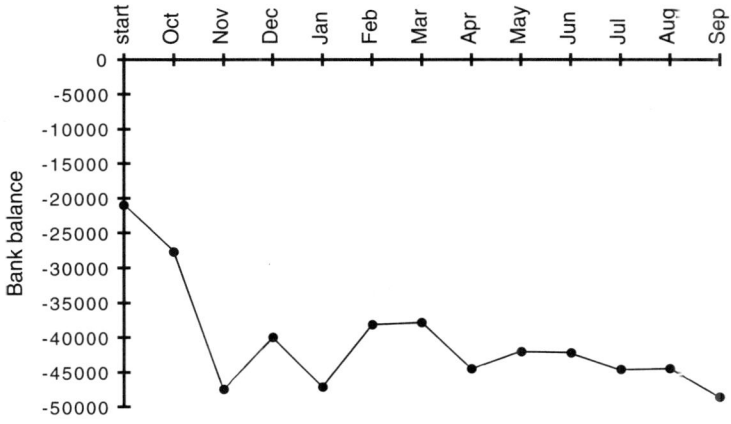

Figure 7.7 *Cash flow graphical profile (based on Figure 7.4)*

A graphical cash flow profile helps put Adam's budget into context (Figure 7.7). One of his objectives (Chapter 2) was to avoid an overdraft of more than £30,000: his bank manager has already indicated that he is not willing to offer a facility of more than £40,000, even with Adam's uncle acting as guarantor What can be done?

The cash-flow budget can be used to identify opportunities for action as well as highlighting problems. Those opportunities can be grouped under four headings:

Delaying payments   It may be possible to delay *purchase* of goods and services (such as machinery bought months earlier than needed in order to claim a discount). Another possibility is delaying *payment* by taking credit, either by the simple expedient of not paying bills on time, or by an alternative form of borrowing such as loan, lease purchase or finance lease.

Advancing receipts   Sales can often be brought forward, selling corn soon after harvest rather than storing it, for instance. Chasing slow payers will also help bring money in.

Boosting cash flow   Increasing cash flow through trading is not easy; you will probably have investigated the obvious opportunities already when you compiled the gross margin budget. This may, however, be the time to reconsider some of the actions you rejected at that stage; cutting labour costs, for instance, or getting rid of a favourite, but cash-hungry beef herd. The most fruitful, if uncomfortable areas are often capital and personal items: could private drawings be cut (the world cruise turned into a camping holiday in Cornwall), capital be injected from private funds, a pet investment project shelved? One of the biggest drains on many farm families is private school fees: is the local comprehensive *really* that bad?

Renegotiating   Many of the above suggestions have costs, financial and personal: lost discounts on early purchase, lost premium for out-of-season produce, credit charges, lost future rewards from long-term investment, reduced job satisfaction. If the cost of borrowing is outweighed by these other costs, the last alternative is to use the cash-flow budget in helping to persuade the bank manager to raise the overdraft limit. The budget allows such persuasion to take place well before the money is actually needed (rather than after the manager has discovered that the limit has been exceeded without his permission).

The above comments are set in the context of an overdraft. Many farmers have bank accounts in surplus for all or most of the year. Although the need for a budget is not quite so pressing here, it can still be invaluable in identifying opportunities for using that surplus: short-term fattening of store lambs over the winter months, for instance, or reducing future tax liability by buying new machines and buildings before the end of the financial year.

To illustrate the potential for reducing cash flow, Figure 7.8 (p. 87–9) takes the Home Farm 'first try' budget and adjusts it as follows:

1   Pig feed brought in smaller lots throughout the year, rather than in bulk and stored.
2   Fertilizer bought in March (when needed) rather than October. If it is *really* needed in October, the fertilizer company may be able to arrange long credit.
3   Machinery cut to £15,000 from £22,000 (and sales to £5000) by a mixture of buying second-hand and making do. Further savings might be possible by using contractors, and leasing would spread the costs.
4   Capital demands reduced by establishing only 1 hectare of new orchard this year, rather than the 4 hectares planned.
5   Apples sold in November rather than stored and sold later.
6   Private drawings cut by £200 per month. Adam will have to face the fact that at least at first he will have to relax his objective of £12,000 drawings a year in order to achieve the other objectives. He still won't be poverty-stricken, especially as his house, transport and some food come with the job.

The result is shown as a graph in Figure 7.9 (page 90). The closing bank balance just strays over £30,000 overdraft, and the interest cost is considerably reduced (by over £3000): this has in turn improved the projected profit (Figure 7.10, page 90). The worries have not evaporated: the balance heads steadily downwards in the last half of the year, and Adam will need outline budgets for the next two years for reassurance that the trend will reverse (more businesses fail in the second than in the first year of their lives). Nevertheless, the picture is far more healthy than that shown in the 'first try' budget.

In reality, many of these actions would incur costs such as loss of discounts. In order to maintain consistency with the gross margins in Chapter 6, these have not been built in to Figure 7.9. Partial budgets (see Chapter 9) can be used to test these effects in isolation, but in the end, both cash flow and profit budgets will have to be revised and reconciled. A computer spreadsheet (see Appendix 5) is ideally suited to this process, but even if you have only pencil and paper the effort is worth it.

CASH FLOW BUDGET YEAR '99x/9y VERSION 2 (revised)

% interest rate: 15

Receipts	#	TOTAL	Oct	Nov	Dec	Jan	Feb	Mar	Apr	May	Jun	Jul	Aug	Sep
Milk	1	72770	2280	3800	8550	10450	10070	8550	6650	6080	5700	5510	5130	3325
Calves	2	7400	500	3500	2000	1000	400							
Cull cows	3	11000										6600	4400	
Sheep	6													
Pigs	7	63000	6300	6300	3150	6300	6300	6300	6300	6300	3150	6300	6300	3780
Poultry	9													
Wheat	10													
Wheat straw	11													
Oats	12													
Apples	13													
Potatoes	14	23000			23000									
Sundries	18	420				220				200				2230
VAT charged	19													
VAT refunds	20													
Capital: grants	21													
machinery sales	22	5000				5000								
Personal receipts	24	3200										3200		
TOTAL		185790	9080	13600	36700	22970	16770	14850	12950	12580	8850	21610	15830	9335

Figure 7.8 Continued

			Oct	Nov	Dec	Jan	Feb	Mar	Apr	May	Jun	Jul	Aug	Sep
Payments:														
Feed: cows	25	12900	3750		3000	3750		1350				1050		
young stock	26													
pigs	27	26982	2800	2418	2420	2418	2418	2418	2418	2418	2418	2418	2418	2418
	28													
Vet and med.: cows	29	2292	212	208	208	208	208	208	208	208	208	208	208	208
pigs	30	1100	100	100	100	100	100	100	100	100	100	100	100	100
L/stock purch.: cows	31	17500										10500	7000	
pigs	32	25000	2500	2500	1750	2500	2500	2500	1750	2500	2250	1750	2500	2500
Misc. dairy costs	33	2750	250	250	250	250	250	250	250	250	250	250	250	250
Misc. pig costs	34	1146	104	104	104	104	104	104	104	104	104	106	104	104
Seed	35	600						600						
Fertilizer	36	6070						6070						
Spray	37	1930								1930				
Misc. crop costs	38	2870	650	75	750	450	350	200	150	75	20		150	50
Wages: permanent	39	17875	1625	1625	1625	1625	1625	1625	1625	1625	1625	1625	1625	1625
casual	40	3700	1000	800	400	400	400	400	50	50	50	50	100	
Power: fuel	41	6360	540	540	540	740	540	540	550	540	740	550	540	540
repairs	42	6875	625	625	625	625	625	625	625	625	625	625	625	625
contract hire	43	600				300							300	400

		TOTAL												
Rent and rates	44	3300						3300						3300
Property repairs	45	200	200											
Overdraft interest	46	2105	935					468			702			851
Loan interest	47	550	550					550						550
Hire purchase	48													
Leasing charges	49	2100	525					525		525			525	
Overhead sundries	50	7975	1725	625	625	625	625	625	625	625	625	625	625	
	51													
Capital: orchard	52	3000			1000	1000	1000							
machinery	53	15000				15000								
capital repayment	54	8200			4100						4100			
Personal: drawings	56	9120	760	760	760	760	760	760	760	760	760	760	760	760
tax	57	3000				1500							1500	
VAT paid	58													
TOTAL		191100	15541	12455	18192	32355	12030	23693	9215	12335	10477	26217	17830	14906
Net cash flow	59	-5310	-6461	1145	18508	-9385	4740	-8843	3735	245	-1627	-4607	-2000	-5571
Opening balance	60	-21000	-21000	-27461	-26316	-7808	-17193	-12453	-21296	-17561	-17316	-18943	-23550	-25550
Closing balance	61	-26310	-27461	-26316	-7808	-17193	-12453	-21296	-17561	-17316	-18943	-23550	-25550	-31121
Monthly interest		263	343	329	98	215	156	266	220	216	237	294	319	389

Figure 7.8 Cash flow budget (revised) for Home Farm

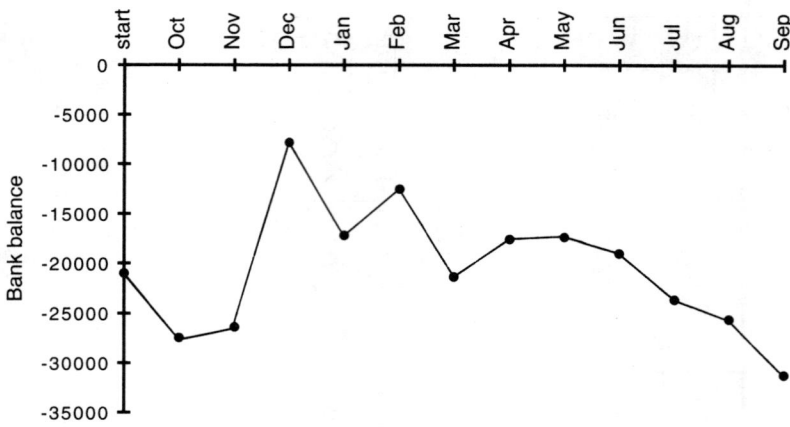

Figure 7.9   *Cash flow graphical profile – revised budget*

	£	£
NET PROFIT before depreciation and finance		34,086
Depreciation: machinery	9,800	
vehicles	2,000	
orchard	520	
NET PROFIT before finance costs		21,766
Finance costs: overdraft interest (from Figure 7.8)	2,956	
loan interest	1,100	
leasing charges	2,100	
NET PROFIT after finance costs		15,610

Figure 7.10   *Net profit adjusted for revised depreciation and overdraft interest*

Further reading

Atkinson, J. M., Hastings, M. R. and Warren, M. F., *Cash Flow Budgeting* (Agricultural Training Board/Seale Hayne College/Manpower Services Commission (The Family Farm Series), 1986, revised 1990). A step-by-step guide to cash-flow budgeting and monitoring.

A budgeted balance sheet

Compiling the budget

The principles of construction and interpretation of a balance sheet have been explained in Chapter 4 of this book. All that remains is to apply those principles to budgeted information.

Compared with other budgets, the budgeted balance sheet is usually easy to compile, since most, if not all of the information required is available from the profit and cash-flow budgets, or the preliminary work for those budgets.

In budgeting a closing balance sheet for a particular year, the likely level of cash surplus or overdraft is taken from the cash-flow budget. Debtors, creditors and stocks have been estimated in preparing the profit budget, and the written-down value of machinery and buildings derives from the depreciation calculations for that budget. Any repayments and/or extensions of hire-purchase, loans or other credit will be shown in the cash-flow budget, as will sales and purchases of land or investments.

Thus, as long as budgets for profit and cash flow are available for the year in question, budgeting a closing balance sheet* is straightforward. If a detailed cash flow budget is not available, an alternative is to use a projected flow of funds statement (see Chapter 4) together with a simple capital budget, i.e. a statement of the initial capital required. This is very much a second-best, but it is better than nothing.

As always, it is essential to 'prove' the accuracy of the calculation by drawing up a capital account, and checking repeatedly for mistakes if capital account and balance sheet disagree. It is a waste of time and effort to perform these checks in a blind fashion. Certain aspects of a balance sheet are more prone to error than others, and should be checked first. Among these are trade debtors and creditors (often given different values in profit budget and budgeted balance sheet); loan repayments (often allowed for in the balance sheet but not in the cash-flow budget, and vice versa); and written-down values of wasting assets, which can easily be miscalculated from the depreciation estimation.

It should also be checked that there has been no revaluation of assets without a

---

*It is often unnecessary specifically to budget opening balance sheets, since in a going concern they are given by the closing balance sheets of the previous years. In a new business the opening balance sheet refers to the present time, thus easing the task of valuation.

corresponding allowance for the 'holding gain' (see Chapter 21). Other points, such as the valuation of stocks, level of bank balance, payments of tax and personal drawings, are easily checked with profit and cash-flow budgets, respectively.

If the cause of the discrepancy has still not been found, there is little alternative but to embark on a full-scale check of all three budgets. Two facts should always be remembered: (a) that until the error is traced you cannot have complete confidence in your budgets (after all, a discrepancy of £10 could be the result of an error of £10,000 in one direction and an error of £10,010 in the other), and (b) that the error is not the result of some mysterious external influence, but lies somewhere within your calculations. It is up to you to find it.

A budgeted balance sheet for Home Farm

Figure 8.1 (overleaf) shows a budgeted balance sheet for Home Farm, based on the calculations of profit and cash flow in Chapter 6 and 7. The written-down values of vehicles and machinery have been adjusted to accommodate the reduced spending recommended in Chapter 7. Note that the capital account is shown here as part of the balance sheet: this is normal practice but remember that it is in fact a separate calculation to the balance sheet. The net capital given by the capital account matches that given by the balance sheet and is final confirmation that all the arithmetic is correct and that profit, cash-flow and balance sheet budgets reconcile.

What does the balance sheet show? The techniques of balance sheet analysis have been described in some detail in Chapter 4, and it is enough here to refer to the summary of the analysis shown in Figure 8.2 (page 94). On the positive side, the budgets anticipate an adequate, if not dramatic return on capital of 16.2 per cent, and a growth of 2.0 per cent in net capital – although this is rather lower than the UK rate of inflation at the time of writing. The percentage owned is likely to improve marginally, and gearing will fall markedly as a large loan repayment is made.

Neither of these ratios is very healthy, however, and the loan repayment will put pressure on the overdraft, with short-term ratios (liquidity and current) falling sharply as a result. This emphasizes even more the importance of planning and controlling cash flow in this business, and the need to increase profits to reduce borrowings. The fixed asset ratio is quite typical for tenanted dairy farms (refer to your local Farm Business Survey results) and will change little over the years.

The flow of funds analysis (Figure 8.3) shows trading providing nearly two-thirds of the cash flowing through the business during the year, with the overdraft providing the bulk of the rest. The resulting £33,320 is split between private uses, paying off part of the mortgage and investment in new assets. The latter should enable the business to be more profitable in future years, but in the short term Adam needs to look for other ways of increasing the cash generated by his business.

29/9/9X	Projected balance sheet at 28 September 199Y		
	Fixed assets:		
10,000	Orchard		12,480
39,000	Machinery and plant		39,200
10,000	Vehicles		8,000
50,050	Dairy herd		53,300
109,050	Fixed assets		112,980
	Current assets:		
	Stocks		
800	Trading livestock: calves	800	
24,750	Trading livestock: pigs	22,500	
3,780	Crops in store: barley grain	4,560	
390	Crops in store: barley straw	360	
8,484	Miscellaneous stores	9,332	37,552
9,080	Trade debtors		8,350
0	Cash in bank		0
0	Cash in hand		0
47,284	Current assets		45,902
	Current liabilities (due within one year):		
6,800	Trade creditors		5,520
21,000	Bank overdraft		31,121
27,800	Current liabilities		36,641
19,484	Net current assets		9,261
128,534	Total assets less current liabilities		122,241
	Creditors due after one year:		
34,000	Mortgage		25,800
	Capital account:		
	Opening net capital	94,534	
	+net profit	15,610	
	+capital injections	3,200	
	−private drawings	−9,120	
	−income and capital tax	−3,000	
	−benefits in kind	−4,783	
94,534	Closing net capital	96,441	96,441
128,534			122,241

Figure 8.1 *Projected balance sheet for Home Farm*

Ratio analysis	Opening	Closing
	%	%
Percentage owned	60.5	60.7
Gearing	36.0	26.8
Acid-test ratio	32.7	22.8
Current ratio	170.1	125.3
Fixed asset ratio	69.8	71.1
Return on net capital		16.2
Growth in net capital		2.0
Growth in assets		1.6
Growth in liabilities		1.0

Figure 8.2 *Ratio analysis for revised projected balance sheet*

FLOW OF FUNDS ANALYSIS			£
SOURCES:	NET PROFIT (LOSS)		15,610
	Depreciation (+)		12,320
	Change in debtors (increase -, decrease +)		730
	Change in creditors (increase +, decrease -)		-1,280
	Valuations (increase -, decrease +)		-2,598
	Benefits in kind (-)		-4,783
CASH FROM TRADING			19,999
ADD:	Capital introduced		3,200
	Sale of land, property, investments		0
	Increase in overdraft		10,121
	Increase in loans		0
	Reduction in cash balances		0
CASH FROM OTHER SOURCES			13,321
	TOTAL CASH AVAILABLE		33,320
USES:	COMMITMENTS		
	Private drawings		9,120
	Tax payments		3,000
	Reduction in loans		8,200
TOTAL COMMITMENTS			20,320
ADD:	Purchase of land, property, investments		0
	Net purchase of buildings		3,000
	Purchase of machinery	15,000	
	Less sale of machinery	-5,000	10,000
	Repayment of overdraft		0
	Increase in cash balances		0
			13,000
TOTAL CASH USED			33,320

Figure 8.3 *Home Farm — flow of funds analysis for revised budget*

Further reading

Atkinson, J. M., Hastings, M. R. and Warren, M. F., *Using your Accounts* (Agricultural Training Board/Seale Hayne College/Manpower Services Commission (The Family Farm Series), 1986, revised 1990).

Barnard, C. S. and Nix, J. S., *Farm Planning and Control*, 2nd edition (London, Cambridge University Press, 1979), pp. 542–51.

Berry, A. and Jarvis, R., *Accounting in a Business Context* (London, Chapman & Hall, 1991), chapter 3.

Bull, R. J., *Accounting in Business*, 6th edition (London, Butterworths, 1990), chapter 2.

Griffis, D., 'Classifying businesses according to their financial health', *Farm Management*, vol. 6, no. 12. A valuable, and now widely-used 'short-hand' analysis of the vulnerability of a farm business.

Shepherd, C. G., 'An analysis of performance by size, type and form of ownership of farms', unpublished Diploma in Farm Management project report, Seale Hayne Faculty, Polytechnic South West, 1991.

Warren, M. F. and Pierpoint, P. R., 'Vulnerability of farm businesses in the far South West of England', *Farm Management*, vol. 7, no. 12.

9

Budgeting for partial change

Introduction

Up to now, we have been concerned with preparing budgets for the whole business. There are times, however, when whole-business budgets are too cumbersome for the problem under consideration. What is needed is a simpler form of budget which may be used to assess the potential financial effect of *partial* changes.

Various types of partial change can be identified. They include expansion of the business (such as the purchase of a few more hectares of land); changes within enterprises (such as changes of variety or breed, and changes in the type or quantity of inputs used); changes in the enterprise mix (such as the substitution of beef for dairy); and changes in items of fixed cost. Related to the latter are changes in the financing of the business.

Although such changes are termed 'partial', to distinguish them from those which influence every aspect of the business, they can have considerable effects on the financial health of the business. Therefore it is vital to have some mechanism for assessing these effects. As always, we are concerned with three financial indicators: profit, cash flow, and capital. The budgets used in this assessment are known collectively as *partial budgets*.

Partial budgets

Partial budget principles

A partial budget is concerned only with those financial items which change as an outcome of a particular decision. Those items may be classified into four groups:

1   Extra returns.
2   Costs saved.
3   Extra costs.
4   Returns lost.

The partial budget is simply a device whereby (1) and (2) may be set against (3) and (4). If the resulting balance is in favour of (1) and (2), the proposed change is likely to be worthwhile. This is a direct application of the principle of opportunity cost (see Appendix 1): testing one course of action by comparing the profit it generates with that lost by not following an alternative course.

The partial budget may be used in two related ways. It may first be used to test the effects on the whole-business budgets of an alternative to the plan embodied in those budgets. Several such alternatives may be under test, resulting in a 'central' whole-business budget with a series of 'satellite' partial budgets, thus avoiding the effort of preparing a new set of whole-business budgets for each alternative to the central plan. An example of this would be where the central budgets included forage maize in the cropping, but where the farmer wished to check the potential of lucerne as an alternative.

The second way of using a partial budget is a means of testing individual decisions in isolation, where there is insufficient time and/or need for the compilation of whole-business budgets. An example of this is the decision on whether or not to sell corn straight off the combine, or to store it in the hope of higher prices later in the year. Another is the decision on whether to employ a contractor for a particular job, or to use one's own labour and machinery. The partial budget's simplicity and suitability for rapid calculations make it ideal for such circumstances.

Ideally, both methods should be used – the latter as an initial screening device to see whether a change is worthwhile in itself; the former as a device for adjusting the central budgets once a change has passed the screening.

Partial profit budgets

The most common, and most useful form of partial budget is the partial profit budget. Once this has been calculated, it is usually easy to see the potential effects of the decision on cash flow and capital. An example of the conventional layout of a partial profit budget is shown in Figure 9.1 (overleaf).

It is important that the budget should begin with a clear statement of the decision under consideration, to ensure that one never loses sight of the main issues. As in the whole-business budget, all items should be specified in full physical and financial detail where possible.

Items that will not be affected by the change should not be included Particular care is needed with items of fixed cost, since in many circumstances a change in the intensity of use of these items does not result in a change in the cost to the business. In the example shown, depreciation of the grain store is not a cost saved, since the building is still owned by the business, even though it may be unused. Similar arguments often apply to regular labour and machinery depreciation; saving the labour of a quarter of a man (or tractor) may result in little cash saving if the man (or tractor) must still be employed to perform the other three-quarters of the work. Significant benefit will arise only if the released labour or machinery can be put to profitable use elsewhere (i.e. has a high opportunity cost).

Some types of decision, such as enterprise substitutions, are more conveniently dealt with by using the gross margin format illustrated in Figure 9.2 (overleaf). This method is economical of effort, and allows clear discrimination between variable and fixed costs. There is a danger of losing sight of the original assumptions underlying the gross margins, however, unless these assumptions are recorded separately.

Whether the conventional or the gross margin form of budget is used, the contents will depend to a certain extent on the way it is to be used. If it is to be used as a

Costs of change	£	Benefits of change	£
Revenue lost		*Extra revenue*	
Barley grain: 4t/ha @ £95	4,560	Lambs: 1.5/ewe @ £45/lamb	12,150
Barley straw: 2t/ha @ £15	360	Ewe premium @ £12/ewe	2,160
		Wool: £3/ewe	540
		Cull ewes @ 25% @ £30	1,350
		Cull rams: 2/year @ 35	70
Sub-total	4,920	*Sub-total*	16,270
Extra costs		*Costs saved*	
Replt. ewes: 30% @ £75	4,050	Seed: 0.13t/ha @ £267/t	400
Replt. rams: 2/year @ 250	500	Fertilizer: 0.42t/ha @ £115/t	575
Feed: 65 kg @ £150/t	1,755	Sprays: £30/ha	360
Vet. and med.: £4/ewe	720	Misc.: £10/ha	120
Misc.: £3/ewe	540	Machinery running costs	900
Extra forage costs	500	Casual labour, harvest	100
Depreciation of building		Overtime	200
£2,000 over 10 years	200	Combine depreciation	
Extra labour		(£3,000 @ 20%)	600
(casual and overtime)	700		
Sub-total	8,965	*Sub-total*	3,255
TOTAL COSTS	13,885	TOTAL BENEFITS	19,525
EXTRA PROFIT before interest	5,640		

Decision   Eliminate 12 ha spring barley, introduce 180-ewe breeding flock.
Housing alterations £2,000.

Figure 9.1   *Partial budget for sheep flock, Home Farm — normalized year*

Costs of change	£	Benefits of change	£
Gross margin lost		*Gross margin gained*	
12 ha spring barley @ £280.4	3,364	180 ewes @ £45.6	8,204
Sub-total	3,364	*Sub-total*	8,204
Extra fixed costs		*Fixed costs saved*	
Depreciation of building		Overtime	200
£2,000 over 10 years	200	Combine depreciation	
Extra labour		(£3,000 @ 20%)	600
(casual and overtime)	700	Machinery running costs	900
Sub-total	900	*Sub-total*	1,700
TOTAL	4,264	TOTAL	9,904
EXTRA PROFIT before interest	5,640		

Decision   Eliminate 12 ha spring barley, introduce 180-ewe breeding flock.
Housing alterations £2,000.

Figure 9.2   *Partial budget in gross margin form*

'satellite' to the central budget, it will be concerned with the specific year covered by the latter. (The exception is where the central budget itself relates to a 'normalized' year.)

In this case, the items included in the partial budget should be calculated as in the central profit budget, using the same depreciation rates and methods, including the full cost of livestock purchases, and allowing for changes in stock values over the year. Interest charges can be estimated from a partial cash-flow budget (see below) but if this is not available, they may be calculated on the initial extra capital (fixed and working) required for the proposed change. (If the change results in a system of lower capital intensity, this may be a cost saved rather than an extra cost.) Purchases of non-wasting assets, such as land, are not of course shown in a budget concerned with net profit; nor are changes in personal or tax items.

If, on the other hand, the partial budget is used as an initial screening device, it is more appropriate to look at a typical or normalized year. This implies using annual average extra costs and benefits. Thus an increase in the number of breeding livestock should be represented by an increase in herd depreciation rather than the full cost of purchase. Depreciation of wasting assets should be calculated by the straight-line method, since diminishing-balance depreciation relates to particular years. All other prices and quantities should be those you would expect in a typical year. Figures 9.1 and 9.2 use this form.

One of three methods can be used to account for changes in the capital employed when compiling a normalized budget. The first is to charge interest on the borrowed capital employed, at the anticipated interest rate. This gives rise to problems of determining just how much of the extra capital is likely to be borrowed. More importantly, it does not cater for differences in the use of the farmer's own capital, which has an opportunity cost.

The second alternative is to include a charge which represents the opportunity cost of *all* the extra capital employed (own and borrowed). The appropriate percentage rate is applied to the extra capital employed, including working capital. Estimation of the extra capital employed is not too difficult, but the estimation of the farmer's opportunity cost of capital is more tricky.

The third, and perhaps neatest solution is to exclude charges for the use of capital from the partial budget, and then use the result to calculate the marginal rate of return on the capital invested. The result may then be compared to the potential rate of return from other uses of the capital (i.e. its opportunity cost) in order to decide whether or not to commit the capital.

All three methods are discussed in Chapter 19 ('Capital Planning'). Figure 9.4 illustrates the second and third approaches, taking the opportunity cost of borrowing to be the interest rate on the overdraft which, in Adam's case, would be used to finance any new venture (i.e. 15 per cent).

Net capital invested includes both fixed and working capital. Fixed capital is easy to understand, being the money invested in items such as buildings, machinery and livestock. Working capital is the money needed to pay the accumulating running costs until cash starts flowing in to offset them. Thus the business would have to finance the costs of sheep production for a year before seeing a return. In the case of the caravan site, Adam expects his first takings about 4 months after starting to incur running costs such as advertising. Set against the extra capital required is the capital that may be released by discontinuing the previous production: thus there is a combine harvester to sell when the barley enterprise is disposed of, and working capital set free when there are no barley running costs to finance any more.

The calculations use 'initial capital', in other words, the total amount invested at the start of the project. It could be argued that since the budgets deal with 'normalized' years, 'average capital' should be used, making allowance for the fact that borrowed money will be paid off steadily (interest calculation) or for the declining value of the assets over the years (return on capital). Apart from the assumption about paying back borrowed money being usually fallacious, the use of average capital tends to give more optimistic results than other more sophisticated methods such as discounted cash flow (see Chapter 19). Use of initial capital errs on the pessimistic side, which is much safer and goes some way to counteract the over-optimism usually built in elsewhere in the budget.

Partial profit budgets for Home Farm

In the previous chapter, it was concluded that Adam should look for ways of improving profitability. The partial budget is ideal for this use, and Figures 9.1 to 9.4 investigate two such possibilities. The initial impression from Figures 9.1 and 9.3 is that the caravan site would be the most profitable. When an estimate of the

Decision Reduce spring barley by 4 ha for 50-van touring caravan site. Works cost £30,000			
Costs of change		*Benefits of change*	
Revenue lost	£	*Extra revenue*	£
Barley grain: 4t/ha @ £95	1,520	50 vans x 120 nights x 60%	
Barley straw: 2t/ha @ £15	120	x £4 per night	14,400
Sub-total	1,640	*Sub-total*	14,400
Extra costs		*Costs saved*	
Running costs: casual labour	800	Seed: 0.13t/ha @ £267/t	139
publicity	2,000	Fertilizer: 0.42t/ha @ £115/t	193
other	500	Sprays: £30/ha	120
Depreciation on initial costs		Misc.: £10/ha	40
over 10 years	3,000	Machinery running costs	200
		Casual labour, harvest	20
		Overtime	80
Sub-total	6,300	*Sub-total*	792
TOTAL COSTS	7,940	TOTAL BENEFITS	15,192
EXTRA PROFIT before interest	7,252		

Figure 9.3 *Partial budget for caravan site, Home Farm – normalized year*

Introduction of sheep flock (Figure 9.1)		
Initial capital:		£
Fixed:	building	2,000
	purchase of livestock	14,500
	less: sale of combine harvester	-3,000
Working:	1 year sheep costs (excluding	
	depreciation and livestock purchase)	4,215
	LESS barley costs over half a year	
	(excluding depreciation) [2,655/2]	-1,328
	TOTAL	20,715
Interest on initial capital @ 15%		3,107
Extra profit after interest (5,640–2458)		2,533
Return on marginal capital (5,640 as a percentage of 16,388)		34%

Introduction of caravan site (Figure 9.3)		
Initial capital:		
fixed:	building and works	30,000
working:	running costs over 4 months	
	(excluding depreciation) [3300/3]	1,100
	LESS barley costs over half a year	-396
	TOTAL	31,100
Interest on initial capital @ 15%		4,665
Extra profit after interest (7,252–4,606)		2,587
Return on marginal capital (7,252 as a percentage of 30,704)		23%

Figure 9.4 *Allowing for capital effects in partial budgets*

interest cost is included, though, the sheep enterprise emerges as the better of the two (Figure 9.4). Each has a return on capital greater than the interest rate, but that of the sheep flock is significantly greater.

The decision cannot rest solely on these budgets. Every budget is subject to the risk that the estimated figures used will turn out to be wrong, and this is especially so when investigating new projects. Adam thus needs to quantify this risk, and make sure that his business can withstand the worst outcome (see Chapter 20).

Secondly, he needs to allow for the 'hassle factor'. The budgets deal with financial matters, and cannot accommodate the likely upheaval in the organization of the farm, and the effect on the personal lives of himself, family and employees. A caravan site involves the intrusion of other people and their demands which, while many farmers enjoy the company, can cause considerable stress. A sheep flock creates seasonal demands, especially at lambing time, which can ruin family life. These and other similar effects, good and bad, need to be weighed against the financial consequences.

Finally, the change will affect cash flow and capital, particularly at the beginning when the project is getting under way. In this case, it needs little examination to realize that each of the projects would put unwarranted strain on the business. Potentially they are worthwhile developments, but require cash injections that would put the business at risk.

Decision Get rid of Home Farm pig herd. Use cottage for self-catering holiday lets			
Costs of change		*Benefits of change*	
Gross margin lost	£	*Gross margin gained*	£
1,000 fattening pigs @ £4.83	4,830	Use of cottage for holiday accommodation (15 weeks @ £200/wk less maintenance and cleaning £500)	2,500
Sub-total	4,830	*Sub-total*	2,500
Extra fixed costs		*Fixed costs saved*	
Depreciation of cottage furniture and fittings (£3,000 over 5 years)	600	Labour: 1 man	10,000
		Electricity and fuels	500
		Misc. fixed costs	600
Sub-total	600	*Sub-total*	11,100
TOTAL	5,430	TOTAL	13,600
EXTRA PROFIT before interest	8,170		

Figure 9.5 *Partial budget for elimination of pig herd: normalized year*

Other projects may not be so clear-cut, though. Figure 9.5 looks at the possibility of getting rid of the pig herd – a profitable opportunity, though with the unpleasant prospect of making a man redundant. Ideally, in order to see whether the change would release enough money to make a significant effect on the overdraft, the cash-flow budget for the business should be reworked. If available, a computer spreadsheet makes this a relatively easy task but a useful short cut is a partial cash-flow budget (Figure 9.6).

The principle of the partial cash-flow budget is the same as that of the partial profit budget, except that only cash items are included, and that it is divided up to show the effect of the change on monthly (or quarterly) patterns of cash flow. Balancing

PARTIAL CASH FLOW BUDGET

Decision: get rid of pig herd plus 1 man, and use cottage for holiday lets

Extra receipts	Total	Oct	Nov	Dec	Jan	Feb	Mar	Apr	May	Jun	Jul	Aug	Sep
Cottage rent	3,000									500	1,000	1,200	300
Payments saved													
Livestock purchase	25,000		2,500	1,750	2,500	2,500	2,500	1,750	2,500	2,250	1,750	2,500	2,500
Concentrate feed	19,344					2,418	2,418	2,418	2,418	2,418	2,418	2,418	2,418
Misc. pig costs	984		20	50	80	104	104	104	104	104	106	104	104
Vet. and med.	950		20	50	80	100	100	100	100	100	100	100	100
Labour	6,664					833	833	833	833	833	833	833	833
Electricity and fuel	320					40	40	40	40	40	40	40	40
Misc. fixed costs	400					50	50	50	50	50	50	50	50
Sub-total (a)	56,662		2,540	1,850	2,660	6,045	6,045	5,295	6,045	6,295	6,297	7,245	6,345

Extra payments	Total	Oct	Nov	Dec	Jan	Feb	Mar	Apr	May	Jun	Jul	Aug	Sep
Cottage maintenance	500								40	80	150	200	30
Cottage furnishing	3,000						1,000	1,000	1,000				
Receipts lost													
Sale of pigs	44,730					6,300	6,300	6,300	6,300	3,150	6,300	6,300	3,780
Sub-total (b)	48,230					6,300	7,300	7,300	7,340	3,230	6,450	6,500	3,810
Effect on net cash flow before interest (a-b)	8,432		2,540	1,850	2,660	-255	-1,255	-2,005	-1,295	3,065	-153	745	2,535

Figure 9.6 *Partial cash flow budget for initial year*

extra cash receipts and cash payments saved against extra cash payments and cash receipts lost gives the effect of the change on net cash flow (before interest is taken into account). This can be related to the central cash-flow budget to indicate the effect of the change on the closing bank balances for each month. If the results are favourable and the project adopted, the central cash-flow budget should be amended accordingly.

In Figure 9.6, the effect of working capital released has an immediate effect through savings in livestock purchase, gathering momentum as more costs such as feed can be saved. The loss of sales from January onwards is partly balanced by savings in wages. The net result in the first year is a saving of over £8000, with the prospect of more in susequent years.

Effect of partial change on capital

Partial budgeting principles are not appropriate to capital calculations, since one is here assessing a stock of wealth rather than a flow of income. Measuring the effect of a partial change on the capital structure of a business is a matter of drawing up a new balance sheet in the light of the partial profit budget, and, if available, the partial cash-flow budget. Such calculations are applicable only where budgets are used to examine the effects of change in a particular year, since a balance sheet shows net capital at a specific point in time.

Further reading

Atkinson, J. M., Hastings, M. R. and Warren, M. F., *Improving Farm Profits* (Agricultural Training Board/Seale Hayne College/Manpower Services Commission (The Family Farm Series) 1986, revised 1990), section 7: 'Making a partial budget'.
Barnard, C. S. and Nix, J. S., *Farm Planning and Control*, 2nd edition (London, Cambridge University Press, 1979), pp. 315–17.

PART THREE

Financial History

So far we have been looking to the future. It would be most unwise to neglect the past, however, and every business needs a means of recording historical information.

A farmer will wish to retain information for four reasons. The first is that history can be a valuable guide to the future – one can learn from past mistakes and make corresponding adjustments when budgeting. The second is that effective control of the business is impossible without records of actual performance to compare with the performance that was originally expected. Thirdly, he is required by law to retain certain information, ranging from gun licences to VAT records. Finally, he may like to keep some information for pure enjoyment: a machinery catalogue, for instance, can afford hours of pleasure even if the farmer has no intention of buying any of the items shown.

The following chapters deal with the recording of the three main financial indicators, starting with cash flow (since the calculation of historic profit and net capital is based on records of cash transactions). A separate chapter is devoted to the supporting or 'back-up' records, in recognition of their importance both as a basis for the main financial records and as management tools in their own right.

10

Recording cash flow

Designing a cash recording system

General considerations

A recording system of any sort, whether for cash, profit, capital or physical records, must have two characteristics. These are that it should be as easy as possible to:

1   Store the information.
2   Retrieve the information from its storage and use it effectively.

These characteristics tend to work against each other, of course. The easiest way of storing information is to throw everything into a huge box, but this would make retrieval of a particular document somewhat difficult. It is worth a great deal of effort when setting up recording systems to find the 'right' compromise for the business concerned and for the person(s) who will be making use of them.

Recording the cash flow of a business implies recording all cash transactions between the business and the 'outside world'. For such records to be used effectively in planning and control, they should ideally be stored in such a way that comparisons may easily be made between historic and budgeted cash flows, and that profit and loss accounts may easily be prepared in gross margin form. They should also provide the information required to meet the legal obligations of the business, especially, in the UK, with respect to VAT and Income (or Corporation) Tax. A business registered for VAT is obliged to submit returns to the Customs and Excise to show the VAT paid and received, etc. All businesses are required to submit accounts to the Inland Revenue for Income/Corporation Tax purposes.

A method of recording is thus needed which is relatively easy to keep up to date and also allows the grouping of transactions in such a way as to ease the task of interpretation by the manager and accountant.

The simplest form of grouping or classification is by the use of a code. Transactions are listed in a cash book, receipts on one page and payments on another. Each type of transaction is given a code, which is recorded in a column alongside each entry. The code 'M' might refer to milk sales, and 'G' to grain sales, for instance. The main codes could be subdivided: 'GW' might be wheat grain sales, 'GB' barley grain sales. A similar system would be used for payments.

Another method of classification is the use of columns. As well as the main lists of transactions and the amounts involved, subsidiary columns are used to collect together similar types of payment and receipt. Thus there could be a column for milk sales, another for grain sales, and so on. On the payment page, columns could be used to distinguish fertilizer purchases from livestock purchases, wages, and other types of payment.

A third means of grouping transactions is by using separate account book pages, or even a separate file, for each type of goods or service.

Selecting the method

In choosing between these methods of book-keeping, the farmer should bear in mind the two fundamental design criteria. Where *ease of entry* is concerned, he will like the simple coding best, since it involves only two lists of numbers, one for receipts and one for payments. The only slight complication is the need to look up the code for each entry.

The next favoured is likely to be the column analysis, since although the main amounts have to be split between columns, and there are several columns of numbers to add up on each page, they are at least all visible on the one page.

The least popular, from the point of view of ease of entry, is likely to be the page by page analysis, where before an entry can be made, the appropriate page must be found. This can be a tedious process if several different types of transaction need recording.

When looking at *ease of retrieval* of the information, it is more difficult to predict opinions. Preferences will here depend largely on the number of transactions, which in turn depends on the size and type of farm. The simple coding system is least easy to use for recovery of information. Particular difficulties arise where a single payment is made in respect of several different items (such as settlement of a merchant's account in respect of fertilizers, feeds and baler twine). Great care is necessary when coding, since the scope for error is large. On the other hand, where the number of transactions is relatively small, these difficulties may be outweighed by the simplicity of the system.

If a very large volume of transactions is expected, classification by page provides the easiest retrieval of information. The most common form of book-keeping (the 'double-entry' method) is of this form. It can be expanded to cope with any volume of business, since the pages can be split between any number of clerks, each responsible for a particular set of pages, or 'accounts'. It incorporates an automatic record of debtors and creditors, which is valuable where the bulk of the trade is on a credit basis. It is also relatively easy to adapt to mechanical or electronic data processing systems.

The flexibility of the double-entry system has made it the first choice of book-keeping methods for commercial and manufacturing businesses for several hundred years. Where a farm business, because of size and/or type of production, generates a large volume of transactions, double-entry book-keeping will be essential.

The needs of most farm businesses, however, are such that their owners find that the analysis column is the most suitable. While the volume of transactions in a typical farm business is too great to allow reliance on a simple coding system, it is insufficient to warrant the extra effort involved in keeping a double-entry system. Nor is the number of credit transactions likely to be large enough for the in-built debtor/creditor recording of the double-entry system to be much of an advantage.

The balance between effort and benefit is dramtically changed if a computer can be used for financial recording. A well-designed and properly set up double-entry accounts program can be easier to operate than a cash analysis book, producing a greater quantity of information in a more useful form. Even a simple spreadsheet can be used to very good effect with a column or coding system. Since only a small proportion of farms in the UK (and even in the USA) own and use computers, however, this chapter concentrates on manual systems, and particularly the column, or *cash analysis* method.

The cash analysis system

Choosing column headings

The first step in establishing a cash analysis system is to buy a *cash analysis book* (CAB). Each page of a CAB includes, on the left-hand side, a broad column for a description of each transaction entered. To the right of this are two thin columns for recording the date of each transaction, and the number of the cheque or paying-in slip concerned. The rest of the page is taken up with a large number of analysis columns. Some publishers produce special farmers' account books where each of these columns has been given a heading. In most cases, however, it is better to choose your own headings to suit your own farm and system of management accounting. A loose-leaf format adds versatility and allows pages to be sent to the accountant while the book itself is retained for continuing use. A good example of a book in this form is the Records Book produced by the NFU and ADAS.

In choosing the headings, it is essential to refer back to the way in which the information is eventually to be used. The legal obligations are fairly easily satisfied by ensuring that space is available for recording VAT (see 'statutory records', below) and that the classification is sufficiently clear for an accountant to follow when he prepares the financial accounts for the Inland Revenue. Perhaps more crucial is to design the classification to ease the preparation of gross margin accounts, the completion of the 'actual' column in the cash-flow budget, and the compilation of a closing balance sheet.

To this end, column headings should be chosen which separate, as far as possible, receipts and payments of one enterprise from those of another, and fixed costs from variable costs. To help in compiling the balance sheet and capital account, all capital, personal and tax items should be kept to the extreme right of the page, clearly separated from the trading items. The columns headings should correspond throughout the headings used in the cash-flow budget; this is made much easier if the classification used in the budget correspond to those used in the profit budget, as suggested in Chapter 7.

In addition to these analysis columns, two further columns are required on each page. One of these is the 'bank' column, which is used to record the amount of cash changing hands. The other is the 'contra' column, the use of which is explained later in this chapter.

The column headings of the receipts and payments analysis pages for Home Farm might be as shown in Figure 10.1. Adoption of any of the developments discussed in Chapter 9 would require the addition of further columns.

Receipts	*Payments*
Bank	Bank
Contra	Contra
Milk	Cattle purchase
Cattle	Dairy feed
Pigs	Dairy miscellaneous costs
Cereals	Pig purchase
Apples	Pig feed
Miscellaneous trading	Pig miscellaneous costs
	Crop costs
	Regular wages
	Casual wages
	Power and machinery
	Misc. fixed costs
	Finance: interest and charges
Capital receipts	Capital payments
Personal and tax	Personal and tax
VAT charged on outputs	VAT paid on inputs
VAT refunds from Customs and Excise	VAT paid to Customs and Excise

Figure 10.1   *CAB column headings for Home Farm*

The number of columns per page limits the possible extent of classification by column. In the above example, for instance, 'crop costs' are allocated a single column, instead of the four (for fertilizer, seed, sprays and miscellaneous) which might be thought ideal. In the limited space available, the four columns could be accommodated only by allowing the payments analysis to spill over to another page. This should be avoided wherever possible, since it makes entry of transactions more difficult, and thus errors more likely.

The problem may be overcome by using a coding system within the columns. The code 'BF' by an entry in the 'crop costs' column might be used to indicate barley fertilizer, and 'GS' to indicate grass seed. As with the 'all-coding' system described earlier in this chapter, it is essential to write an index to these columns in the front of the CAB.

Some farmers prefer to classify inputs entirely by enterprise, resulting in payments analysis columns for dairy variable costs, barley variable costs, and so on, with codes used to identify different types of input within the columns. This method tends to make retrieval of information slightly easier, at the expense of slightly more difficult entry. The choice between the two alternatives is largely a matter of personal preference, the main thing being to ensure that both CAB and cash-flow budget use the same system.

Entry of transactions

For the time being, we will assume that all receipts are paid directly into the bank, and all payments are made by cheque. This simplifies the recording process and minimizes the scope for error (naturally some cash in hand or 'petty cash' will be required for small transactions – this is dealt with separately). When starting a new account book, the first entry must be that of the opening bank balance; on the receipts page if a credit balance, and on the payments page if an overdraft, with the words 'Opening balance' written in the 'Details' column, the date in the 'Date' column and the amount in the 'Bank' column.

Whenever the cash changes hands, the date and the details of the transaction should be recorded on the stub of the cheque or paying-in book. The details should include the number and type of item, and the name of the other party to the transaction. At least once per month, the farmer should go through the chequebook and paying-in book stubs, transferring the date, details and stub number into the relevant page of the CAB. The sum of money paid or received is entered into the relevant analysis column. Entries may be required in several columns if the cash payment or receipt covers several items. Figure 10.2 (overleaf) shows the entry of the first four payments made by Adam Haynes in December 198X, together with the entry of the opening balance of £26,302 overdraft.

Contra transactions

Often a firm supplying goods or services to the farm will also purchase items from the farm. Examples are the merchant who buys corn as well as selling fertilizer, and the machinery dealer who takes an old tractor in part-exchange for the new. In such cases, the account will be reckoned up at a convenient time (probably the end of the month) and the business owing the most money will send a cheque for the balance to the other. This is known as a *contra transaction*. Figure 10.3 (overleaf) gives a diagrammatic representation of an example where a farmer has, during a particular month, sold £1000-worth of wheat to a merchant, and has bought £600-worth of feed from the same firm.

A single cheque thus represents both a receipt and a payment. To maintain the accuracy of the classification, these two elements must be separated and recorded on the relevant pages. This is achieved through use of the *contra column*. In Figure 10.3 the farmer receives a cheque for £400, which is entered in the 'Bank' column of the receipts page. The value of the wheat sold is £1000, so this is entered in the 'Wheat' column. The balance of £600 is entered in the 'Contra' column; it is simply a way of explaining the discrepancy between the two previous figures.

Cheques paid:

926521 J. Bird: 53 weaner pigs £1,325 (zero-rated for VAT)
926522 Cleverdon Feeds: 18 tonnes pig meal £2,790 (zero-rated)
926523 Robert Martin: supply of fence-posts £100 (supplier not registered for VAT)
926524 A. Jellings: vet services for dairy (£507) and pigs (£190) (at standard rate of 17.5% VAT)

Date	Details and supplier	Cheque no.	1.00 Bank	5 Dairy Misc. Costs	6.00 Pig Purchase	7.00 Pig Feed	8 Pig Misc. Costs	13 Misc. Fixed Costs	14 Finance Interest & charges	15 Capital Payments	16 Personal & Tax	17 VAT paid on inputs
1/12	Opening balance (overdraft)		26,302.00									
5/12	J. Bird: 53 weaners	521	1,325.00		1,325.00							
	Cleverdon feeds: 18t pig meal	522	2,790.00			2,790.00						
7/12	R. Martin: fence posts	523	100.00					100.00				
	Jellings: vet services	524	818.98	v 507.00			v 190.00					121.98

Figure 10.2   *Entry of transactions in cash analysis book*

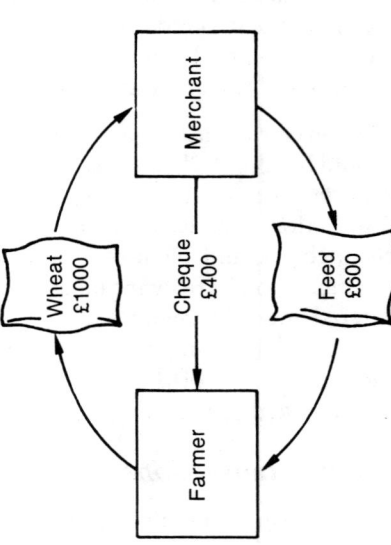

Figure 10.3   *Contra-transaction*

At the same time, the farmer buys feed to the value of £600. He thus enters £600 in the 'Feed' column of the payments page, but enters nothing in the 'Bank' column since no cheque has been sent. Again, the 'Contra' column is used to explain the discrepancy between the amounts in the bank and analysis columns (see Figure 10.4).

Receipts page

Date	Details	Stub	Bank	Contra	Wheat
4/8	A. Merchant (10 t wheat at £100/t)	123	400	600	1000 ⓖ

Payments page

Date	Details	Stub	Bank	Contra	Feed
4/8	A. Merchant (5 t dairy feed at £120/t)			600	600 ⓓ

Figure 10.4 *Entry of a contra transaction in the CAB*

The use of a contra column allows contra transactions to be recorded with the minimum disturbance to the cash analysis system, and allows easy checking of accuracy. In particular, it is worth noting that the figures in the contra column of the receipts page are identical to those of the payments page. This provides a useful check on accuracy when the accounts are summarized at the end of the month (see below).

Discounts

Discounts are of two types. The first is the *trade discount*, given as an incentive for bulk purchase, or to build up goodwill with a regular, even if not large, customer. The second is the *cash discount* given for settlement of an account within a stipulated time. There is rarely any point in recording either type of discount, since the information is of little value in itself. It is sufficient to record the amount of money paid, net of discount, in both bank and analysis columns of the CAB. Where an account includes more than one item, the discount should be allocated between them by simple proportion.

The monthly totals

At least once a month, time should be set aside for 'doing the books'. This process should include the totalling of each column, the finding of a closing bank balance, and the checking of the result by both internal tests and by reconciliation with the bank statement.

The first step is to rule off each page below the last entry, and find the total of each column, including the bank and contra columns. Two accuracy checks may then be made:

1   The total of the receipts column should be identical to the total of the payments contra column.
2   When the bank column total on each page (excluding the opening balance) is added to the contra column total, the result should be identical to the sum of the totals of the remaining columns (each receipt or payment is entered twice; once in the bank and/or contra column, and again in one or more analysis columns).

If these checks do not work out, the entries for the month must be checked systematically until the error is found. Then the completeness of the recording can be checked by reconciling with the bank statement.

Reconciliation with the bank statement

Cash analysis is the farmer's attempt to keep track of changes in his bank account. The bank keeps its own records, a copy of which may be sent, on request, to the farmer at convenient intervals. This is the *bank statement*.

The existence of two sets of records of the same bank account provides a further opportunity to check the accuracy of recording. The first step is to ask the bank to send statements at a time in each month which is convenient for the farmer to complete the accounts for that month (usually the end of the month). The cash analysis results and the bank statement may then be compared as soon as the former are complete.

The chances are that the two will not agree, for one or more reasons:

1   The bank may have an error in recording (unlikely but possible).
2   The farmer may have made an error in recording (rather more likely).
3   The bank may have omitted certain items, such as cheques which have not yet been presented by the recipient.
4   The farmer may have omitted certain items, especially those where cheques are not involved, such as standing orders, direct debits, and deduction of bank interest and charges.

The simplest way of identifying the reason for any discrepancy is to go through the bank statement, ticking off the entries which also appear in the cash analysis book. Any entries which appear in the bank statement but not in the CAB may be checked, pencilled in the bank column below the bank balance, and a new balance found in the relevant analysis columns.

The balance can then be found between the receipts bank column total and the payments bank column total, and entered on the page with the smallest total. A credit balance is entered on the payments page, and an overdraft is shown on the receipts page. Any entries which appear in the CAB but not in the bank statement may similarly be checked, pencilled in on the statement, and a new balance found. The two balances should now agree. If they do not, they must be checked systematically until the error is found. The results of the cash analysis may then be used with reasonable confidence in cash-flow control (Chapter 1?) and as a basis for the preparation of profit and capital statements.

The month-end totalling and checking process is illustrated for Home Farm, December 198X, in Figures 10.5, 10.6 and 10.7.

After the closing balance has been reconciled with the bank statement, the accounts are ruled off and the balance 'carried down' to open the accounts for the following month. The opening balance is always entered on the opposite page to

MidWest Bank Plc

Statement of Account

MR. A HAYNES (FARM) A/C
HOME FARM
ANYWHERE

Account Number   367554321

Date	Particulars		Payments	Receipts	Balance	
	Opening balance				26302.00	OD
4-Dec		125629		4269.00	22033.00	OD
8-Dec		926521	1325.00		23358.00	OD
		926522	2790.00		26148.00	OD
11-Dec		926523	100.00		26248.00	OD
		926526	595.00		26843.00	OD
		926525	551.91		27394.91	OD
19-Dec		926524	818.98		28213.89	OD
	CHARGES TO 1 DEC		122.00		28335.89	OD
	INTEREST TO 1 DEC		822.00		29157.89	OD
		926527	610.00		29767.89	OD
20-Dec	MILK MARKETING BOARD			9111.82	20656.07	OD
21-Dec		926528	248.34		20904.41	OD
	LOAN ACCOUNT			4650.00	25554.41	OD
27-Dec		125631		18952.00	6602.41	OD
		125630		1805.94	4796.47	OD
		125633		58.75	4737.72	OD
		125632		399.50	4338.22	OD
28-Dec		926530	880.00		5218.22	OD
		926529	1172.06		6390.28	OD
31-Dec	A. HAYNES (PERS A/C)		760.00		7150.28	OD
	Reconciliation:					
	less unpresented cheques rec'd.					
		634			−1674.00	
	plus unpresented cheques paid					
		531			3401.63	
		532			768.45	
	Adjusted balance				9646.36	√

Figure 10.5 *Home Farm bank statement for December 199X*

Cheques paid:

926521   J. Bird: 53 weaner pigs £1,325 (zero-rated for VAT)
926522   Cleverdon Feeds: 18 tonnes pig meal £2,790 (zero-rated)
926523   Robert Martin: supply of fence-posts £100 (supplier not registered for VAT)
926524   A. Jellings: vet services for dairy (£507) and pigs (£190) (at standard rate of 17.5% VAT)
926525   Treachers Ltd: dairy supplies (£345.36 + 17.5% VAT) and pig supplies (£136.65 + 17.5% VAT) less 3% cash discount
926526   Cash for wages: regular £380.00, casual £215.00
926527   Cash for wages: regular £385.00, casual £225.00
926528   Fisher Garage: diesel fuel £216.89 + 17.5% VAT less 3% cash discount
926529   Brassleys Agricultural Engineers: Tractor gear-box and clutch repair £1050.00 less 5% trade discount + 17.5% VAT
926530   Cash for wages: £780.00 regular, £100 casual
926531   D. Jewett: purchase of tractor, £3,545.89 + 17.5% VAT less 5% cash discount, less sale of tractor, £500 + 17.5% VAT
926532   A. Smith: apple packaging materials £654 + 17.5% VAT

Date	Details and supplier	Cheque no.	1 Bank	2 Contra	3 Cattle purchase	4 Dairy Feed	5 Dairy Misc. Costs	6 Pig Purchase	7 Pig Feed	8 Pig Misc. Costs
1/12	Opening balance (overdraft)		26,302.00							
5/12	J. Bird: 53 weaners	521	1,325.00					1,325.00		
	Cleverdon Feeds: 18t pig meal	522	2,790.00						2,790.00	
7/12	R. Martin: fence posts	523	100.00							
	Jellings: vet services	524	818.98				V 507.00			V 190.00
	Treachers: dairy & pig supplies	525	551.90				M 335.00			M 132.55
	Cash for wages	526	595.00							
13/12	Cash for wages	527	610.00							
	Fisher Garage: diesel etc.	528	248.34							
20/12	Brassleys: tractor repair	529	1,172.06							
	Cash for wages	530	880.00							
	ACME auctions: commission			89.07			M 75.80			
30/12	D. Jewett: purchase of tractor	531	3,401.63	587.50						
	A. Smith: apple packaging	532	768.45							
	Totals before reconciliation		39,563.36	676.57	0.00	0.00	917.80	1,325.00	2,790.00	322.55
	Reconciliation adjustments:									
	MMB (fees)			142.18			M 121.00			
	Personal drawings		760.00							
	Bank interest and fees		944.00							
	Loan repayment		4,650.00							
	Adjusted totals		41,267.36	818.75	0.00	0.00	1,038.80	1,325.00	2,790.00	322.55

9 Crop costs	10 Regular wages & NI	11 Casual wages & NI	12 Power & machinery	13 Misc. Fixed Costs	14 Finance Interest & charges	14	15 Capital Payments	16 Personal & Tax	17 VAT paid on inputs
				100.00					121.98
									84.35
	380.00	215.00							37.96
	385.00	225.00	F 210.38						174.56
			R 997.50						
	780.00	100.00							13.27
									620.53
							3,368.60		114.45
654.00									
654.00	1,545.00	540.00	1,207.88	100.00	0.00		3,368.60	0.00	1,167.10
					944.00	4,100.00		760.00	21.18
					550.00		4,100.00		
					1,494.00				
654.00	1,545.00	540.00	1,207.88	100.00	100.00		7,468.60	760.00	1,188.28

Figure 10.6 *Home Farm – payment analysis for December 199X*

Cheques received:

125629 Carpenters, butchers: 52 cutter pigs £4,269.00 (zero-rated)
125630 ACME Auctions: sale of 19 calves (zero-rated), £1,895.00 less commission £75.80 +17.5% VAT
125631 Williams Fruits: apples £18,952.00 (zero-rated)
125632 Robin Clutterbuck: hedge-cutting, £340.00 + 17.5% VAT
125633 J. Bull: firewood, £50.00 + 17.5% VAT
125634 Customs and Excise: VAT refund, £1,674.00

Date	Details and customer	Ref. no.	1 Bank	2 Contra	3 Milk	4 Cattle	5 Pigs	6 Cereals	7 Apples	8 Misc. Trading	9 Capital Receipts	10 Personal Receipts	11 VAT charged on outputs	12 VAT refund from C & E
1/12	Carpenters, butchers	629	4,269.00				4,269.00							
20/12	ACME Auctions: 19 calves	630	1,805.94	89.07		1,895.00								
	Williams Fruits: apples	631	18,952.00						18,952.00					
	Robin Clutterbuck: hedge cutting	632	399.50							340.00			59.50	
	J. Bull: firewood	633	58.75							50.00			8.75	
30/12	Customs and Excise: VAT refund	634	1,674.00											1,674.00
	D. Jewett: tractor (part-exchange)			587.50							500.00		87.50	
	Totals before reconciliation		27,159.19	676.57	0.00	1,895.00	4,269.00	0.00	18,952.00	390.00	500.00	0.00	155.75	1,674.00
	Reconciliation adjustments:													
	MMB: 46023 litres milk		9,111.82	142.18	9,254.00									
	Adjusted totals		36,271.01	818.75	9,254.00	1,895.00	4,269.00	0.00	18,952.00	390.00	500.00	0.00	155.75	1,674.00
	Closing bank balance (overdraft)		9,646.35											
			45,917.36											

Figure 10.7 Home Farm – receipt analysis, December 199X

that on which the previous month's closing balance appears. Thus an opening overdraft is shown on the payments page, and an opening credit balance on the receipts page.

Petty cash

So far it has been assumed that all transactions take place via the bank. In most businesses, however, it is useful to have some cash in hand for small expenses, such as the purchase of half a dozen bolts from the local ironmonger's, or the employment of a schoolboy on Saturday mornings. If such small or *petty cash* transactions do take place within a business, it is essential to record them. A number of small transactions can accumulate to a large sum and their omission will distort the picture shown by the accounts.

A basic requirement of any petty cash system is a petty cash box, the use of which helps avoid business money being mixed up with beer money, or being deposited in various forgettable places around the farmhouse. Where petty cash transactions are infrequent, it is possible to record them directly in the CAB, using a 'Petty cash' column in addition to 'Bank' and 'Contra', and analysing in the usual way. With a typical volume of petty cash transactions, however, it is more convenient to use a separate petty cash book; it avoids the CAB being cluttered with myriads of small transactions, and can be small enough to fit in the cash box.

Although some farm businesses may receive small amounts of cash from the sale of eggs, hay, potatoes, etc., it is best to restrict the system to payments only. Receipts should be paid directly into the bank or, if cash sales are frequent, a separate box and cash book should be used. The alternative is a complex recording system, which is prone to error.

The petty cash book should have at least two columns per page; one for the total amount paid, and one for the VAT paid (Figure 10.8 overleaf). Given an accurate description of each transaction, and any VAT invoices, transfer of the details to the CAB at the end of the month is straightforward. It can be made easier by adding, if space permits, further columns to allow for more extensive classification.

The most popular way of managing petty cash is the 'imprest' or 'float' method. The farmer decides how much petty cash he is likely to need between visits to the bank. This amount, plus an allowance for contingencies, is drawn from the bank and deposited as a float in the cash box. The initial withdrawal from the bank (and any subsequent increase in the float) is recorded in the CAB as a capital payment, since it represents the establishment of a separate capital reserve. Before the next visit to the bank, the petty cash book is balanced and the cash in the box is counted. The two sums should tally: if they do not, there is something wrong with the accuracy of the farmer's recording, the honesty of his employees, or his ability to keep his own spending money distinct from the business money.

Enough cash is drawn from the bank to bring the float up to the original level. This amount represents the petty cash paid out during the period. The cheque

Date	Details	Amount	Casual labour	Car	Other	VAT paid
21/8	Bale carting	20.00	20.00			
23/8	Headlight unit (etc.)	4.60		4.00		0.60
30/8	TOTALS	85.00	60.00	20.00	2.00	3.00
30/8	Cheque drawn	85.00				

Figure 10.8 *Petty cash book – example layout*

may thus be entered in the CAB payments page 'Details' column as 'Petty Cash' and analysed out according to the information in the petty cash book (see Figure 10.9, page 122).

Statutory records

Value Added Tax

Value Added Tax (VAT) is a tax on sales imposed throughout the European Community and elsewhere, but described here in the UK context. This is not the place to describe the tax in great detail, but it is important to recognize certain characteristics of the VAT system. VAT distinguishes between four different types of goods and services:

1   Standard-rated items.
2   Zero-rated items.
3   Exempt items.
4   Items which are outside the scope of VAT.

Examples of each are shown in Figure 10.10 (page 123).

The producer of a standard-rated item must charge tax, at the relevant rate, on the sale of that item, but may, at the same time, reclaim any tax he has paid on the purchases of inputs used to produce the item. He pays the balance between receipts and payments of VAT to the Customs and Excise, who administer the tax. If receipts in a particular period are less than payments, he may claim a refund. Thus the net direct financial effect on the producer's business is zero (although the indirect effect is to increase the price of his products and thus depress sales). This procedure is followed at every stage of the production and marketing process, the final consumer paying the accumulated tax (see Figure 10.11, page 124).

The producer of a zero-rated item is not required to charge VAT on sales of that item, but is allowed to reclaim the tax paid on inputs used in producing them.*
The producer of an exempt item is not required to charge VAT on its sale, but may not reclaim VAT paid on inputs used in producing that item.

Producers with a taxable turnover of less than a stipulated amount (£33,600 per annum at the time of writing) are not required to register for VAT, i e. they do not have to charge VAT on any sales, and are not able to reclaim tax paid on inputs. For businesses where most sales are taxable at the higher or standard rates, it pays to avoid registration if possible. Farmers are concerned mainly with the production of food products, which are zero-rated. Since this implies that they will be paying more tax on inputs than they receive from sales, it is worth most farmers registering for VAT in order to claim the refunds.

The VAT system uses the businessman as an intermediate tax-collector. To prevent fraud, the law requires painstaking recording of each transaction made by a registered producer. This involves the issuing of special invoices, the storing of all invoices and related documents for three years, the regular completion of tax returns, and the ability to demonstrate that these returns are accurate.

---

*With the exception of tax paid on cars and business entertaining expenses.

Date	Details	Stub	Bank	Casual labour	Vehicle expenses	Misc.	VAT paid
30/8	Petty cash	123	85.00	60.00	20.00	2.00	3.00

Figure 10.9 *Petty cash – entry in CAB*

Standard Rate	Zero rate	Exempt
Fertilizers/sprays/manures	*Food production*	*Bank charges and interest* (paid or received)
	Including:	Building Society interest
Machinery	Produce (e.g. wheat, potatoes, beef, milk, fish, game birds)	Cottage rents (not holiday)
Including:		Finance charges
New plant, machines and implements	Products (e.g. butter, cheese)	Insurance (business)
Car repairs	Livestock (e.g. cattle, sheep, pigs, poultry)	Land
Machinery repairs		Letting land for crops
Workshop, tools, spares	Feed (e.g. cattle feed, pig feed, poultry feed)	Postages
Hire of machinery		Timber felling rights
Road fuels	Seeds (e.g. wheat, potatoes, sugar beet)	Wayleaves
Other fuels for business use (e.g. tractor diesel, gas, electricity, coal and coke)		*Items outside scope* (*excluded from return*)
	Others	VAT payments and refunds
Non-food produce	Grain and potato futures	Wages, PAYE and NI
Including:		Insurance claims
Flowers, flower seeds		Compensation
Bulbs		Life assurances/pensions
Trees and wood		Private payments and income
Wool		Dividends
		Grants and subsidies
Repairs		Loans and repayments
Including buildings (except protected buildings), roads, fences, electrical		Cars
		Business rates
Professional services		Levies (e.g. PMB)
Including:		NFU subscriptions
Solicitors, accountants		Vehicle licences & MoT fees
Consultants' fees		
Auctioneers' commission		
Vet. and med.		
Leasing services		
General services		
Including:		
Recording fees and A.I.		
Contracting		
Water and sewerage for business use		
Others		
Crop & livestock sundries		
Holiday accommodation		
Provision of meals		
Hot take-away meals		
Horses, sheepdogs		
Petfood		
Advertising		
New building work		
Building conversions		
Building extensions		

Figure 10.10 *Example of VAT classifications (see HM Customs and Excise Notice No. 701, Scope and Coverage)*

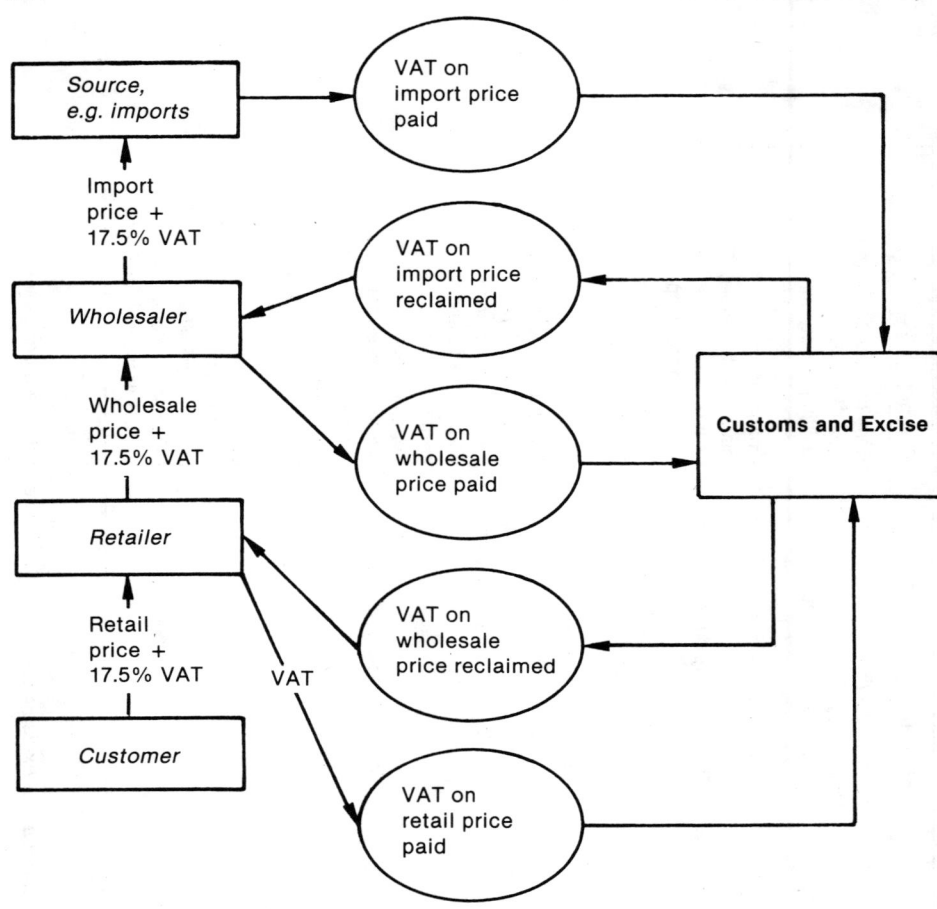

Figure 10.11   *Standard- and higher-rate VAT — operation*

These requirements affect the farmer's recording of transactions in two ways. First, the farmer will wish to record the effect of VAT on his cash flow. Therefore he will require two VAT columns on each of the payments and receipts pages of his CAB. On the receipts page he will need columns for 'VAT received' and 'VAT refunds from Customs and Excise' and, on the payments side, columns for 'VAT paid on inputs' and 'VAT paid to Customs and Excise'.

Second he will wish to make the completion of the VAT return as easy as possible. The VAT return is a document that must be completed every three months and sent to the Customs and Excise.* The information required includes:

*A producer may elect to make monthly returns, as long as (a) he keeps it up for at least a year, and (b) he has not registered voluntarily. This can be quite an advantage for a farmer, since it enables earlier claiming of VAT refunds. An annual accounting scheme now allows tax payers with an annual taxable turnover of less than £300,000 to pay by direct debit. It is only useful for net payers of tax, and is thus of little value to most farmers.

1 VAT received on sales.
2 Deductible VAT paid on inputs (charged on the amount before cash discount).
3 Net payment due to, or reclaimed from, Customs and Excise.
4 The value of all outputs before cash discounts given.
5 The value of all taxable inputs before cash discounts received.

Items (1), (2) and (3) are catered for by the CAB columns described above, the additional information can be supplied by modification of the cash analysis book.

(a) *Modified cash analysis* This entails adding further analysis columns to the receipts and payments pages. One column is added to the payments page, for recording the value of inputs charged at higher, standard and zero rates. Two columns are added to the receipts analysis, one to record the value of zero-rated sales, and the other for the value of exempt sales. These extra columns are *not* part of the cash analysis, and should be carefully ruled off from the other columns (see Figure 10.12, pages 126 – 7).

Anyone faced with the practicalities of designing a financial recording system for a farm business is strongly recommended to use Atkinson, Hastings and Warren (1990), a step-by-step guide to cash analysis and VAT recording.

Records for income tax

The Inland Revenue, in assessing an individual's liability for Income Tax in a given year, will ask him to complete a tax return. In the case of a businessman, it will require some verification of the accuracy of this return. One way of doing this would be for the Inland Revenue to exercise its right to investigate the farmer's books of account, including the CAB. It is more convenient for both sides, however, if the farmer makes available his profit and loss account and balance sheet for the year in question.

If these latter accounts are prepared by the farmer himself, the Inland Revenue may still refuse to take them at face value. It is normal practice, therefore, to employ an 'outsider' to the business to undertake this task. This person should, preferably, be a member of a professional accountancy institute which endeavours to ensure that its members adhere to a strict code of conduct. The fact that such qualified outsider has prepared the accounts will give the Inland Revenue a degree of extra confidence in their accuracy.

It follows that the CAB must be as clear as possible to others, as well as to oneself – an accountant's time is expensive. This in turn implies the need for care in both the design of the CAB and the entry of transactions, and for the regular, i.e. at least monthly, reconciliation of the accounts.

PAYMENTS ANALYSIS

Date	Details and supplier	cheque no.	1 Bank	2 Contra	17 VAT paid on inputs	18 VAT paid to C & E	19 VAT RETURN ONLY Standard & zero-rated	20 VAT RETURN ONLY Exempt & out of scope
1/12	Opening balance (overdraft)		26302.00					
5/12	J. Bird: 53 weaners	521	1325.00				1325.00	
	Cleverdon Feeds: 18t pig meal	522	2790.00				2790.00	
7/12	R. Martin: fence posts	523	100.00					100.00
	Jellings: vet services	524	818.98		121.98		697.00	
	Treachers: dairy & pig supplies	525	551.90		91.88		525.00	
	Cash for wages	526	595.00					595.00
13/12	Cash for wages	527	610.00					610.00
	Fisher Garage: diesel etc.	528	248.34		37.96		216.89	
20/12	Brassleys: tractor repair	529	1172.06		174.56		997.50	
	Cash for wages	530	880.00					880.00
	ACME auctions: commission			89.07	13.27		75.80	
30/12	D. Jewett: purchase of tractor	531	3401.63	587.50	594.13		3500.00	
	A. Smith: apple packaging	532	768.45		114.45		654.00	
	Totals before reconciliation		39563.36	676.57	1148.22		10781.19	2185.00
	Reconciliation adjustments:							
	MMB (fees)			142.18	21.18		121.00	
	personal drawings		760.00					760.00
	bank interest & charges		944.00					362.00
	loan repayment		4650.00					4650.00
	Adjusted totals		45917.36	818.75	1169.40		10902.19	7957.00

RECEIPTS ANALYSIS

Date	Details and customer	Ref. no.	1 Bank	2 Contra	11 VAT charged on outputs	12 VAT refund from C & E	13 VAT RETURN ONLY Standard & zero-rated	14 Exempt & out of scope
1/12	Carpenters, butchers	629	4269.00				4269.00	
20/12	ACME Auctions: 19 calves	630	1805.94	89.07			1895.00	
	Williams Fruits: apples	631	18952.00				18952.00	
	Robin Clutterbuck: hedge cutting	632	399.50		59.50		340.00	
	J. Bull: firewood	633	58.75		8.75		50.00	
30/12	Customs and Excise: VAT refund	634	1674.00			1674.00		1674.00
	D. Jewett: tractor (part-exchange)			587.50	87.50		500.00	
	Totals before reconciliation		27159.19	676.57	155.75	1674.00	26006.00	1674.00
	Reconciliation adjustments: MMB: 46023 litres milk		9111.82	142.18			9254.00	
	Adjusted totals		36271.01	818.75	155.75	1674.00	35260.00	1674.00
	Closing bank balance (overdraft)		9646.35					
			45917.36					

Figure 10.12 *Cash analysis book modified for VAT analysis*

Further reading

Cash analysis

Atkinson, J. M., Hastings, M. R. and Warren, M. F. *Keeping the Books* (Agricultural Training Board/Seale Hayne College/Manpower Services Commission (The Family Farm Series) 1986, revised 1990).

Critchley, R., The North of Scotland Agricultural College Home Study Series (Aberdeen, North of Scotland Agricultural College):
Business Growth and Your Farm Accounts (1985).
Financial Management: Case Study 1 (1986).
Financial Management: Case Study 1, Supporting Material (1986).
Understanding Your Farm Accounts (1982).

Hosken, M. and Brown, D., *The Farm Office*, 4th edition (Ipswich, Farming Press, 1991).

Value Added Tax

HM Customs and Excise, *Value Added Tax: Scope and Coverage*, HMCE Notice No. 701 (HMSO).

HM Customs and Excise, *Value Added Tax: General Guide*, HMCE Notice No. 700 (HMSO).

Sinclair, W. I., *Allied Dunbar Tax Guide* (London, Longman).

Double-entry book-keeping

Bull, R. J., *Accounting in Business*, 6th edition (London, Butterworths), chapter 5.

Etor, J. and Muspratt, M., *Keep Account: A Guide to Profitable Bookkeeping* (London, Pan, 1982). Easier to follow than most book-keeping texts.

Wood, F., *Business Accounting 1*, 5th edition (London, Longman, 1989).

11

Recording profit and capital

Preparing a profit and loss account

Adjustment for debtors and creditors

Given a well designed cash analysis book, the compilation of a profit and loss account should be straightforward. In the Home Farm example used in the preceding chapter, the 'trading' columns concerned with the productive activity of the business were kept together on the left-hand side of each analysis page, carefully segregated from the capital, personal and tax columns. In compiling a profit and loss account for a given period (say a year), the monthly totals in each of these trading columns are summed to give an annual total for each column. Each of these annual totals may then be transferred to the appropriate place in the profit and loss account.

It is convenient to make the necessary adjustment for opening and closing debtors and creditors (including prepayments, accruals, etc.) before this transfer takes place. Thus after the cash analysis has been ruled off for the year, two extra lines are included to allow for the deduction of opening debtors and creditors from the relevant columns, and the addition of closing debtors and creditors (these may be obtained from examination of invoices outstanding, but a separate monthly record of trade debts outstanding can save a lot of searching). The result of this calculation will be an adjusted total for each analysis column, ready for transfer to the profit and loss account (see Figure 11.1 overleaf).

It may be that an opening debtor refuses or becomes unable to pay his debt. This *bad debt* must then be 'written off' by entering it in the profit and loss account as an expense, and omitting it from both the closing debtor adjustment in the CAB, and the 'trade debtors' item in the closing balance sheet.

Compiling a profit and loss account in conventional form

The format of a conventional profit and loss account was discussed in Chapter 3. As a rule, it is insufficiently detailed for precise control, but it can be used to give a relatively quick check on profitability before more comprehensive enterprise accounts are prepared.

To compile this form of account, the adjusted annual totals of the trading columns in the CAB are listed under their column headings, expenses on the left of the page, receipts on the right. Depreciation is calculated as described in Chapter 5, and is

PAYMENTS ANALYSIS

Date	Details and supplier	cheque no.	1 Bank	2 Contra	3 Cattle purchase	4 Dairy Feed	5 Dairy Misc. Costs	6 Pig Purchase	7 Pig Feed	8 Pig Misc. Costs
	opening balance for year (overdraft)		21000							
	ANNUAL PAYMENTS SUMMARY (sum of monthly totals, excluding opening balance)		218624	3514	18260	11362	6258	27024	28950	2444
	Adjustments:									
	– opening creditors					4000			2800	
	+ closing creditors					3021	258	3510	3100	
	Adjusted totals				18260	10383	6516	30534	29250	2444

RECEIPTS ANALYSIS

Date	Details and customer	ref. no.	1 Bank	2 Contra	3 Milk	4 Cattle	5 Pigs	6 Cereals	7 Apples	8 Misc. Trading
	ANNUAL RECEIPTS SUMMARY (sum of monthly totals)		205522	3514	77059	16089	65975		18952	4897
	Adjustments:									
	– opening debtors				2280	500	6300			
	+ closing debtors				2174		5836			
	Adjusted totals				76953	15589	65511		18952	4897

Figure 11.1 Home Farm – adjusting CAB for debtors and creditors

entered as an expense on the left of the page. The value of benefits in kind is taken from records (if they exist) or estimated. The opening valuation of stocks is given (it is the same as last year's closing valuation), and it only remains to estimate the closing value of stocks (see 'Valuing Stocks' below).

The result will be two columns of figures, the difference between their totals being the net profit or loss; this is the profit and loss account, as depicted in Figure 3.1.

Compiling a profit and loss account in gross margin form

The particular value of the gross margin form of account is that it can provide a wealth of management information (see Chapter 6). This feature naturally adds to the difficulty of compiling the account. Nevertheless, if the CAB layout has been designed with gross margin accounting in mind, the task need not be daunting. In the CAB examples used in the previous chapter, the columns were arranged so as to keep fixed costs separate from variable costs. A judicious blend of classification by column and by code was recommended, to enable rapid identification of all the output and variable inputs relating to a particular enterprise.

The first step in the compilation of this type of account is to extract from the CAB all the receipts and variable cost payments relating to each enterprise. Where a column is highly specific (such as that for milk receipts), it will be sufficient to take the 'milk' column annual total, adjusted for opening and closing debtors and creditors. Where columns are shared, and codes are used within the columns, there is no alternative to searching the CAB records for the whole year, extracting all items identified by a particular code. The total thus derived must then be adjusted for those debtors and creditors which relate specifically to the subject of the code.

Once the picture of adjusted cash receipts and payments has been built up for each enterprise, adjustments may be made for transfers between enterprises. This will require reference to the physical 'back-up' records such as livestock movement records and barn records. If records of benefits in kind have been kept, these may be used to enter the home consumption of produce in the output of each enterprise. Usually these items are relatively so small that an estimate is sufficient. Finally, adjustments for changes in valuation may be made to enterprise output and variable inputs where necessary.

The gross margin for each enterprise is then calculated by deducting variable costs from enterprise output. As in the budget, all components of the gross margin should be expressed throughout per hectare or per head. All livestock enterprise gross margin accounts should show the final margin expressed both per head and per unit of area used by the enterprise (per forage hectare for grazing livestock; per square metre for intensive livestock). If capital, or even labour, are limiting resources, the gross margin may be expressed per £100 capital employed, or per 100 man-hours (see Appendix 1).

The use of worksheets (such as those shown in Chapter 6) makes the process of drawing up an enterprise gross margin account considerably easier.

Most of the fixed costs can be taken from the relevant adjusted column totals in the

CAB. The main exception is depreciation, which must be calculated by reference to the opening value of buildings and machinery, and to purchases and sales of such assets during the year (shown in the 'capital' columns in the CAB). A machinery register can be helpful in this calculation (see Chapter 12). Benefits in kind which relate to items of fixed cost should be deducted from the appropriate sub-total (usually miscellaneous fixed costs).

If the total fixed cost is now deducted from the total gross margin of the business, after allowance for any unallocated variable costs, a net profit or loss will result. This should be identical with that derived from the cruder conventional format. If it is not, checking for errors should begin with those revenues and expenses which are not recorded in the CAB, particularly changes in stock valuations, transfers between enterprises, and benefits in kind. It is very easy, when allocating these items between enterprises, to make an error or an omission. Inter-enterprise transfers are particularly prone to error: check that the transfers of a product out of one enterprise match the transfers of that product into other enterprises, in both quantity transferred and in unit price.

Compiling a profit and loss account in 'full costing' form

Chapter 6 indicated that there are some situations in farming where the use of full costing may be justified. The most common example is that of intensive livestock production, where most of the costs are specific to the enterprise concerned.

Compilation of a full absorption costing is similar to that of a gross margin account, the calculation of the 'specific' fixed costs following the same pattern as the calculation of variable costs. There will be some costs, however, which cannot be allocated in this way – the 'general overheads' such as office expenses, use of the farm Land-Rover, managerial salaries, and so on. A decision has to be made as to how those overheads are 'absorbed' by the various enterprises. The proportion of overheads absorbed by each enterprise may be determined by its financial contribution to farm output, its share of land occupied, its share of direct labour costs, or any other formula that the farmer thinks appropriate. There is no 'right' basis of absorption; whatever method is used is likely to be fairly arbitrary. Provided that the general overheads are a small proportion of the total costs, this should not matter greatly.

While a full costing gives more precise detail than a gross margin account, and is useful for historic analysis, it is important to remember its limitations as a basis for decision-making (see Chapter 6) and to recognize the superior value of gross margin accounting in this respect.

Reconciliation of profit with cash flow

Whichever method is used to calculate the historic net profit, the result should be reconciled with the cash analysis results as described in Chapter 7. As with all such checks, if the figures do *not* reconcile, the two accounts must be checked and rechecked until the error is found.

'Financial year' and 'crop year' enterprise accounts

The above discussion is concerned entirely with the calculation of accounts for the financial year. The financial year calculation is important in many ways, not least in providing a vital link in the cash flow/profit/capital reconciliation chain, and in forming a basis for the estimation of likely tax liability for the year.

The financial-year basis may not be the ideal for decision-making, however, since the timing of the financial year can give rise to a distorted picture of the performance of an enterprise. An example is that of a breeding sheep flock on a farm where the financial year ends on 31 March. The financial-year gross margin will include the sale of the previous year's crop of lambs, together with the variable costs of producing the current crop. The same applies to winter cereal crops.

Even in the absence of inflation, it can be very difficult to draw conclusions about the performance of the enterprise. A difference between years in climate, or in the size of the enterprise, will confuse the message of the account.

Where the financial year of the business finishes part-way through the production year or 'crop year' of an enterprise, therefore, a *crop year* account should be prepared in addition to the financial year version. The process can be summarized thus:

1   Take the two financial year accounts which span the crop year in question.
2   Remove from them all revenues and expenses relating to the crop years before and after the crop year in question.
3   Add in any revenues and expenses arising in other financial years, but relating to the crop year in question.

Adjustment (3) is not always necessary, but may arise as a result of advance buying, e.g. of fertilizer, or of long storage of output before sale.

In the interests of timely decision-making, it is desirable to prepare the crop year gross margin as soon as possible after the end of that year. Where crops are stored beyond the end of the crop year, or where some livestock is still unsold, it will be necessary to estimate the likely value of the sales, using realistic, if conservative, valuations. The resulting gross margin should be corrected as soon as the sales or transfers are complete.

As an example of the preparation of a crop year gross margin account, take a winter wheat crop in a business whose financial year ends in December. An appropriate 'crop year' would run from 1 October to 30 September (see Figure 11.2 overleaf).

The gross margins for the financial years 199X and 199Y are shown in Figure 11.3, highly summarized. Note that it is impossible to express these sensibly in £ per hectare, since the various items of output and cost arising in a given financial year relate to different areas of land.

To arrive at a crop year gross margin, we can remove the sales of the 199X financial year, together with the top-dressing, the fungicide, and the baler twine. All relate to the previous crop year. We can also remove the seed, seed-bed

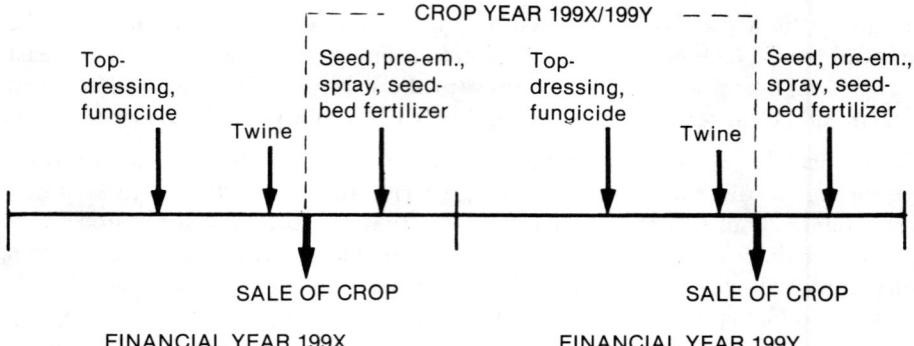

Figure 11.2 *Illustration of financial and crop years*

	Year ending 31 December 199X	Year ending 31 December 199Y
Hectares harvested	30	35
Output (total)	£	£
Grain	21,000	17,500
Straw	1,500	1,050
	22,500	18,550
Variable costs (total)		
Seed	1,400	1,120
Fertilizer, seed-bed	1,225	1,280
Fertilizer, spring top-dressing	900	1,225
Sprays, fungicide	1,500	2,100
Sprays, pre-emergence herbicide	1,050	1,280
Miscellaneous (baler twine, etc.)	300	350
	6,375	7,355
GROSS MARGIN (total)	16,125	11,195

Figure 11.3 *Financial year gross margin for winter wheat*

fertilizer and pre-emergence spray costs from the 199Y financial year, since these have been incurred in respect of the following crop.

Assuming that there are no revenues or expenses relating to this crop and arising outside the two financial years shown, the crop year gross margin would be as in Figure 11.4.

The result is an account which can be used with ease in enterprise analysis (see Chapter 14). It is worth noting that the use of an October to September financial year minimizes the need for such adjustments.

	£ total	£/ha
Output		
Grain	17,500	583
Straw	1,050	35
	18,550	618
Variable costs:		
Seed	1,400	47
Fertilizer, seed-bed	1,225	41
Fertilizer, top-dressing	1,225	41
Sprays, fungicide	2,100	70
Sprays, pre-emergence herbicide	1,050	35
Miscellaneous (baler twine, etc.)	350	12
	7,350	245
GROSS MARGIN	11,200	373

Figure 11.4 *Crop year gross margin (30 ha winter wheat grown)*

Whatever the financial year-end, crop-year adjustments are not necessary in 'continuous-production' livestock enterprises such as pigs, poultry and, for most purposes, dairy. Particular difficulties surround the calculation of enterprise accounts for trading livestock enterprises with long production cycles, such as rearing beef or dairy replacements. The easiest solution is to calculate the account on the basis of the financial year. For instance, in an established heifer-rearing enterprise, with 30 animals transferred per year to the dairy herd at three years old, one would expect the financial-year account to show:

1 Value of 30 heifers transferred out.
2 Cost of purchase or transfer in of 33 calves (allowing for mortality).
3 Cost of rearing 33 heifers in their first year.
4 Cost of rearing 31 heifers in their second year.
5 Cost of rearing 30 heifers in their third year.

If numbers stay more or less the same from year to year, this will give a reasonable approximation of the current cost of rearing heifers. If numbers change significantly from year to year, or one wants to determine what a batch of animals actually costs, the figures used should ideally be those relating to an entire production cycle, rather than the cross-section described above. Whichever method is used, the components of the account should be expressed per finished animal sold or transferred, rather than per animal in the enterprise as a whole.

Valuing farm stocks

General comments

At the end of each financial year it is necessary for a valuation to be made of the farm stocks. This valuation is required for the calculation of both net profit and net capital.

The *prices* used in these valuations will depend on the use to which the accounts are to be put. For accounts used in the assessment of income tax liability, the farmer is allowed to use the lower of the *cost of production* or the *net realizable value* of the stocks, i.e. the anticipated market value after deduction of storage, transport and marketing costs. Where the cost of production is not known with accuracy, the farmer may use 75 per cent of a 'reasonable' market value of home-bred sheep and pigs, 60% for cattle, and 85 per cent for crops in store. Breeding livestock may be given a cost of production value when they enter the flock or herd, and kept at that value until they are culled. An alternative is to remove them from the profit and loss account altogether by using the 'herd basis' method of valuation (see Appendix 3).

Although beneficial from the point of view of minimizing the impact of taxation, these methods can be unsatisfactory for management purposes. A farmer needs a realistic indication of how his stocks have changed in value over the year, if he is to identify the relative contribution of each enterprise to net profit. This implies that, wherever possible, he should use net realizable value as the basis of valuation for management accounts.

There is a danger, with this method, of valuing stocks at the peak of a very short-term price fluctuation. If the price slumps again before the stocks are sold in the next financial year, a distorted distribution of profit between years will result. To avoid this it is wise to err on the conservative side when valuing.

Price is not the only uncertain factor in valuing − it can often be difficult to determine *quantities*, especially of harvested crops stored in bulk. Where possible such items should be weighed on storage; although some loss of weight is likely to occur during storage, weighing will at least provide the basis for a reliable estimate at the time of valuation. Where this is not possible, either because of the cost of weighing devices or the nature of the material, e.g. silage, it is necessary to determine the volume and density of the material and thus estimate the final weight. For relatively standard items, such as grain, specimen densities are published in various farm management handbooks. For other items, such as silage, sample weighings of measured volumes must be taken.

It is sound policy to employ a qualified valuer every two or three years, even if not specifically required to by the Inland Revenue, as a check on the accuracy of valuations.

Valuation of specific types of stocks for management purposes

Farm stocks were earlier (Chapter 3) grouped in the categories of:

Breeding livestock;
Trading livestock;
Crops in store;
Crops in ground, manurial residues, etc.;
Purchased stores.

Breeding livestock may be regarded as fixed assets, and thus there is much to be said for removing changes in their valuation from the profit and loss account altogether, accounting only for their net replacement cost or 'depreciation'.* The alternative is to value the animals at their net realizable value, which can be reasonably estimated as about half-way betweeen the cull price and the price of a good replacement animal.

Trading livestock are difficult to value, particularly those that are immature. Again they should be valued for management purposes at net realizable value, which will probably be determined by a mixture of the farmer's experience of local markets, and intelligent guess-work. Livestock markets can be volatile, and it is wise to be conservative in times of high prices.

Crops in store can be classified into saleable and unsaleable crops. The former include grain, potatoes, seeds, straw, hay, and so on. Pricing is rarely a difficulty here, as long as one remembers to make the appropriate allowances for storage, transport and marketing costs, and for possible deterioration in storage. The unsaleable crops in store include silage, for which there is no ready market due to its bulk. Without a reliable market value, one is forced back to using cost of production, or more specifically, the *variable* costs of production.

It can be argued that the use of opportunity cost would be more realistic, e.g. the profit obtainable from the best alternative use of the land conserved, less the cost of a ration composed of bought-in fodder and giving the same level of nutrients. While this principle should certainly be used for specific decisions in forage crop policy (via partial budgets), it is rarely likely to be worth the effort in valuation, since we are here concerned with *changes* in valuation over the year. The net effect of choice of method on profit is likely to be small compared with the effort involved in calculating the opportunity cost. The same argument applies to the inclusion of the fixed costs of production in the valuation.

Crops in ground are rarely saleable (exceptions being grass and fodder crops which can be let for keep, and cash crops at point of harvest), and are normally valued at their variable cost of production. Crops near to harvest may be valued at their net realizable value, less a substantial discount for the risk of calamity before harvest.

If it is thought that a significant change in manurial values has taken place over the previous 12 months, valuation tables may be used to calculate the net effect of the change (see Further Reading). In view of the relatively small values involved, and the effort involved, it is normally more sensible to keep the values the same from one end of the year to the other, leaving any revaluing to the valuer on one of his biennial or triennial visits. A modification of this is to revalue both opening and closing valuations by the percentage change in fertilizer price levels during the year. This will keep the values fairly realistic, while avoiding the appearance of 'paper' profit.

Purchased stores are valued at their cost of purchase.

---

*This is the practice followed in the herd basis method of valuation mentioned earlier. Although it was designed to reduce the effect of inflation on tax liability, it is possible to use it for management accounts.

Enterprise: **Fattening pigs**   Ha or head? 939   Year 199x/9y

Version 1

Products:	Bacon pigs							
	Qty	£	Qty	£	Qty	£	Qty	£
Cash received	1,015	65,975						
Closing debtors	93	5,836						
−Opening debtors	−100	−6,300						
Sales	1,008	65,511						
Transfers out								
Benefits in kind								
Closing valuation	481	24,050						
−Opening valuation	−550	−24,750						
OUTPUT	939	64,811						

Inputs:	Bought weaners		Conc. feed		Transport		Other		Vet/med, etc.			
	Qty	£	Qty	£	Qty	£	Qty	£	Qty	£	£	£
Cash paid	1,016	23,514	225	28,950	1		625		480	1,339		
Closing creditors	110	3,510	18	3,100								
−Opening creditors			−20	−2,800								
Purchases	1,126	27,024	223	29,250	1		625		480	1,339		
Transfers in												
−Benefits in kind												
Opening valuation												
−Closing valuation												
VARIABLE COST	1,126	27,024	223	29,250	1		625		480	1,339		

MISCELLANEOUS VALUATION CHANGES	Breeding livestock		Crops in gd.	Total
	no.	£	£	£
Closing valuation				
−Opening valuation				
Valuation change				

Fattening pigs			GROSS MARGIN		
Ha or head 939	Total Quantity	Qty/ha or /head	£ per unit quantity	£ Total	£/ha or /head
Bacon pigs	939.0	1.00	69	64,811	69.02
misc. valn. changes	xxxxxxx	xxxxxxxx	xxxxxxxx		
OUTPUT				64,811	69.02

VARIABLE COSTS	Total Quantity	Qty/ha or /head	£ per unit quantity	£ Total	£/ha or /head
Bought weaners	1,126	1.20	24	27,024	28.78
Conc. feed	223	0.24	131	29,250	31.15
Transport	1		625	625	0.67
Other	1		480	480	0.51
Vet/med, etc.				1,339	1.43
VARIABLE COST				58,718	62.53
GROSS MARGIN				6,093	6.49

Figure 11.5 *Actual gross margin of pig herd, Home Farm 199X/9Y*

Figures 11.5 and 11.6 show the actual results for the Home Farm pig enterprise and for the farm as a whole − jumping forward nine months from the previous chapter. To ensure easy comparison with the budgets in Chapters 6, 7 and 8, it is here assumed that Adam Haynes implemented none of the developments investigated in Chapter 9.

	Per head or ha	Total	Total
Gross margins	£	£	£
Pigs	6.5	6093	
Dairy	653.0	52213	
Barley	263.0	3156	
Apples	2584.0	10337	
			71799
Unallocated revenue items			
Misc. trading receipts			4897
Misc. valuation changes			4998
TOTAL GROSS MARGIN			81694
Fixed costs			
Regular labour			18450
Machinery and vehicles: running costs			18500
depreciation			11500
Buildings and property: repairs			
depreciation			565
Rent and rates			6600
Misc. fixed costs:			7476
Interest: overdraft			2374
other			3200
LESS benefits in kind, input items			−4250
TOTAL FIXED COSTS			64415
NET PROFIT			17279

Figure 11.6 *Home Farm financial summary − actual results 199X/9Y*

Recording capital

The balance sheet

The various formats of the balance sheet were fully described in Chapter 4. Once the format has been determined, it remains to complete the lists of assets and liabilities, and find the net capital. If the CAB and profit and loss accounts have been compiled as above, and rigorously checked at every stage, this should be easy.

29/9/9X	Projected balance sheet at 28 September 199Y		
	Fixed assets:		
10,000	Orchard	13,572	
39,000	Machinery and plant	37,998	
10,000	Vehicles	8,000	
50,050	Dairy herd	55,000	
109,050	Fixed assets		114,570
	Current assets:		
	Stocks		
800	Trading livestock: calves	700	
24,750	Trading livestock: pigs	24050	
3,780	Crops in store: barley grain	4231	
390	Crops in store: barley straw	480	
8,484	Miscellaneous stores	13202 42,663	
9,080	Trade debtors	8,010	
0	Cash in bank	0	
0	Cash in hand	0	
47,284	Current assets	50,673	
	Current liabilities (due within one year):		
6,800	Trade creditors	9,889	
21,000	Bank overdraft	30,588	
27,800	Current liabilities	40,477	
19,484	Net current assets		10,196
128,534	Total assets less current liabilities		124,766
	Creditors due after one year:		
34,000	Mortgage		25,800
	Capital account:		
	Opening net capital	94534	
	+net profit	17279	
	+capital injections	4500	
	−private drawings	−10400	
	−income and capital tax	−2512	
	−benefits in kind	−4435	
94,534	Closing net capital	98966	98,966
128,534			124,766

Figure 11.7 *Actual balance sheet for Home Farm*

Starting with the assets, the cash in hand is shown by the petty cash book, and the cash in bank (if any) by the closing balance in the CAB. Closing debtors and closing valuation of stocks have already been used in the calculation of profit. The written-down value of machinery, buildings and improvements may be derived from the depreciation calculations. The value of land and investments may be derived from the opening balance sheet, adjusted for any sales and purchases shown in the 'capital' section of the CAB.

The liabilities are even easier. Overdraft (if any) is taken from the CAB. Creditors, like debtors, have already been calculated. Loans may be calculated by taking the amount outstanding at the beginning of the year, and adjusting for any repayments or new receipts of loan finance, as recorded in the 'capital' section of the CAB.

Total liabilities taken from total assets gives the closing net capital of the business. Figure 11.7 shows the actual balance sheet for Home Farm at the end of September 199Y.

The capital account

As always, it is vital to check the balance sheet through the capital account (see Chapter 4). Opening net capital is given by the opening balance sheet. Private contributions are shown by the CAB column headed 'Personal receipts'. Grants will be shown in the 'capital receipts' column, but be careful to avoid including grants which have already been shown in the balance sheet as deductions from the cost of buildings and machinery before depreciation. Private drawings and tax are easily obtained from the relevant CAB columns, and benefits in kind have already been calculated for the profit and loss account.

The result of the calculation should be identical with that of the balance sheet. If not . . . you know what to do.

Further reading

See the reading list for Chapter 6.

Valuation of stocks

Berry, A. and Jarvis, R., *Accounting in a Business Context* (London, Chapman & Hall, 1991), chapter 6.

Bull, R. J., *Accounting in Business*, 6th edition (London, Butterworths, 1990), chapter 7.

Gamble, B. T., *The Farming Business* (London, Institute of Chartered Accountants, 1986), chapter 7.

Hosken, M. and Brown, D., *The Farm Office*, 4th edition (Ipswich, Farming Press, 1991).

Her Majesty's Stationery Office, *Landlord and Tenant: The Agriculture (Calculation of Value for Compensation) Regulations, 1978*, Statutory Instrument No. 809 (HMSO). The tables in this (or a more recent edition, if available) can be a useful guide to the valuation of manurial residues etc.

12

The 'back-up' records

Introduction

The financial records discussed in the preceding chapters are designed to give clear, simple summaries of the performance and state of the business. These summaries are based on raw information of considerable volume and variety: if they are to be reliable, the business needs a foolproof system of gathering and storing this raw or 'back-up' information.

For ease of discussion, this chapter makes a somewhat arbitrary distinction between three types of back-up record: transaction documents (such as invoices and statements); physical records (of matters relating to production); and 'background information' (the rest). An examination of methods of dealing with paperwork concludes the chapter.

Transaction records

A typical transaction between farmer and supplier, e.g. of fertilizer, may go through the following stages:

1   The farmer seeks and receives a price quotation for the quantity and type of goods required.
2   If the quotation is acceptable, the farmer places an order.
3   The supplier, on receipt of the order, packs and despatches the goods to the farm.
4   The supplier sends the farmer an invoice or bill.
5   The supplier sends the farmer a statement of account at the end of the month, showing the total amount owed by the farmer (allowing for all goods supplied during the month, any credits to the account, and the amount owed at the beginning of the month).
6   The farmer sends a cheque in full or part settlement of the account, some time after his receipt of the statement.

In most cases it is likely that stages (1) and (2) will be conducted by telephone. Where transactions are frequent, it is a sensible procedure to use order forms with carbon or pressure-sensitive paper, so that the farm has a copy of the order to check against the goods delivered. Even where orders are made by telephone, they should ideally be confirmed in writing. It is not unknown for verbal messages to become distorted.

The supplier usually responds to the order by making out an invoice set. This is a bundle of forms, printed on pressure-sensitive paper. The details of the order are transcribed on to the top form (the *invoice* or bill) which is then given or sent to the customer to confirm the goods supplied and their cost. The second copy may be retained for the supplier's own records. The third and fourth copies may be sent with the goods as delivery notes, one to be retained by the farmer and the other, after being signed by the farmer as confirmation of the correct delivery of the goods, sent back with the lorry driver. Slightly different arrangements apply if the supplier uses a haulier, post, or public transport, but these make little effective difference to the documentation received by the farmer. An example of an invoice form is shown in Figure 12.1.

The statement of account shows any balance outstanding at the end of the previous month, followed by a list of the invoices issued within the current month. If goods have been returned, e.g. faulty or wrongly supplied goods, or returnable containers and pallets, one or more credit notes (a sort of invoice in reverse) will also be recorded. The total of these figures represents money owed by the farmer to the supplier. The statement will also state the terms of trade, i.e. when payment is expected, and what discounts, if any, are given for prompt payment.

The examples used above assume the farmer to be the customer. In principle it is sensible for the farmer to operate a similar system for his own sales. In practice most of the standard farm outputs are taken from the farm before the details of sale are fully known; milk, livestock (whether sold at auction or by deadweight), grain, sugar beet, and so on. In these cases, the farmer is notified of the details of sale by means of a *self-billed invoice*. The proceeds of the sale may even be paid directly into the farmer's bank account by *direct debit*. The typical farmer thus has to issue invoices for a relatively small number of items. It is unlikely that he will want a complex set of documents; a two-copy set, one for the customer and one for himself, will probably suffice.

The documents that a farmer will collect as a result of each transaction are useful both as short-term checks (e.g. order against invoice, invoice against delivery note, delivery note against goods supplied, invoices against statement) and as more permanent reminders of the quantity and type of goods bought and sold. In their latter role they provide valuable source material for financial records, and should be filed carefully (see section on paperwork later in this chapter).

Physical records

Physical records as a base for financial records

Physical records are concerned with the source and disposal of materials and services. A certain amount of physical information is required for both the compilation and the analysis of financial records. Without information concerning fertilizer rates, for instance, it may be impossible to determine accurately the

A. MERCHANT LTD
1 Fore Street
Anywhere
Barsetshire
Tel: 0123 99900

INVOICE D/N:

NO. **319**

A. Haynes Esq.
Home Farm, Anywhere

DATE   18.6.9X

QTY.	YOUR ORDER NUMBER 123	UNIT		GOODS		VAT	
		150	00	1,500	00	262	50
		130	00	1,950	00		
	Packing and Carriage						
	VAT Reg. No. 007 999 123 TERMS Strictly Monthly	SUB TOTALS		3,450	00	262	50
		VAT at 17½%		262	50		
		TOTAL		3,712	50		

Figure 12.1 *Invoice form – example*

variable costs of the various crop enterprises. Without accurate information concerning the number of pigs reared per litter it is difficult to draw useful conclusions from the management accounts of a pig breeding herd.

The physical records necessary for compilation and analysis of enterprise accounts include:

(a) *For each crop:*
  Area grown of each variety.
  Yield and quality of main product (by variety).
  Yield and quality of secondary product(s).
  Disposal (sales and transfers) of main and secondary products.
  Types and rates of use of seeds, fertilizers, sprays, etc.
  Use of casual labour and contract hire of machinery.
  Use of regular labour and own machinery (full costings only).
  Other useful information – such as soil analysis results, type and timing of
    cultivations, application of farmyard manure, etc.

(b) *For each trading livestock enterprise:*
  Sources (purchases and transfers) of young stock.
  Weight of animals on entry to herd or flock.
  Disposal (sales and transfers) of the finished animals.
  Weight and quality of the finished animals (where sold for slaughter).
  Mortality.
  Type and quantity of concentrate fed.
  Type and quantity of forage fed.
  Use of casual labour and contract hire of machinery.
  Use of regular labour own machinery (full costings only).
  Other useful information – such as dates of housing and turning out,
    veterinary records, weaning dates, grazing days, pedigree documents,
    service dates and pregnancy diagnosis for replacement breeding stock.

(c) *For each breeding livestock enterprise:*
  Number and type of progeny born and reared during the year.
  Quantity and quality of other products, e.g. milk, eggs, wool.
  Disposal (sales and transfers) of progeny and other produce.
  Mortality of progeny.
  Culls and deaths of breeding stock.
  Sources (purchases and transfers) of replacement breeding stock.
  Type and quantity of feeds (concentrate and forage).
  Use of casual labour and contract hire of machinery.
  Use of regular labour and own machinery (full costings only).
  Other useful information – such as dates of service and parturition, dates of
    weaning, dates of housing and turning out, veterinary records, pregnancy
    diagnoses, grazing days, pedigree records, etc.

(d) For fixed cost analysis:
   Number of overtime hours worked by regular labour.
   Number of hours of use of machinery, especially tractors.
   Purchases and sale of machinery, equipment and buildings.
   Service and repair records of machinery and equipment.

Not all of the records mentioned above are applicable to every enterprise, of course, and it may be that particular enterprise types require records that do not appear in the lists given.

Many of the listed items may be obtained from the transaction documents described in the previous section. These include records of quantities and quality of produce sold, and quantities of inputs which are specific to a particular enterprise, such as a fertilizer used solely for winter wheat, or a feed used only for fattening pigs. How the remaining items are recorded depends largely on the needs of the particular enterprises, and is largely a matter of organization and common sense. The golden rules of recording are:

1   Make the records easy to keep and easy to use.
2   Build in checks on accuracy, where possible.
3   Never keep any record which is unlikely to be used effectively.

Four types of physical record are sufficiently important to describe in detail. The first is a *field record*, which consists of a loose-leaf file or card index, with the details of crop inputs and outputs, cultivations, and other relevant matters recorded for each field on a separate page or card. Ideally, the record should also contain information relating to one or two previous years, since past experience is often a useful guide to present decisions. At the beginning of the production year for a crop, a new page or card can be inserted, and the oldest of the previous years' records removed and filed safely elsewhere.

For forage crops, the field record may include some items relevant to livestock, such as grazing days. Alternatively, this type of information may be kept in a separate *enterprise record* for each livestock enterprise, together with records of physical inputs (especially feed) and outputs and general information. An integral part of any livestock enterprise record should be a *livestock movement record (reconciliation)*. The movement of livestock on and off the farm, and between enterprises, is a source of much potential confusion. Where substantial numbers of various types of livestock are kept, it is well worth keeping a monthly check; otherwise a quarterly or half-yearly check may suffice. Where the latter is the case, the record may include dates of transfer of stock between enterprises, as a guide to establishing appropriate transfer prices.

An example of a livestock reconciliation form is shown in Figure 12.2 (overleaf); the farmer may of course design his own to suit his particular circumstances.

The use of reliable *barn records* helps to overcome two other potential sources of confusion: the disposal of stored crops and the allocation of feeds between livestock enterprises. Such a record should provide for the noting of all major items coming into store, particularly straw, bulk fodder, cash crops and fertilizer. It

	Opening Valuation		Purchases		Transfers in		Sales		Transfers out		Deaths	Closing Valuation	
	No.	£	No.	£	No.	£	No.	£	No.	£	No.	No.	£
Dairy cows	89	44,500			24	14,400	19	7,600				94	47,000
Calves	4	400			92	Born	60	6,000	30	3,000	2	4	400
Dairy heifers i.c.	24	14,400			33	14,850			24	14,400		33	19,800
Heifers (yearlings)	13	3,900			27	5,400	3	750	33	14,850		4	1,200
Heifers under 1 yr	23	4,140			30	3,000			27	5,400		26	4,680
Sub-total		67,340											73,080
Ewes	556	16,680	25	2,500	90	3,150	57	1,140			15	99	17,970
Rams	24	1,920	4	400			4	80			3	21	1,680
Lambs	764	19,100			868	Born	732	21,960	90	3,150	10	800	20,000
Sub-total		37,700											39,650
Sows	46	4,600			30	3,300	14	980			1	61	6,100
Boars	3	300	1	100			1	40				3	300
Weaners	39	975			1,020	Born			1,000	25,000	5	54	1,350
Baconers	388	17,460			970	24,250	998	59,845			4	356	16,020
Maiden gilts	9	990	10	1,200	30	750	2	200	30	3,300		17	1,870
Sub-total		24,325											25,640
TOTAL		129,365											138,370

Figure 12.2 *Livestock reconciliation – example for a farm with several livestock enterprises*

should also enable the recording of all disposals of these stored goods, particularly those used in growing next year's crops or in feeding of livestock. Where several livestock enterprises are fed with home-mixed rations, care must be taken to ensure that each batch of feed is recorded at the time of mixing.

The addition of simple records of opening and closing stocks allows regular checks on the accuracy of recording, by reconciliation with the field and enterprise records. This also helps in detecting waste and pilfering, and eases the task of valuing stock at the end of the year.

Where items are stored in bulk, e.g. grain, potatoes and concentrate feed, it is impossible to record accurately without some form of weighing mechanism, and the value of the barn records will suffer as a result. Up to now the adoption of such devices has been relatively slow, partly because of expense. Current developments, such as the electronic load cell, seem likely to reduce the real cost of weighing, and thus the validity of this excuse.

Physical records in short-term control

Financial records are compiled at relatively wide time intervals. Where enterprise accounts (such as gross margins) are concerned, the calculations often cannot be made until the end of the production cycle, by which time it is too late to apply the lessons learnt to the current crop. Where production is continuous (such as milk and eggs) it is possible to make more frequent calculations of margin over concentrates (value of produce less cost of concentrate feed), but at best this is likely to take place on a monthly basis.

This limits the value of financial records in controlling the progress of an enterprise from day to day, week to week. Many operational decisions have to be made to very short deadlines. In such cases, control must be based on physical records.

The scope for short-term control in crop enterprises is limited, since the production cycle is long and it is difficult to measure the response of the crop to various treatments. Records help little here – the farmer has to rely largely on visual examination of the crop, coupled with accumulated experience (either his own or an adviser's).

Trading livestock, too, often have long production cycles, e.g. two to three years for a dairy heifer, or 18 months for semi-intensive beef. In this case, however, it is easier to measure the response of output, e.g. liveweight gain, to inputs (particularly feedstuffs). Regular check weighings of livestock may be made, and both liveweight gain and feed conversion compared with targets (based on standards and/or past experience). If a significant discrepancy appears, appropriate adjustments may be made to the feeding policy.

The output of breeding livestock (in terms of progeny and eggs, etc.) may also be monitored and compared to feed consumption in order to show up short-term problems. Records of pig litter sizes or dairy cow yields, for instance, may give warning of trends which otherwise go unnoticed by the stockman. The records may be put to more positive use in maximizing margin over concentrates, as in the 'brinkmanship' system of dairy herd management.

A further dimension is added by the need to maintain the productive capacity of the herd or flock. Thus in many breeding livestock enterprises it will be necessary to keep detailed records of the breeding cycle of each animal, so that the stockman may anticipate likely dates for services, pregnancy diagnosis and parturition. Such information, together with the output performance and veterinary record of each animal, will also be of value in culling decisions.

The use of physical records in short-term control is most highly developed in large-scale intensive livestock enterprises. This applies particularly to poultry, rabbits and pigs, and to a lesser extent to large dairy herds. In these circumstances, the scope for individual attention to animals or birds is limited by the sheer number in the care of the stockman. The use of physical records becomes a part-substitute for the close relationship between man and beast which is possible in a smaller herd.

An extreme example of this is the daily recording of water consumption which is practised in many intensive poultry houses. Such recording would be of little value if used solely as a basis for enterprise accounts, since the value of the water used is so small that the effort of daily recording would not be justified. On the other hand, a significant deviation of water consumption from the norm gives the stockman a warning to look out for trouble (such as environmental problems, disease, or a leaking pipe). It also gives the vet or technical adviser valuable information for diagnosis.

Other examples include the daily consumption of food, daily mortality, daily production of eggs and similar produce, and the quality of produce (such as the grading of eggs).

Where records are needed for short-term control, there is an extra need to make the job of keeping and using the records as easy as possible. By their nature, they will often be maintained by someone other than the farmer. The 'other person' will almost certainly have less incentive than the farmer to record clearly and accurately, and to take note of unexpected changes. The best way of increasing incentive is to keep the job simple.

To encourage accurate *record-keeping*, use should be made of clear, unambiguous record forms, displayed in an unmissable position, well lit, and with a pencil provided (the occasional 'lost' pencil is a small price to pay for reliable records). To help in *interpretation* of records, graphs and other visual aids can be highly valuable, especially if they have the target performance marked on them. Colour can be used on records sheets to highlight the items that are really vital to check.

Background records

In addition to specific records of transactions and the technical performance of enterprises, there are a number of records which contribute in a general way to the financial management of the business. These range from price lists and press cuttings to insurance policies and loan agreements, and little need to be said about them except in the context of filing (see next section on paperwork).

There are two principal exceptions to this; the wages book and the machinery register. The *wages book* is the source of the single figure which appears in the cash analysis book as a weekly or monthly expense. If the book is well set out, it can help the farmer in the calculations of the various deductions from worker's pay, both statutory (PAYE and National Insurance contributions) and voluntary (milk, eggs, cottage rent, Christmas Club, etc.). It provides the basis for the pay advice slip which should accompany the wages when paid, as well as keeping the cash analysis entries simple.

The *machinery register* records information relevant to the cost of ownership of farm machinery, and eases the calculation of depreciation charges, written-down values, and profits or losses on sale. It may also be expanded to allow the recording of major repairs and maintenance, and hours worked over given periods. Although this information is often recorded in tractor log-books, it is useful to have a central record in case a log-book is mislaid. Where the farm is large enough to justify a workshop, and even the employment of a fitter, more elaborate recording may be necessary. Such records should ideally be kept in the workshop rather than the office, with the fitter or head tractor-driver responsible for their upkeep.

Organizing paperwork – method versus madness

It will be seen from the preceding sections that even a small farm business can generate a considerable volume of paperwork. Sooner or later all this paper will find its way into the files, into the post, or into the waste-paper basket. Two problems present themselves: how to file information so that it can be retrieved quickly and easily, and how to organize the flow of paper through the office so that nothing is lost or delayed.

The word 'filing' conjures up images of rows of filing cabinets, tended by secretaries. To file information simply means to store it, though. The 'files' may be anything from a cardboard box, through loose-leaf folder to microfilm; the method used depends on the size of business. For the small or medium-sized farm business, a system based on lever-arch loose-leaf files will probably be adequate. A three or four drawer filing cabinet will cost more initially, but will last longer and may be more convenient.

Whatever the container, some method of classification will be needed to permit the retrieval of stored documents. Ideally, this classification should relate in some way to the headings in the cash analysis book. Files could thus be started for each of the various enterprises and/or types of input and output, and for the various categories of fixed costs. Retrieval can be further eased by the use of systematic

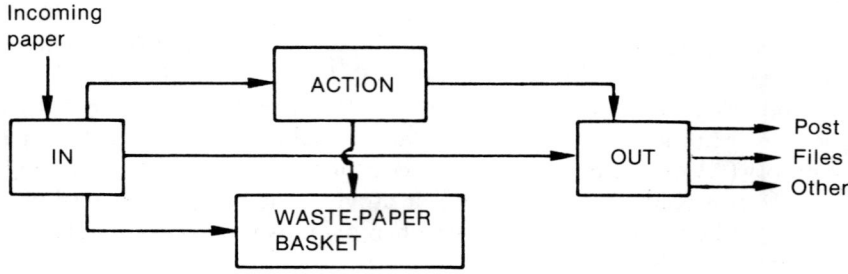

Figure 12.3 *Paperwork system*

indexing; popular methods are by alphabetical order of subject, and by numerical code.

Whatever indexing system is used, there will be times when a document relates to two or more file headings (such as an invoice which includes fungicide sprays for referencing is required. In its simplest form this need consist only of a note in each of the related files, reminding the farmer where the document may be found. More complex systems may be devised using card indexes.

It is of little use having a wonderful filing system if the documents never get to the file. Without a systematic processing of paperwork through the office, vital documents can easily be 'lost' in disorganized piles of paper. The consequences can be financially detrimental (such as the loss of a discount for prompt payment on a large order) or just embarrassing (such as the time when the adviser arrives to talk about the dairy and the milk record sheets cannot be found).

The first requirement of an office* system (see Figure 12.3) is a waste-paper basket. In addition at least three receptacles are needed. These can be standard office trays, but there are many alternatives; bulldog clips, cardboard boxes, or just tidy piles. The first tray (or other receptacle) is used to receive all incoming paper, such as the day's post. Another accumulates paper which has been dealt with, and which is destined for the files or the post. The tray in between acts as a repository for all items which are awaiting action. Paper thus comes into the 'in' tray, stays there only until is is examined, after which it is transferred either to the waste-paper basket, or to the 'action' tray to await further developments, or to the 'out' tray for filing, posting, or other disposal.

A useful supplement to the 'action' tray is a looseleaf diary. This has two advantages over the conventional form of diary. The first is that one can always keep a 'rolling' twelve months in the diary – as soon as one month has gone by, its pages can be removed and new pages inserted at the other end of the diary. The

---

*The term 'office' is used to denote any area set aside for paperwork, whether a purpose-built room or a desk in the corner of the spare bedroom. The essential features are comfort, convenience and quiet.

second, more important feature is the facility for clipping documents into the diary at certain dates. Thus if a large bill is due to be paid in twenty days' time, it can be filed so that on the payment day, the diary is opened to reveal that document. The same process can be used for amounts due to be received, licence renewal forms, and similar documents. This provides a more positive reminder than an action tray full of papers.

Because of their volume, and their financial significance, special care is needed in dealing with transaction documents. If the volume of transactions is sufficiently great, it may even be worthwhile installing a duplicate set of trays solely for such documents. The important points are first, to keep together all documents relating to a particular supplier or customer, and second, to avoid filing any documents before payment has been made or received. Thus, for purchases, the order copy should wait in the action tray for the invoice, delivery note, statement and other related documents; as these arrive they should be checked against each other and pinned to the order. When the cheque is written out, its number and amount can be recorded on the top sheet and the whole bundle of papers transferred to the 'out' tray ready for filing. Naturally the payment details will be recorded on the cheque stub, for transfer to the cash analysis book at a later date. A similar procedure should be followed for sales documents.

As with any unwelcome work, it is advisable to make dealing with paperwork an integral part of the general routine. A suitable analogy relates to trips to the dentist – it is tempting to 'forget' about the six-monthly check-ups, but if you do so the consequences can be painful. Similarly, paperwork can be made less of a chore, and more efficient, if it is incorporated into the daily timetable (say half an hour after breakfast) instead of saving it all up for a rainy day.

End-note

You are likely to be the only person making use of records of your farm. Even in a one-man business, it is possible for the owner to fall sick or have an accident, and have to rely on other people to run the unit. It is therefore vital that the records should be made easy to keep and to interpret, as described above.

Employees may need training and initial supervision to cope with tasks that seem simple to you, but may be totally foreign to them. In order to encourage careful recording, it is good policy to explain why the various records are necessary, and to share with employees the lessons that you learn from those records.

A positive attitude to recording can be encouragd by providing a herdsman, say, with an 'office' area, where he can complete records in relative comfort, and which gives paperwork a higher status in the employees' eyes. Such an area can often be formed within the dairy or other such buildings, and need not cost more than a good coat of paint, a second-hand table and chair, a noticeboard, and some basic office equipment.

Further reading

General

Hosken, M. and Brown, D., *The Farm Office*, 4th edition (Ipswich, Farming Press, 1991). Still the standard work on this topic, and highly recommended.

Physical records

Barnard, C. S. and Nix, J. S., *Farm Planning and Control*, 2nd edition (London, Cambridge University Press, 1979), pp. 516–19.
Speedy, A. W., *Sheep Production* (London, Longman, 1980).
Whittemore, C. T., *Pig Production* (London, Longman, 1980).

PART FOUR

Controlling the Business

Earlier in this book it was suggested that the financial management of a business could be described in terms of 'planning and control'. Adam Haynes has used budgets in planning the financial affairs of Home Farm. As he puts those budgets into operation, he should start operating a system of financial control

'Control' was earlier defined as the comparison of actual and expected performance, and the taking of any necessary corrective action. This process can, and should, be undertaken with respect to each of the three financial indicators: cash, profit and capital.

When using any of the control techniques described in the following chapters, it is essential to remember that one is seeking clues that might help in the solution of a problem, rather than the solution itself. As L. E. Rockley* says in the context of performance ratios:

> [Performance comparisons] are but demonstrations of matters needing further scrutiny. They rarely give the final answers to any problem by themselves alone; it is the ensuing scrutiny of the underlying reasons for change which should present management with a plan of action to correct any undesirable developments.

Finance for the Non-accountant, 3rd edition, (Business Books, 1979).

$\boxed{13}$

Monitoring cash flow

Why monitor cash flow?

Of the three financial indicators, the most sensitive, and probably most important to monitor is cash flow. Few businesses, at least in farming, are likely to produce profit and capital statements at intervals of less than six months, if that. The cash-flow budget and the cash analysis book, on the other hand, are normally drawn up on a monthly basis. A monthly comparison of cash-flow budget and cash analysis results can enable problems to be spotted much sooner than a six-monthly or yearly analysis of profit or capital. The earlier such potential problems are noticed, the sooner remedial action may be taken.

The penalty of *not* monitoring cash flow regularly and frequently could be at best the loss of an opportunity, and at worst the loss of a business. As an example of the first, take Farmer A, whose budgeted cash-flow profile for 199X is shown in Figure 13.1. Farmer A's results are a little better than he had budgeted at the end of month 8.

If Farmer A does not take the trouble to monitor his cash flow, it will not be a disaster. His bank statement will show a larger cash surplus than expected, and he

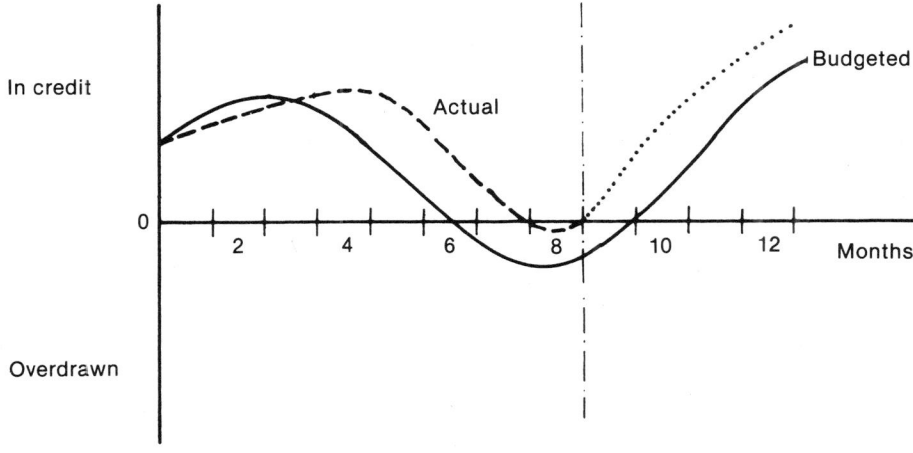

Figure 13.1 *Budgeted and actual cash-flow profiles, Farmer A*

157

may then begin to think about doing something useful with that cash rather than let it lie in the current account. The chances are, though, that by the time realization dawns, many of the opportunities for short-term investment will have been missed. If he had monitored cash flow carefully, he might well have spotted the likelihood of such a discrepancy arising long before it showed up as an increased surplus. He would then have had plenty of time to make plans for buying store lambs, storing grain that little bit longer, or even diverting money to a deposit account for a few weeks.

As an example of a more extreme problem, take Farmer B, whose budgeted cash-flow profile for 199X is shown in Figure 13.2.

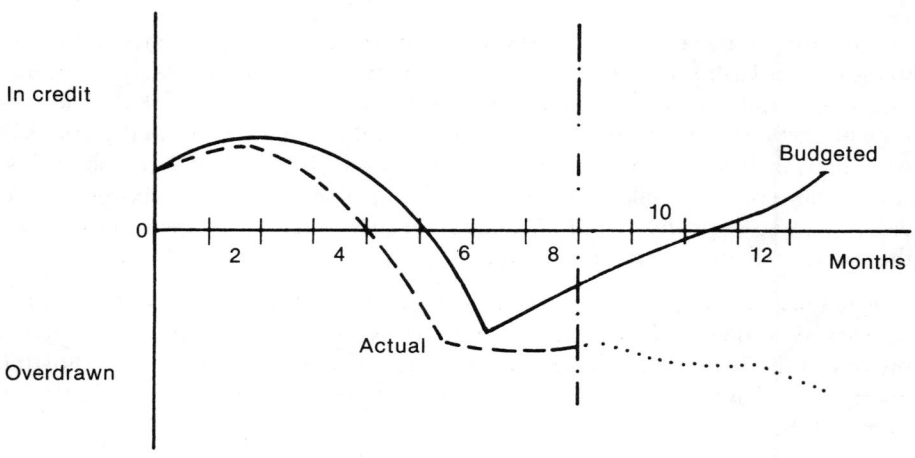

Figure 13.2   *Budget and actual cash-flow profiles, Farmer B*

Whether because of bad luck, bad management, or a combination of the two, Farmer B is having a bad year. If he monitors cash flow carefully, he has a good chance of noticing danger signals at an early stage, and can have contingency plans ready in case his worst fears are justified. These contingency plans might include delaying expansion, bringing sales forward and/or delaying purchases, selling land or cottages, and making an early appointment to discuss the matter with his bank manager.

It would be understandable if Farmer B decided that he could not face the financial realities shown up by the budget/actual comparison. The problem is unlikely to go away of its own accord, however, and if he ignores it, the crunch could come at a time when it is too late to change plans or to maintain the confidence of the bank and other lenders. Result: another farming bankruptcy.

In all businesses, then, whether successful or struggling, there is much to be gained from monitoring cash flow.

CASH FLOW BUDGET		199x/y		**VERSION** 2			
% interest rate 15		OCTOBER		NOVEMBER		DECEMBER	
		budget	actual	budget	actual	budget	actual
RECEIPTS							
Milk	1	2280	2280	3800	3651	8550	9254
Calves	2	500	500	3500	4028	2000	1895
Pigs	7	6300	6300	6300	5214	3150	4269
Apples	14					23000	18952
Sundries	18				256		390
VAT charged	19				132		156
VAT refunds	20						1674
Capital: grants	21						
machinery sale	22				500		500
TOTAL RECEIPTS		9080	9080	13600	13781	36700	37090

		OCTOBER		NOVEMBER		DECEMBER	
PAYMENTS							
Feed: cows	25	3750	4000			3000	
young stock	26						
pigs	27	2800	2800	2418	2295	2420	2790
	28						
Vet and med: cows	29	212	140	208	190	208	507
Vet and med: pigs	30	100	120	100	205	100	190
L/stock purch: cows	31						
L/stock purch: pigs	32	2500	2500	2500	2090	1750	1325
Misc. dairy costs	33	250	320	250	180	250	532
Misc. pig costs	34	104	115	104	115	104	133
Misc. crop costs	38	650	350	75	127	750	654
Wages: permanent	39	1625	1785	1625	1584	1625	1545
casual	40	1000	1026	800	829	400	540
Power: fuel	41	540	410	540	684	540	210
repairs	42	625	426	625	492	625	998
contract hire							
Property repairs	45			200			
Overdraft interest	46					935	944
Loan interest	47						550
Hire purchase	48						
Leasing charges	49			525	525		
Overhead sundries	50	625	930	1725	1100	625	100
machinery purchase	53						3369
capital repayment	54					4100	4100
Personal: drawings	56	760	850	760	850	760	760
tax	57						
VAT paid	58		492		633		1188
TOTAL PAYMENTS		15541	16264	12455	11899	18192	20435
Net cash flow	59	-6461	-7184	1145	1882	18508	16655
Opening balance	60	-21000	-21000	-27461	-28184	-26316	-26302
Closing balance	61	-27461	-28184	-26316	-26302	-7808	-9647
Monthly interest		343	352	329	329	98	121

Figure 13.3 *Cash flow budget/actual comparison, Home Farm*

Comparison of actual and budgeted results

The comparison of budgeted and actual results is made easy by the incorporation of 'actual' columns into the cash-flow budget (see Chapter 7). The figures needed to complete these 'actual' columns are derived from the monthly totals of the analysis columns in the cash analysis book (Chapter 10). If these column headings have been chosen wisely they will correspond very closely to the headings used in the cash-flow budget. The process then becomes one of a simple transfer of figures from cash analysis to budget. This transfer should ideally take place as soon as the monthly reconciliation of the cash analysis book has taken place. Figure 13.3 (page 159) shows this process completed for December 199X/9Y for Home Farm, using figures from the cash flow budget (Figure 7.8) and the reconciled cash analysis (Figure 10.5 and 10.6).

Once the 'actual' column for a particular month has been completed, it can be compared with the corresponding budget column. The golden rule applying to all financial comparisons is to start with the general and work down to the particular. In the case of cash-flow control, this implies starting with a comparison of actual and budgeted closing bank balances for the month under consideration. The next stage is to examine the main factors which contribute to the bank balances, i.e. opening balance, total cash receipt and total cash payments. Then the individual items of receipts and payment should be investigated, concentrating on those which (a) are financially large, and (b) show a significant variance.

A systematic approach of this kind avoids the farmer becoming bogged down in minutiae and losing sight of the overall financial picture as a result. Figure 13.4

Figure 13.4 *Working from the general to the specific in monitoring cash flow*

illustrates the process: analysis should start with the items at the top of the page and work down as far as the detail of the figures will allow. Memory is fallible, and it is useful to make a brief monthly record of events which led to discrepancies between budgeted and actual results; this can be jotted down on the back of the budget, or in a spare space in that month's column. This record is valuable not only for short-term control, but also in providing guidance for the preparation of next year's budgets.

Interpreting the results

Having examined the discrepancies, the farmer must decide what action, if any, to take. If the various discrepancies more or less balance each other out, he may decide to keep the business on its present course. If he decides that corrective action is necessary, then he should prepare revised budgets to show the effect of the changes on cash flow in particular, but also on profit and capital. If the changes are small, outline or partial budgets will be sufficient; otherwise a complete revision will be necessary.

Even if there is no major change of policy during the year, the cumulative effect of many small discrepancies over several months may result in the actual position bearing very little resemblance to the budget by half-way through the year. The closing bank balance may be very close to the target, but the way in which that balance has been derived may differ greatly from the budget. If this is the case, the budget should be revised to correct such anomalies and make the budget a more realistic and useful document. If the cash-flow budget is treated as a 'rolling' plan as described in Chapter 7, this revision will be undertaken automatically at regular intervals.

In the example shown in Figure 13.3, relating to Adam Haynes's first three months' trading, the overdraft is £1839 higher than budgeted. This may not seem a large difference but if it represents a trend that will continue for the rest of the year, it is a matter for concern. The difference arises particularly from the month of December: the closing balance for the previous month is very close to that budgeted.

Looking at the receipts analysis, it is possible to identify variations in individual items which more or less cancel each other out. The large shortfall on apple receipts (over £4000) is partly compensated by increases in pig and milk receipts and some sundry receipts. The VAT charged and refunds, however, merely balance out VAT payments made over the last 3 months, leaving non-VAT receipts about £2000 less than budgeted.

Total payments are up £2243 on budget in December – about £1100 excluding VAT. Much of this is due to the unscheduled purchase of machinery. If this is merely bringing forward a purchase that was budgeted for a later month, the effect of this will be temporary. If, on the other hand, the purchase was not anticipated, it will adversely affect the results throughout the rest of the year.

The absence of a payment for dairy feed has the effect of reducing payments by £3000 compared to the budget. This effect is not likely to last, however. It would be unrealistic to suppose that the farm did not need any dairy concentrates in November and December, and it is a reasonable assumption that the bill remains behind the kitchen clock, waiting to be paid. In that case, the next month's cash flow will be correspondingly poorer than budgeted: in effect, December's cash position is £4839 worse than budget, rather than £1839. Other factors may not show up on the comparison, yet need taking into consideration. Adam has just placed an order for a £2500 farm computer system, for instance. It was not in the budget, so Adam needs to bear this in mind when projecting the results for December forward over the rest of the year.

The £550 difference in loan interest payment arises from a mistake in the original budget, where payments were anticipated in March and September, rather than December and June. In this case the adverse effect will be rectified in March, but budgeting mistakes are not always so small or so temporary: it has been known for a farmer to omit the entire rental payment from the first year's cash-flow budget, with painful consequences. Regular cash-flow monitoring can help the farmer to identify such problems at an early stage in the year, and he can embark on corrective action before it is too late.

Some differences are nevertheless useful prompts to further investigation. The 'vet and med' bill for the cows is more than twice that budgeted, for instance, a fact that might focus Adam's suspicions and encourage him to review the health status of his herd.

Annual cash-flow monitoring

Examination of cash-flow performance over a whole year can be valuable, although it is not as immediate as monthly monitoring, or as comprehensive as profit comparisons. Adam Haynes's first year cash flow is summarized in Figure 13.5, with variances shown in both money and percentage terms.

Since December 199Y (we are jumping forward in time from the previous section) Adam has managed to keep a tight rein on cash flow, with the result that the closing balance is just under that budgeted. This has partly been achieved by an increase in capital injections from his own personal reserves ('personal receipts' in the budget), but the result should, nevertheless, reassure the bank manager at the impending annual review of Adam's account. Lower wages and miscellaneous fixed costs have helped to balance higher power costs: some economies have been possible on dairy feed. The low apple receipts remain a problem, balanced by higher sundries and machinery sales. There are few dramatic variances, however.

The comparison takes no account of money owed, or of goods in store: capital and personal transactions obscure the picture of trading performance. In other words, what is needed for an effective annual appraisal is an examination of net profit.

		Total		Difference	
		budget	actual	£	%
Receipts:					
Milk	1	76,095	77,059	964	1.27
Calves	2	7,400	6,258	-1,142	-15.43
Cull cows	3	11,000	9,831	-1,169	-10.63
	4				
Sheep	5				
	6				
Pigs	7	66,780	65,975	-805	-1.21
	8				
Poultry	9				
	10				
Wheat	11				
Wheat straw	12				
Oats	13				
Apples	14	23,000	18,952	-4,048	-17.60
Potatoes	15				
	16				
	17				
Sundries	18	2,650	4,897	2,247	84.79
VAT charged	19		2,174	2,174	
VAT refunds	20		11,867	11,867	
Capital: grants	21				
machinery sales	22	5,000	7,523	2,523	50.46
	23				
Personal receipts	24	3,200	4,500	1,300	40.63
TOTAL		195,125	209,036	13,911	7.13

		Total		Difference	
		budget	actual	£	%
Payments:					
Feed: cows	25	12,900	11,362	-1,538	-11.92
pigs	27	29,400	28,950	-450	-1.53
Vet and med.: cows	29	2,500	3,346	846	33.84
pigs	30	1,200	1,096	-104	-8.67
L/stock purch.: cows	31	17,500	18,260	760	4.34
pigs	32	27,500	23,514	-3,986	-14.49
Misc. dairy costs	33	3,000	2,912	-88	-2.93
Misc. pig costs	34	1,250	1,348	98	7.84
Seed	35	600	895	295	49.17
Fertilizer	36	6,070	6,524	454	7.48
Spray	37	1,930	2,198	268	13.89
Misc. crop costs	38	2,920	3,257	337	11.54
Wages: permanent	39	19,500	17,250	-2,250	-11.54
casual	40	3,700	4,251	551	14.89
Power: fuel	41	6,900	7,500	600	8.70
repairs	42	7,500	9,900	2,400	32.00
contract hire	43	1,000	1,100	100	10.00
Rent and rates	44	6,600	6,600		
Property repairs	45	200		-200	-100.00
Overdraft interest	46	2,956	2,374	-582	-19.69
Loan interest	47	1,100	1,100		
Hire purchase	48				
Leasing charges	49	2,100	2,100		
Overhead sundries	50	8,600	7,476	-1,124	-13.07
	51				
Capital: orchard	52	3,000	4,137	1,137	37.90
capital repayment	54	8,200	8,200		
Personal: drawings	56	9,120	10,400	1,280	14.04
tax	57	3,000	2,512	-488	-16.27
VAT paid	58		14,041	14,041	
TOTAL		205,246	218,624	13,378	6.52
Net cash flow	59	-10,121	-9,588	533	-5.27
Opening balance	60	-21,000	-21,000		
Closing balance	61	-31,121	-30,588	533	-1.71

Figure 13.5 *Budget/actual comparison, whole year*

Further reading

Atkinson, J. M., Hastings, M. R. and Warren, M. F., *Cash Flow Budgeting* (Agricultural Training Board/Seale Hayne College/Manpower Services Commission (The Family Farm Series), 1986, revised 1990). A step-by-step guide to cash-flow budgeting and monitoring.

14

Monitoring profit and capital

The importance of monitoring profit

Although the monitoring of cash flow from month to month may be vital to the survival of the business, it is not enough on its own to ensure the continued prosperity of the firm. Without taking account of money owed to the business, for instance, or produce that is still unsold and in store, it is impossible to derive a clear impression of the efficiency of the farm as a working unit. For this it is necessary to monitor profits.

The monitoring of profits is not as sensitive a control measure as the monitoring of cash flow. Although it is possible to draw up monthly profit and loss accounts (and common practice in manufacturing firms), the long production cycles of most agricultural products make it unlikely that the benefit will be worth the effort. Possible exceptions are those items whose production most closely resembles a factory system, such as eggs, poultry and milk.

It is likely that the monitoring of profits will be an annual process for most enterprises. Ideally, it should take place as soon as the crop is harvested or the livestock sold, so that any lessons learnt may be applied, without delay, to subsequent production. This will certainly mean the farmer compiling his own management accounts, rather than waiting for the accountant's version. It may also mean anticipating the sale price of produce which is likely to be sold some time after the end of the crop year.

Broadly speaking, there are three complementary ways of monitoring profits each relying on a comparison of some sort. The first is by comparison with the results of previous years; the second by comparison with other farms; and the third by comparison with budgeted profits, i.e. budgetary control.

Certain comments may be made with respect to all three types of comparison, to avoid repetition. First, as with cash flow, the process should be systematic. The major summary figures should be investigated first, working progressively down to the smallest details in the account. The process is illustrated in Figure 14.1 using a profit and loss account in gross margin form as an example. Analysis should start with the items at the top of the page, and work down the page as far as the detail of the account will allow.

Second, since the analysis is intended as a foundation for decision-making, attention should be concentrated on those components of the account which:

1   Can be influenced by the farmer within the time period concerned.
2   Are financially significant.

*Hectares for grazing livestock; sq. metres for intensive livestock (where applicable)

Figure 14.1 *Working from the general to the specific in analysis of profit and loss accounts*

Thus, in a given year, there may be little a farmer can do to influence his rent bill, or even his regular labour costs. Most prices are set outside the business – the farmer is a 'price-taker'. It is unwise to spend time analysing such items when that time could be spent more profitably in analysing items which *are* affected by the farmer's decisions. It is similarly foolish to spend hours trying to find ways of reducing a comparatively minor cost when an equivalent time spent on a larger cost might bring substantially greater rewards.

This is not to say that other items should be completely ignored. Changes in minor costs can be valuable indicators of major problems, and information about the effect of factors outside the farmer's influence (such as changes in price levels) can help him to adapt his strategy to the business environment. It is merely that such items should take second place in the analysis.

Finally, the opening remarks to Part Four should be borne in mind. The comparisons provide only clues – not whole answers. The answers arise only from combining these clues with a thorough knowledge of the farm in question, and of the principles of agricultural husbandry.

Comparison with previous years

The method of analysis

Comparison of profits between years can be used with a profit and loss account of any form. Little needs to be said about the mechanics of the comparison, except to reiterate the need for a systematic approach. Where possible, the current year's results should be viewed in the light of those of several previous years, rather than just one. In this way the farmer may avoid making judgements which are influenced by abnormal features of any one year.

Benefits and limitations

Comparisons with previous years have an advantage over inter-farm comparisons in relating to a single farm rather than to a group of roughly similar businesses. They show the progress of the business between years, in terms of both major expansion and general improvements (or decline) in productivity. They also show the impact of price movements, both general (i.e. inflation), and specific.

Unfortunately, it is often difficult to distinguish between the two effects and to tell how much an improvement in a margin is due to increased efficiency, as opposed to increased product prices. In times of inflation the farmer is likely to be forced back on to comparison of the physical components of the account, such as yields and input quantities.

A further limitation of this approach is that it is more backward-looking than either of the others. The past can be a valuable guide for future decisions, but it is dangerous to rely on it absolutely. Nevertheless, in view of the fact that it is specific to the business under scrutiny, measures progress and uses figures that are almost always readily available, inter-year comparison remains an important source of information.

Inter-farm comparisons (1): conventional profit and loss account

The method of analysis

The technique of inter-farm comparison relies on comparing the farmer's own profit and loss account with those of other, similar farms. If this technique is to be used at all, it should normally be based on profit and loss accounts in enterprise account form. There are times, however, when the only profit information available is in the form of a conventional account.

The form of account analysis used in the manufacturing and commercial worlds is concerned largely with sales – in relation to profit, capital, creditors, and so on. This emphasis on sales performance is not entirely appropriate for farming businesses, since the farmer has little control over the amount he can sell or the price he receives. Once he has committed himself to a production system, his aim must be to produce as much output as possible of a given quality, at the minimum cost. Farm account analysis is thus concerned largely with the efficiency of production, rather than sales.

The usual source of comparison information is the *Farm Business Survey* (FBS). Each regional centre of the FBS (usually attached to the agricultural economics department of a university) collects financial information from a range of farms each year. The results are published annually in the form of a regional farm management handbook. Results are displayed for each of the main farming types in the region, and by farm size.

In order to ensure that their statistics give a fair reflection of farming efficiency, the FBS researchers 'standardize' the profit information that they receive. Their intention is to avoid the results being distorted by factors which are not directly dependent on the standard of farm management. In order to make a fair comparison between his own profit and loss account and the FBS figures, the farmer must 'standardize' his account in the same way. The revised account will give the *net farm income* (NFI) and the *management and investment income* (MII) of the business.

NFI is calculated as follows:

Take   Net profit
include   An extra expense to represent the value of any unpaid labour (not including that of the farmer and spouse);
exclude   (a) Any non-farm revenue and expense.
         (b) Any interest charges paid.

(c) Any revenue and expense connected with the ownership of land (e.g. repairs and maintenance, mortgage payments, receipt of rents). A notional rent should take the place of these items for any land which is owned, rather than rented, by the farmer.

MII is calculated by estimating the value of any physical work done on the farm by farmer and spouse, and deducting this from NFI (see Figure 14.2)

	£	£
Net profit		10,000
Less: Son's labour	− 2,000	
Less: Sundry external receipts	− 500	
Plus: Interest paid	2,000	
Plus: Land expenses	500	
Less: Rents received	− 1,500	
Less: Notional rent for land owned	− 1,000	− 2,500
NET FARM INCOME		7,500
Less: Value of farmer's physical labour		− 2,000
MANAGEMENT AND INVESTMENT INCOME		5,500

Figure 14.2 *Calculation of NFI and MII — example*

The MII per hectare may now be compared with that shown in the FBS handbook for similar farms in the same area. In attempting to explain deviations between his MII and that of the comparison, the farmer should work through the various items of revenue and expense in the same way. These will not be classified by enterprise, so the management information which can be derived is somewhat limited.

Various supplementary 'production standards' can be used in an attempt to remedy this deficiency, such as crop yields per hectare and livestock stocking rates. Those relating to fixed costs can be valuable, particularly the calculation of gross output or gross margin per £100 labour and/or power cost.

The 'standards' used, and their calculation, can vary from one FBS region to another. Before calculating such standards, it is wise to check the glossary of terms in the FBS handbook.

Finally, MII may be compared with the capital employed. Since the standardization of the account removes all land-owning considerations, the appropriate measure of capital is taken to be 'tenant's capital'. Various definitions of tenant's capital are in use, the most common being the average of the opening and closing valuations of stocks, machinery and equipment. MII and tenant's capital are then combined in the calculation of *return on tenant's capital*, using the formula:

$$\frac{\text{MII}}{\text{Tenant's capital}} \times 100 = x \%$$

This can then be compared with the FBS results.

Benefits and limitations

The primary benefit of whole-farm account analysis is that it extracts decision clues from an otherwise unhelpful document. Where records are limited, this benefit can be substantial.

Against this must be set the significant limitations of both the method and the comparison figures. The *method* is based on a whole-farm approach. The result is that there is little scope for investigation of individual enterprises. Another criticism is that most of the comparison is aimed at determining the efficiency of one input, land, whereas the efficiency of use of other inputs, notably capital, is often more important.

The chief problem with the *comparison figures* themselves is their broad grouping of farm types and areas. Each FBS regional unit surveys a large number of farms. For convenience of presentation the results have to be classified into a relatively small number of groups. The 'average' results for each group thus arise from a wide variety of farms – some on good soil, others on poor; some with root crops, others with none, and so on. It follows that it is difficult for the farmer to be sure that he is comparing like with like. Further limitations arise from the inevitable delay between collection and publication of the data, and from doubts over the 'representativeness' of the sample of farms used in the survey.*

In short, it is not worth bothering with this technique unless the only source of profit information is a conventional profit and loss account.

Inter-farm comparisons (2): profit and loss accounts in enterprise account form

The method of analysis

In this form of analysis, enterprise accounts in either gross margin or full-absorption costing form are compared with 'typical' accounts for similar enterprises. These 'typical' accounts will have been compiled from survey data, from the

*See, for instance, Barnard, C. S., 'Data in agriculture', *J. Agric. Econ.*, vol. 26, pp. 310–17, September 1975.

results of enterprise costing schemes, or by reference to standard performance figures.

A common source of survey data is the Farm Business Survey; other sources are investigations carried out by commercial firms (such as feed and fertilizer suppliers); by the advisory and development services; and by researchers in universities, colleges, and research institutes.

Enterprise costing schemes are run by various organizations, such as the Meat and Livestock Commission (MLC) (beef, sheep and pigs); commercial firms (such as feed suppliers); the Genus Management Services; the National Farmers' Union (NFU) (eggs and poultry); and various advisers and management consultants. The results may be made available only to subscribers to the scheme concerned, but are often widely published. A particularly useful type of scheme is that using comparisons between a relatively small group of farmers within the same locality.

'Standard' accounts are not built up directly from survey data, but from the opinions of experts as to the typical performance which might be expected from a reasonably well-run enterprise. They are particularly useful where survey data is out of date, insufficiently detailed, or in other ways unreliable. The various sources of standards include MLC publications, the Cambridge University Pig Management Scheme, the NFU poultry bulletins and, with forecast prices, farm management handbooks such as those produced by J. S. Nix, Agro Business Consultants, and the Scottish Agricultural Colleges.

If a step-by-step analysis is followed, as recommended at the beginning of this chapter, few difficulties should arise. It is necessary occasionally to make judgements on a highly-summarized account, with little detail supplied. In such circumstances it is vital to ascertain the way in which the account was compiled. In a gross margin account, for instance, the inclusion of casual labour and/or contractors' charges in the account of one enterprise can make the margin look poor in comparison with another where all the labour and power is supplied from within the business.

In comparing gross margin accounts it is easy to forget the existence of fixed costs, although there is often great scope for economy in labour and power costs. These should be investigated in the first place using the FBS comparisons described earlier, followed if necessary by the more detailed analysis described in Chapter 18.

For continuous-production enterprises such as milk and egg production, it is possible to make interim checks on performance by comparing such measures as the *margin over concentrates* (i.e. value of milk or egg sales minus cost of concentrate feed), or the quantity of concentrate feed used per unit of physical quantity of output (e.g. kilogrammes of concentrate feed per litre of milk or per dozen eggs). Although these are crude as measures of financial performance, they are quick and easy to calculate, and sensitive indicators of flock or herd health and management.

Benefits and limitations

The main benefit of this form of analysis is the ability to compare the economics of one's own farm enterprises with the performance that other farmers are currently achieving. As long as enough detail is provided in the comparison figures, a 'lower-than-typical' margin can be explained by careful examination of output and costs. This may, in turn, lead to corrective action being taken to prevent similar discrepancies occurring in future. Since each enterprise is investigated individually, the grosser limitations of the whole-account method are avoided.

On the other hand, it is difficult to avoid the problems inherent in the use of comparison with a 'typical' farm. Survey and costing scheme data is likely to be drawn from a wide range of farm types and, as with the whole-account comparisons, it is difficult for the farmer to be sure that he is comparing like with like. There is inevitably a delay between collection of the data and its publication (often more of a problem with surveys than with costing services). Where collection of information depends on the willing co-operation of farmers, it is often difficult to be sure that the information is truly representative (more of a problem with costing services than with surveys). The wide range of types of contributing farms may make difficulties in providing full physical detail in the comparison accounts.

The use of 'standard' accounts can overcome the problems of delay and detail. This is only gained, however, at the expense of reliability, since one is dependent on the compiler's opinion as to what level of performance is 'typical' or 'acceptable'.

The clues provided by this technique are of higher quantity and quality than those provided by the whole-farm technique, but they must still be treated with considerable caution.

Budgetary comparisons

The method of comparison

In attempting to control the finances of a farm business, it is far more relevant to make comparisons with targets set for that specific farm than with the performance of a 'typical' farm. This is the process of budgetary control which was discussed in the previous chapter with respect to cash flow. The method is one of simple comparison between the profit and loss account and the profit and loss budget; it can be used with profit statements of either conventional or enterprise account form, although the latter will, of course, give a more comprehensive view. It is also possible to use summary enterprise checks (such as margin over concentrates) as interim control measures.

As with the other forms of comparison, it is essential to use a systematic approach (see Figure 14.1).

Benefits and limitations

This method compares figures relating to the same farm, in the same time period and with as much physical detail as the farmer himself cares to supply. It thus avoids most of the problems associated with comparisons between years and/or between farms. A more positive benefit is that, since the budget will have (or should have) been prepared with the farmer's objectives firmly in mind, the budgetary comparison is a valuable check on the degree to which those aspirations have been achieved. Its contribution to the planning/control process is thus far more direct than that of the comparisons with a wide range of other farms, each of which may have different objectives from those of one's own farm.

The limitations of this technique are minor compared to the other forms of comparison. The most significant problem is likely to be insularity. If the farmer relies entirely on comparisons within his own farm, and never takes the trouble to compare with standard or survey data, there is a danger that he will be ignorant of opportunities to improve profits by bringing outputs and/or costs into line with those on comparable farms. This can be avoided by use of a judicious blend of both inter-farm and budgetary comparisons, the one helping the interpretation of the other.

Variance analysis

Principles and method

The primary aim in any form of account comparison must be to identify discrepancies between one account and another. It is often difficult to decide exactly *how* these discrepancies arise, however. Three factors are at work: volume, i.e. the number of head or hectares; unit quantity, i.e. yield or input per head or per hectare; and price.

As an example, the revenue from the sale of weaners in a pig breeding herd will vary according to the average number of sows in a herd during the year, the number of pigs weaned per sow, and the average price obtained for each weaner. Unless some attempt is made to isolate the effects of these on a comparison, valuable management clues may be lost. To use the above example, the actual revenue may be £5 more than the comparison. This £5 could be the result of a 'favourable variance' (say £1005) arising from better prices, and 'unfavourable variances' arising from poor sow performance (– £950) and low sow numbers (– £50). A serious management problem is thus masked by a fortunate increase in prices. This is an extreme example, but it demonstrates the danger of relying on the *measurement* of discrepancies, without any attempt to *explain* their origins.

Such explanations may be provided by the use of *variance analysis*. The principles of the technique can be illustrated, for a simple 'two-way' example (i.e. excluding

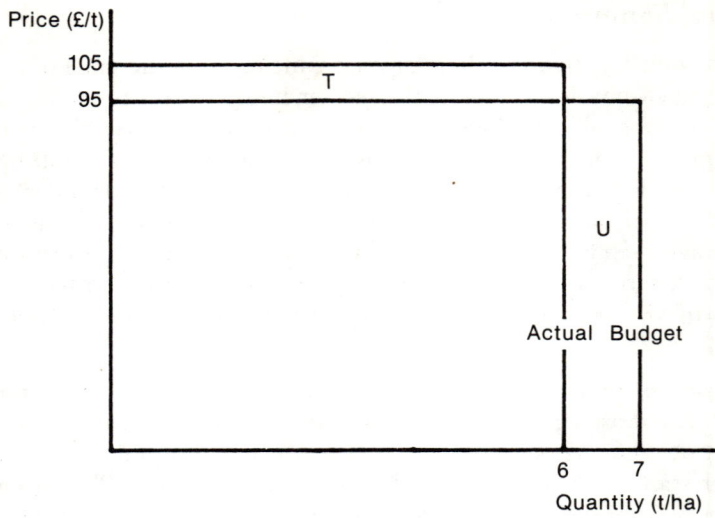

Figure 14.3 *Price/quantity diagram for a wheat crop*

the effect of volume variances), by means of a price/quantity diagram. Figure 14.3 relates to the revenue per hectare of a wheat crop; price is shown on the vertical axis, unit quantity on the horizontal axis, and revenue (price × quantity) is shown by the area of the resulting rectangle. Two revenue rectangles are shown on the same diagram, one representing the actual performance obtained, and the other the comparison (described here as the budget, but it could be from survey, standard, or previous-year data).

It may be deduced that the effect of the unfavourable variance in quantity is represented by the small rectangle marked 'U' (i.e. − 1 t × £95). Similarly the effect of the favourable variance in price is given by the small rectangle marked 'T' (i.e. £10 × 6 t). The measurement and explanation of variances may now be restated as:

	£
Actual revenue: 6 t at £105/t	630
Budget revenue: 7 t at £95/t	665
Difference	− 35
Variance due to unit quantity: −1 t × £95	− 95
Variance due to price: + £10 × 6 t	+ 60
Total variance	− 35

From this may be derived a general formula for the calculation of two-way variances:

Variance due to unit quantity
= Difference in unit quantity × Budget price

Variance due to price
   = Difference in price × Actual unit price

The technique may be extended to the analysis of three-way variances, so as to incorporate the effects of volume variances. If the wheat crop above was grown on only 30 ha instead of the 35 budgeted, the difference in total revenue would be:

$$(£630 \times 30 \text{ ha}) - (£665 \times 35 \text{ ha}) = -£4375$$

Variance due to volume (of hectares or head)
   = Difference in numbers × Budget unit quantity × Budget price

Variance due to unit quantity
   = Difference in unit quantity × Actual numbers × Budget price

Variance due to price
   = Difference in price × Actual numbers × Actual unit quantity

Thus the − £4375 revenue difference of the example may be explained by:

	£
Variance due to volume (− 5 ha × 7 t/ha × £95/t)	− 3325
Variance due to unit quantity (− 1 t × 30 ha × £95/t)	− 2850
Variance due to price (+ £10 × 30 ha × 6 t/ha)	+ 1800
	− 4375

The formula may be used in exactly the same way to explain variances in items of expense. It is important to remember, of course, that a negative variance in expense is a favourable variance.

Benefits and limitations

Little needs to be said about the benefits of using this technique. Its use enables the influences of volume, unit quantity and price to be identified separately. This enables the farmer to see how much his profits have been affected by the quality of his management (usually reflected by volume and unit quantity variances) as opposed to chance (usually the main influence on prices, as far as the farmer is concerned). Several items of revenue and/or expense may be analysed simultaneously, and the results related. In the example used for Figure 14.3, for instance, analyses could have been made of differences in fertilizer costs, and the results related to the yield variance. In this way the farmer gains a comprehensive insight into the economics of his business.

Of the limitations, one will be immediately obvious; the time-consuming and complicated nature of the calculations. This need not be a great problem as long as the farmer restricts his analysis to those items which are large enough, in money terms, to bother with, and which are well 'off-target' with respect to volume and/or unit quantity.

A second problem lies in the application of a precise formula to date which is often rather imprecise. This applies particularly to inter-farm comparisons. Much of the

Figure 14.4   *Favourable variances in both price and quantity*

discussion in earlier sections was concerned with doubts over the validity of using survey or standard data as a guide to the performance of one's own farm. Use of variance analysis in such circumstances has the danger that the results will attract an unjustified aura of precision. This does not mean that the technique should not be used; merely that the farmer must continually remember that he is looking for clues rather than answers.

The final limitation arises from doubts over the formula itself. This formula has gained wide acceptance in farm management circles, and is described (if not explained) in a variety of publications (see, for instance, those listed under Further Reading). It works perfectly when a favourable price variance is combined with an unfavourable unit quantity variance. With any other combination of variances, however, it gives distorted results, as can be seen from Figures 14.4–14.6. Figure 14.4 shows the effect of favourable variances in both price and quantity. Areas V and X are clearly the result of variances in price and quantity, respectively, but

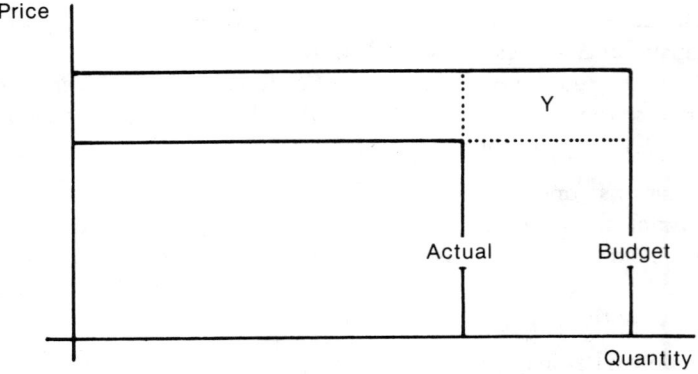

Figure 14.5   *Unfavourable variance in both price and quantity*

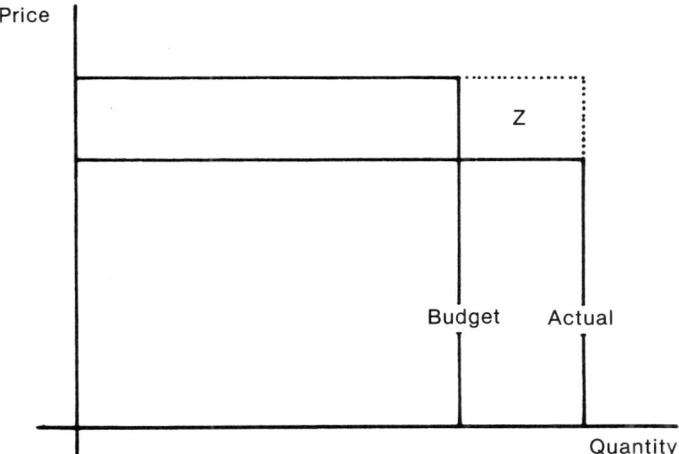

Figure 14.6 *Favourable quantity variance combined with unfavourable price variance*

area W cannot be attributed to either, since it results from the interaction of price and quantity variances. The formula, however, attributes this area to price alone (try it and see).

In Figure 14.5, which shows the result of *un*favourable variances in both price and unit quantity, a similar interaction is represented by area Y. This time the formula attributes it all to unit quantity variance.

Figure 14.6 shows a favourable variance in quantity combined with an unfavourable price variance. The diagram suggests that the price variance is given by difference in price × budget quantity, and the quantity variance by difference in quantity × actual price. The formula, however, states that these should be, respectively, difference in price × actual quantity, and the difference in quantity × budget price. The formula thus exaggerates the influence of both price and quantity by equal amounts, i.e. area Z.

There are two sensible solutions to this difficulty. The first is to use the formula regardless, and assume that the resulting inaccuracies are likely to be small. The other is to refer to sketch diagrams rather than to use the formula. This has the advantage that one does not need to memorize the formula, but is only practicable for 'two-way' analysis. The irrational solution would be to avoid using the technique; despite its limitations it remains a highly valuable aid to the analysis of profit statements.

Profit monitoring for Home Farm

We have available the budgeted and actual financial summaries (Figures 6.18, 7.10 and 11.6) and the budgeted and actual pig gross margin accounts (Figures 6.15 and 11.5) for Home Farm's first year of trading. This allows an illustration of the techniques described above, although in 'real life' it would be important to use previous-year and inter-farm comparisons as well as budgetary control, and all the enterprises would come under scrutiny. It is important to note at this stage that the variances can just as easily arise from inaccurate budgeting in the first instance as from the quality of management during the year: another argument for continuous monitoring, particularly during the first years.

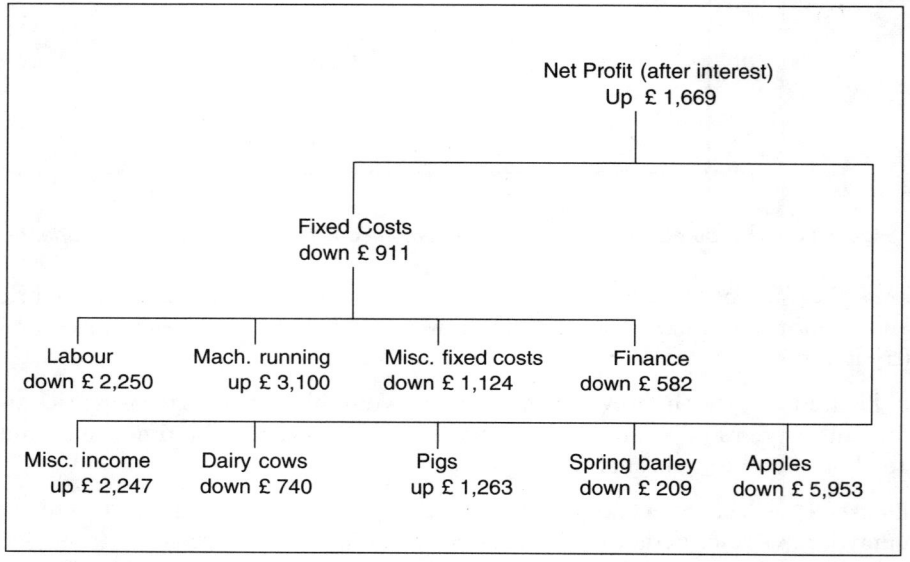

Figure 14.7 *Breakdown of actual/budget comparison, financial summary*

The comparison of results for the whole farm is summarized in Figure 14.7. The diagram shows that net profit is up by £1669 compared with budget, this being brought about by reduced fixed costs and increased gross margins in equal measure. Increased machinery running costs have been balanced by reduced labour costs, plus positive variances in both miscellaneous fixed costs and finance charges (the latter partly due to improved cash flow).

As we have already seen, the apple enterprise had a particularly bad year, and there has been downward pressure on the dairy and barley gross margins. In the light of this, improvement in the pig enterprise and in miscellaneous income are welcome news. However, miscellaneous stores have accumulated over the year (this, note, would not have appeared in the cash flow) and their increase in value is sufficient to increase total gross margin by £758 compared to the budget. These items have incurred expense, but have not yet been used. They are therefore legitimate components of the profit calculation, although care should be taken in their valuation to allow for deterioration and wastage.

The whole-farm analysis gives an overview of performance, but begs questions.

Why, for instance, were machinery costs so much higher than the budget? What brought about the improvement in the pig enterprise? For this we need to look more closely at the components of the budget, and this process is illustrated for the pig gross margin in Figure 14.8. This shows clearly that the main positive influence is an increase in output per pig, one big enough, even allowing for increased variable costs and reduced numbers, to improve the margin by £1263. Various interpretations can be put on these differences: they could have arisen from Adam's careful management of the pigs during the year, or his ineptitude could have been concealed by a fortunate increase in pig meat prices. This is where variance analysis can help.

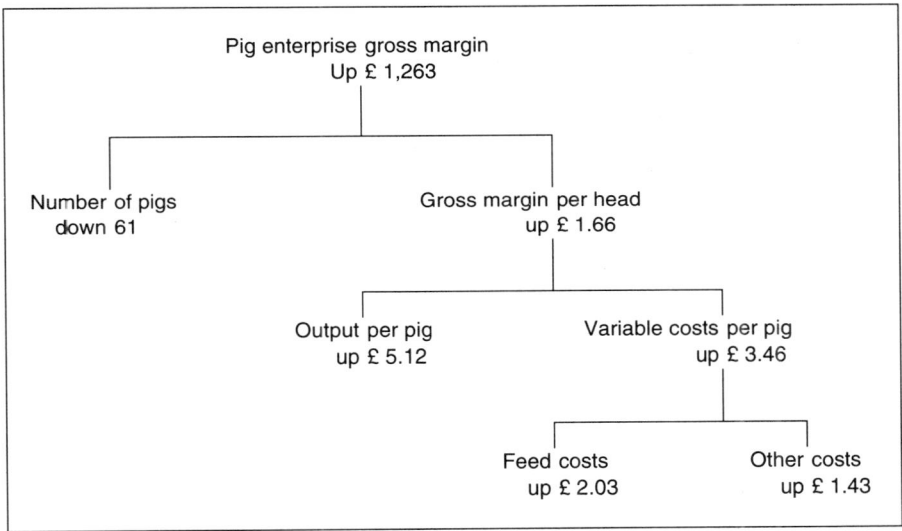

Figure 14.8 *Breakdown of actual/budget comparison, pig enterprise*

A two-way analysis on pig output, for instance, is as follows:

	£
Variance due to difference in numbers: -61×63.90	-3898
Variance due to difference in price: $+£5.12 \times 939$	$\underline{4808}$
	$\underline{\underline{910}}$

The full extent of the damage done by the shortfall in numbers can now be seen: nearly £4000. It may be, of course, that the improved price is partly a result of lower numbers and less stress through overcrowding. The point is that Adam now has a clear indication of the effect of that policy.

The most important cost factor is concentrate feed, and for this a three-way analysis is needed (a third factor of quantity per pig is involved here). Using the formula given earlier, this analysis would be as follows:

	£
Variance due to difference in numbers: -61×0.208 t $\times$ £140	-1776
Variance due to difference in quantity fed: $+0.0295$ t $\times$ 939 $\times$ £140	3876
Variance due to difference in price: $-$£8.83 $\times$ 939 $\times$ 0.2375 t	-1969
	131

This analysis shows clearly that the drop in numbers (whose cost is explored in the two-way analysis above) and the drop in price (more likely to have arisen outside the business than from Adam's management) have obscured the full effect of an increase in the consumption of feed per pig – nearly £4000. Again, this may be part of Adam's policy to improve performance by producing a heavier, better-quality animal, or it could be poor feed management, but we cannot draw any firm conclusions without talking to Adam and seeing the unit at first hand. At least Adam now has precise information with which to interpret the past results and to plan for the future.

As well as examining the other components of the budget in this way, Adam would be wise to compare his results with previous years and with local comparison figures in the manner described earlier.

Monitoring capital

There are two aspects to the monitoring of capital. The first is the examination of the actual balance sheet using ratio analysis, flow of funds analysis, etc. The techniques concerned have been fully explored in Chapter 4 and need no further discussion. The results of this examination are useful both in themselves and as a basis for the budget/actual comparison which forms the second aspect of the monitoring process.

One way of tackling this latter comparison is as follows. Firstly the net capital figures are compared, budget against actual. Then the main ratios are compared: liquidity, percentage equity, gearing. If significant discrepancies appear, the various groups of assets and liabilities should be examined. The flow of funds statements (budget and actual) will prove useful in detecting the root cause of any discrepancy.

Although the capital position of a business is, in most circumstances, a far less sensitive indicator of its financial health than are cash flow and profit, the process described above still merits the description 'control'. The time periods are much greater, but the logic is the same as that behind cash-flow control. By careful monitoring, it is possible to spot unfavourable trends developing while there is still time to rescue the situation. Conversely, favourable movements may be detected early enough to capitalize on them.

Ratio analysis	Opening	Closing	Budget
	%	%	%
Percentage owned	60.5	59.9	60.7
Gearing	36.0	26.1	26.8
Acid-test ratio	32.7	19.8	22.8
Current ratio	170.1	125.2	125.3
Fixed asset ratio	69.8	69.3	71.1
Return on net capital		17.5	16.2
Growth in net capital		4.7	2.0
Growth in assets		5.7	1.6
Growth in liabilities		7.2	1.0

Figure 14.9 *Ratio analysis for actual balance sheet, Home Farm*

In Figures 8.1 and 11.7 we have already seen the opening, budgeted closing and actual closing balance sheets for Home Farm, and Figure 14.9 shows a summary of the main features. Essentially there has been little change in the main ratios, although the movements are generally positive. The net capital has increased beyond expectations, however, as a result of greater movement than anticipated in both assets and liabilities. This, together with the small positive messages from the cash flow and profit results, should enable Adam to proceed with cautious optimism – as long as he maintains the process of budgetary control for the following years.

Figure 14.10 completes the analysis with a flow of funds statement. Trading is seen to be the main source of cash flowing into the business, though it has needed a cash injection and increased overdraft in addition. Apart from the commitments represented by private drawings (could there still be scope for economy here?), tax payments and loan repayments, much of the cash has been spent on reinvestment in machinery and orchard, investment which should bear (literally) fruit in succeeding years.

FLOW OF FUNDS ANALYSIS		£
SOURCES:	NET PROFIT (LOSS)	17,279
	Depreciation (+)	12,065
	Change in debtors (increase −, decrease +)	1,070
	Change in creditors (increase +, decrease −)	3,089
	Valuations (increase −, decrease +)	−9,409
	Benefits in kind (−)	−4,435
CASH FROM TRADING		19,659
ADD:	Capital introduced	4,500
	Sale of land, property, investments	0
	Increase in overdraft	9,588
	Increase in loans	0
	Reduction in cash balances	0
CASH FROM OTHER SOURCES		14,088
TOTAL CASH AVAILABLE		33,747
USES:	COMMITMENTS	
	Private drawings	10,400
	Tax payments	2,512
	Reduction in loans	8,200
TOTAL COMMITMENTS		21,112
ADD:	Purchase of land, property, investments	0
	Net purchase of buildings	4,137
	Purchase of machinery 16,021		
	Less sale of machinery −7,523	8,498
	Repayment of overdraft	0
	Increase in cash balances	0
		12,635
TOTAL CASH USED		33,747

Figure 14.10 *Home Farm − flow of funds analysis for 199X/9Y*

Further reading

Barnard, C. S. and Nix, J. S., *Farm Planning and Control*, 2nd edition (London, Cambridge University Press, 1979), pp. 530–42.

Norman, L., Turner, R. A. E. and Wilson, K. R. S., *The Farm Business*, 2nd edition (London, Longman, 1985). The first part of the book includes a blow-by-blow account of whole-farm comparative analysis: pp. 146–268 contain a valuable collection of enterprise studies.

PART FIVE

More on Planning and Control

Unfortunately, the financial management of a farm is rarely as straightforward as the previous chapters have implied.

In Part Five some of the possible complications are considered, starting with a look at planning in its widest sense, building up a farm business system from scratch. It then moves on to examine particular management problems, including the planning of livestock enterprises, the planning and control of labour and machinery, investment appraisal, and coping with risk and uncertainty.

15

The planning process –
a wider view

Introduction

In the interests of simplicity, the preceding chapters have viewed management, especially the planning process, in a very narrow way. Discussion of planning has been confined to the budgeting of a given system; little distinction has been made between the long and short terms; and it has been assumed that the objectives of a business can be described completely in financial terms.

It is now time to take a broader look at the planning process, with the aim of selecting and budgeting the *optimal* system for the business, rather than the uncritical rebudgeting of an existing business system.

Reference back to the decision-making process outlined in Chapter 2 provides a useful starting-point for this 'broader look'. It is repeated below, with some of the steps further divided:

1 Set objectives.
2 Forecast likely changes in the external environment of the business.
3 Consider the constraints which are likely to limit the range of alternative actions open to the business (including those imposed by limited availability of resources).
4 Consider all the alternative plans which could be expected to achieve the objectives, given the forecasts and constraints.
5 Select the plan which appears to have the greatest chance of achieving the objectives.
6 Implement that plan.
7 Ensure the existence of a procedure for the periodic monitoring and revision of plans.

The planning process

Setting objectives

Up to now we have considered objectives only in financial terms, and without distinguishing between long- and short-term goals. In fact the owner of a business is likely to have a mixture of objectives, some financial and some non-financial relating to a variety of time periods.

Long-term or 'strategic' objectives are the overall goals of the business, unlikely to change for several years, even a lifetime. It is rare that a strategic goal can be achieved in one jump, and it is likely that a series of short-term or 'tactical' objectives will need to be set, each contributing in some way towards the attainment of the long-term goals.

To give an example, a farmer may have a long-term objective of setting each of his three sons up in farming. To achieve this goal, he may have to achieve a large number of intermediate tactical goals. Some of these may be concerned with increasing profits from his own business, in order to finance the venture; some with acquiring suitable plots of farmland; some with minimizing the effects of capital taxation.

Non-financial objectives come in a host of varieties. A farmer may have a strong desire to own land, to have the best Hereford bull in the county, to be highly regarded in the local community, to conserve the flora and fauna of his holding. He may want a business that occupies him 24 hours a day, or one that will tick over happily while leaving him with half the week for fishing, going to market, or visiting his mistress. He may place importance on bringing his son into the business early so that he can retire, but on the other hand he could be determined to keep hold of the reins as long as he is able. He may aspire to the chairmanship of the county NFU, or to a seat on the local Bench. The list is endless.

If such non-financial objectives are not considered, there is a risk of planning a business which proves to give the owner little or no satisfaction – and what is the point in possessing such a business? They will always be subject in some degree to the financial objectives, however, since if the business collapses financially, *none* of the objectives can be achieved.

Setting objectives is rarely easy. Among the difficulties are those of:

1   Ensuring that *all* objectives are explicitly considered.
2   Ensuring that objectives are realistic.
3   Ensuring that objectives are clear.
4   Resolving conflict between objectives.

The *explicit consideration* of all objectives requires a methodical approach if the farmer is to avoid the danger of omitting an objective which, though crucial to the business, escapes his mind at the planning stage. One way of avoiding this is to run through a checklist such as the one below:

1   *Personal:*
    – leisure and pleasure
    – family considerations
    – prestige
    – others

2   *Financial:*
    – profitability
    – stability
    – adaptability

3   *Physical:*
    - innovation (techniques and products)
    - productivity (of land, labour and capital)

4   *Responsibility:*
    - to employees
    - to local community
    - to society in general

This list is by no means exhaustive, but provides a foundation on which the farmer may build his own, more detailed schedule.

Even a checklist may fail to ensure the explicit consideration of all objectives, one of the principal reasons being lack of honesty. It may seem peculiar to refer to honesty in describing one person's attempt to decide what he wants from the business, but in fact lack of such honesty is common. It is often linked with the fact that some objectives are disturbing or distressing to consider.

An example of this might arise where a young farmer has taken over a farm business from his ageing father. A major consideration in this situation must be to minimize the threat to the business imposed by the likely impact of capital taxation after the father's death. The prospect of this event may be so distressing that both father and son blinker themselves to its inevitability. They ignore it and hope that everything will work out fine when the time comes. But such issues *must* be faced squarely, despite the emotional discomforts involved, if a policy for preserving the business is to be formulated.

The problem of *realism* is that of setting targets which are capable of achievement, without being too easily achieved. The farmer who sets himself impossible targets risks constant self-dissatisfaction and frustration. This leads to loss of interest in the performance of the business, and probably a deterioration in the standard of management as a result. Objectives which are too easily attained, on the other hand, are of little value in the management of a business. Once the objective is achieved, what then? The business is floundering again through want of direction.

Clarity of objectives usually requires some form of quantification. It is no use giving a stranger the objective: 'Meet me in London on Wednesday.' If the objective is to be achieved it must be more precise, e.g. 'Meet me under the clock at Charing Cross Station at 3.30 p.m. on Wednesday.' Business objectives must similarly be precise.

This is easier with financial objectives (where there is a convenient unit of measurement) than with some non-financial objectives. In some cases it may be neither possible nor desirable to state objectives in quantifiable terms. An example might be the intention to maintain good relations with the neighbouring farmers and villagers. While this may be an important objective (with implications for methods of slurry handling and the siting of intensive livestock units), it would be unreasonable to attempt to state it more precisely. Such examples will usually be in the minority, however, and every effort should be made to express objectives in measurable terms.

It is almost inevitable that *conflict* will arise between the various objectives of a business. Two common forms of conflict are those between long- and short-term objectives, and between financial and non-financial objectives. An example of the former might be provided by the farmer mentioned earlier, who was anxious to set his sons up in farming. If his own business has a succession of bad seasons, there is a chance that he will be faced with the choice between this long-term objective and the shorter-term one of keeping his own business intact.

A familiar example of the conflict between financial and non-financial objectives is that of the young farmer who has a strong wish to spend at least one day a week with his family. He quickly finds that he has to work all day, every day, to keep the farm going. The alternative is to hire additional labour, which will push the overdraft well beyond the limits of safety. He has to hold one of the objectives in abeyance – the financial or non-financial. If he wants to stay in business it will be the latter.

Determining the relative priorities of conflicting objectives is not always as clear-cut a process as in the examples given. There is no easy solution; in the end it comes down to the judgement of the farmer.

Finally, it is important to remember that objectives and their priorities change with time. For this reason, a critical review of objectives should be undertaken as an integral part of the annual planning procedure.

Forecasting future events

Little needs to be said here about forecasting, since the topic has been discussed elsewhere in this book (Chapter 6). The only new consideration is that, since we are now thinking in terms of both non-financial and financial objectives, the forecasts need to consider a wide range of aspects of the external environment of the business, and not just those which impinge on its financial status.

Determining constraints

The freedom of action of any manager is limited in various ways. A major limit or 'constraint' will be the quantity of resources available. Adam Haynes, for instance, has only a certain area of land, a certain quantity of cash, and a certain level of technical expertise at his disposal. Other constraints will be imposed by a variety of factors, including the personal preferences of the farmer (and wife and family), the law of the land, the wishes of the landlord and/or bank manager, the requirements of good husbandry, and so on. Some will be linked closely with the objectives of the business.

A list of the main constraints on Adam Haynes's business might well look like this:

1   The system must be relatively easy to operate, and not be too time-consuming.
2   Borrowing should not exceed £30,000 in either of the first two years.

3 The permanent pasture must never be ploughed.
4 Each of the remaining fields must be sown to grass for at least three years in every seven.
5 Winter wheat must not be grown in any field for more than two years in any five.
6 The land is not suitable for root or rape crops.

There would doubtless be other constraints beside these. Those determined by Adam's non-financial objectives, such as (1) and (2), are subject to the remarks made above concerning the relative priority of financial and non-financial objectives.

As with objectives, the relative importance of the various constraints changes over time. A farmer may be limited in the short-term by the size of his farm, but as neighbouring property becomes available for purchase or rent, land area may become less of a restriction. In order to prevent constraints being taken for granted year after year, they should be subject to periodic review.

Formulating alternative plans

One of the most common faults in management is 'tunnel vision'; the inability or unwillingness to consider any action other than the one first thought of. It is closely connected with another common problem, the 'emotional decision'. This is a decision made entirely on the grounds of a 'gut feeling'. The feeling might be that you must have XYZ tractors, even if they are the most expensive available, or that you must buy that 20 ha parcel of land next door, as it may never come up for sale again. It is not that such gut feeling should be ignored; merely that they should be viewed in the light of the other possibilities. A vital stage of the planning process is thus the consideration of a range of courses of action.

It is easy to talk of considering a wide range of alternatives, but less easy to do it. This is partly a matter of lack of knowledge; partly a matter of lack of imagination. It is impossible for one man (especially a busy farmer) to be fully informed about all the possible opportunities for development of his business. It can be very difficult (especially after a day's hard physical work) for him to stretch his mind to make maximum use of the knowledge that *is* available.

The only remedy for the first problem is to make every effort to keep well informed by the means discussed in Chapter 6, and be prepared to pick the brains of others.

Neither is there an easy way of solving the second problem. The main requirement is to keep as open a mind as possible. One way of doing this is to adopt the suggestion of Humble (1972) and ask, 'What business am I really in?' An attempt to find an honest answer to this deceptively simple question can often provide the idea that transforms an adequate business into a highly successful one. For example, the farmer who has always thought of himself as first and foremost a stock farmer (perhaps because his father and grandfather were stock farmers) may thus come to realize that his crop production is of a higher quality than his livestock production. This may in turn break mental barriers to the transfer of resources (such as land and capital) away from the stock towards the crops.

Similarly, the person who thinks of his business as a farm with a caravan site attached may come to realize that it is in fact a leisure business with a farm attached, and concentrate on developing the former as a more effective way of achieving his objectives than further development of the farming enterprises.

Another way of generating a wide range of ideas is to gather a group of other people, e.g. family, friends or neighbours, round a pot of tea or a crate of beer, tell them the problem in hand, and ask for as many suggestions as possible within a given time. No suggestion should be commented on, nor should apparently wild or fanciful ideas be discouraged − everything should be noted down. When the flow of suggestions has dried up, each of the ideas noted should be discussed at greater length. Often ideas which at first seemed crazy will, on consideration, begin to look interesting. The resulting list of possible plans will almost certainly be more comprehensive than one person could have produced on his own.

Selection of the optimal plan

This is such a large topic that a separate chapter (Chapter 16) has been devoted to it. For the moment it is enough to make the following points: (a) the process of selection should be a rational and ordered one; (b) in order that selection may be ordered, the consequences of adopting each of the alternative plans should be carefully examined; and (c), although the main criterion of judgement between the alternative plans will usually be financial (due to the strength of the financial objectives), non-financial consequences should be carefully considered.

Implementation and monitoring of the selected plan

If you have read the preceding chapters, you will be well aware that you must be prepared for actual events to turn out differently to your expectations. You will also have read many times of the importance of continual monitoring of the progress of plans in order to ensure that the business is still on the path to attain its objectives, and to enable corrective action to be taken if this is not the case. There is little else that a book can tell you about this part of the process − you have to learn it through experience.

Strategic and tactical plans

Since objectives can be classifed by time into strategic and tactical objectives, it follows that plans for their achievement can be similarly classified. Strategic plans are likely to cover periods of several years, while tactical plans will probably relate to no more than 12 months at a time. This is more than just a theoretical distinction − it can be very helpful in matching action to objectives.

As an example, one of the options open to Adam Haynes is the introduction of a heifer-rearing enterprise to provide him with replacements for his dairy herd. A strategic plan prepared to show the impact of such a policy would indicate the likely impact of the new system, when established, on Adam's long-term objectives. Associated tactical plans, supported by budgets, would show the effect on the business during the period of establishment. In choosing between this and the alternative policies open to him, Adam would thus be able to examine first the long-term consequences of its adoption. If the strategic plan looked promising, he could then go on to check on the short-term implications of the tactical plan. The information is presented in a way that encourages ordered, logical decision-making.

Ideally, strategic plans should be revised every year. In this way they become 'rolling' plans, rather than being limited to a fixed period. Tactical plans should be formulated at the same time but are likely to need further revision as the year unfolds.

Involving other members of the organization

A business is run by and for people. The farmer who is unmarried, a sole proprietor, and employs no other labour but his own is lucky in the sense that he has only himself to organize and motivate. As soon as other people – family, employees, partners – become involved, the problems arise of ensuring that the objectives of the business reflect those of *all* those concerned with the ownership of the business, and that the efforts of all the members of the organization contribute toward these business objectives.

One of the most effective ways of coping with these problems is to make sure that those 'other people' are involved in the planning process. Objectives should be agreed (not just discussed) with those who are going to have to achieve them, and the resulting plans should be the result of not just the farmer's efforts, but also those of the people who are responsible for their implementation. This process can take place at various levels; the stockman need only be concerned with a narrow range of plans, relating to physical performance, while the assistant manager should probably be involved in the formulation of objectives and plans for the business as a whole.

This aspect of management deserves more space than can be afforded in a book concerned primarily with financial management techniques. Its best-known manifestation is 'management by objectives', and the writings of Humble (1972), and Giles and Stansfield (1990), are strongly recommended. Other methods adopting similar approaches are 'corporate planning' (Argenti 1980), and the familiar 'budgetary control' expanded to provide a mechanism of organization and motivation in larger and more complex businesses than Home Farm, e.g. Lucey (1983). All of the books quoted are very 'readable', and will well repay the effort of buying or borrowing them.

Further reading

General

Giles, A. K. and Stansfield, J. M., *The Farmer as Manager*, 2nd edition (Oxford, CAB International, 1990). See especially part 2: 'Management Functions'.
Bowman, C. and Asch, C., *Strategic Planning* (London, Macmillan, 1987).

Management by objectives and similar techniques

Argenti, J., *Practical Corporate Planning* (London, Allen & Unwin, 1980).
Giles and Stansfield, *op. cit.*, chapter 3.
Humble, J. W., *Improving Business Results* (London, Pan Books, 1980).
Lucey, T., *Management Accounting* (Eastleigh, Hampshire, DP Publications, 1983), chapter 10: 'Budgetary Control'.

16

Selecting the optimal plan

Introduction

The selection of the 'best' plan from a range of alternatives needs, as suggested in the previous chapter, a rational and ordered procedure. A variety of techniques is available to help the farmer in this task.

The short-list and budget method

This method relies on the farmer sifting through the wide range of alternative plans and subjectively choosing a few that look attractive. The selection should always include a plan based on the continuation of the present system, for comparison. The chosen few are then subjected to closer scrutiny. Given the importance of financial objectives, this scrutiny must include the preparation and comparison of budgets for each of the short-listed plans, based on normalized figures. The non-financial aspects of each plan should then be examined before a final decision is reached. Both strategic and tactical aspects of each plan should be considered.

Even after this procedure has been followed, it may still be difficult to choose between two or more of the short-listed alternatives. A possible example on Home Farm would be the choice between a plan involving the expansion of the dairy herd and the introduction of a dairy follower herd (attractive on financial grounds), and one involving the selling of the dairy herd and its substitution by arable crops and beef (less attractive financially, but perhaps closer to satisfying the non-financial objectives). In this situation it may be helpful to compare formally the strengths and weaknesses of the two plans. A simple example of this device is shown in Figure 16.1 (overleaf).

The actual list is likely to be rather longer than this, although in the interests of clarity it should be limited to strategic factors.

The analysis of strengths and weaknesses, opportunities and threats (SWOT) can clarify the issues in difficult choices, but it cannot overcome the fundamental limitations of the short-list and budget approach. In particular, the selection of the initial short-list relies on subjective, and often arbitrary judgement. Moreover, the work involved in preparing budgets for even a small range of plans can be considerable, although this can be reduced by the use of partial budgets round a 'central' whole-farm budget (see Chapter 9).

	Expand dairy	Scrap dairy
Strengths	High profit More even cash flow Some dairy buildings and equipment available	More opportunity for leisure Reduced long-term borrowing
Weaknesses	High gearing Needs constant attention More quota needed	High cash deficit in summer Lower profit More grain storage needed
Opportunities	Sale of pedigree heifers Manufacture of 'farm-house' dairy products	Possibility of large seed wheat contract Potato quota available
Threats	Agricultural policy on milk production Declining demand for dairy products	Possible disease risk if cereal production intensified

Figure 16.1   *Example of SWOT analysis*

Gross margin planning

One way of refining the selection process is to plan the business on an enterprise basis. The enterprise which seems likely to make the biggest contribution towards the objectives is put into the plan and increased as far as the constraints will allow. Then the enterprise with the second best contribution is put in, and so on. Because of the difficulties of quantifying non-financial objectives, this process tends to be restricted to financial objectives, and the maximization of profit in particular. The economic principle on which it is based is the theory of equi-marginal returns (see Appendix 1).

The first step is to decide which of the key resources (land, labour, capital or management skill) most limits the scale of production in the business in question. In a small, densely populated country (such as Britain) the most limiting resource is frequently land, especially in the short and medium-term. In the long-term, however, it is possible to buy all other resources given enough capital, which thus becomes the most limiting resource. The latter argument may not apply on the small family farm, where there is often a strong reluctance to employ non-family labour. Labour could here be the most limiting resource, particularly in the short run.

Next, a list of all the feasible enterprises is made, and the normalized gross margin per unit of the most limiting resource calculated for each enterprise. These gross margins should be based on forecast data for the period of the plan, though past performance and local standard performance data may be used as a guide in forecasting.

Now the enterprise having the largest gross margin per unit of the limiting resource is identified and put into the plan. It is increased in size as far as possible within the constraints. Then the enterprise having the second largest gross margin per resource unit is introduced and increased until it, too, is stopped by one of the constraints. The process continues until one of the key resources is entirely used up. If this is the most limiting resource, the object of the exercise has been achieved, although it may be possible to increase total profits further by introducing an enterprise which does not use any of that resource, e.g. intensive poultry when land is limiting.

If it is one of the other resources which has been exhausted, an enterprise must be found which uses relatively small amounts of the exhausted resources, and can be substituted, without reduction in total gross margin, for an enterprise which is already in the plan and which uses relatively large amounts of this resource. The process then continues as before.

In the simplest form of the procedure, constraints are considered in an informal, intuitive manner – they are 'borne in mind'. This is known as *gross margin planning*. As a simple example, take an arable farm of 72 ha, where four enterprises are being considered, and where land is the most limiting resource. Their budgeted normalized gross margins are:

Winter wheat	£500
Spring barley	£350
Potatoes	£800
Sugar beet	£600

Potatoes, having the largest gross margin per hectare, are selected first, and the farmer will have as big an area as possible. He knows that his potato quota is only 15 ha, so after introducing that area of potatoes he will have to turn to sugar beet. This is similarly brought into the plan as far as possible. The farmer knows that this is going to put pressure on labour use in the autumn, and reckons that 10 ha is the most that he can risk. Winter wheat and spring barley are brought into the plan in the same way. The result will be a rough plan which can then be juggled to arrive at a workable farm system.

Like all management techniques, gross margin planning has its limitations. In the first place, it is often difficult to decide which of the key resources *is* the most limiting. Then there is the problem that the 'agricultural' gross margin is a compromise; to be classified as 'variable', a cost must not only be variable in the true sense, but also easily allocated. This excludes from the gross margin many costs (such as tractor fuel and overtime) which will in fact change as the proportions of the enterprise are varied in the plan. The gross margins used in the technique can be adjusted to take account of this, but it can be a difficult and arbitrary process.

Another worry is the assumption that the 'fixed' costs (even after adjustment) remain constant irrespective of the combination of enterprises. This may be true of some fixed costs, such as rent, but others represent 'lumpy' or integer inputs. These are inputs whose costs are fixed only up to a certain scale of operations; if it is necessary to expand production beyond this point an additional unit of the input must be purchased, or a substitute of larger capacity purchased. A particular combine harvester might be able to cope with 50 ha of cereals per year; expanding the cereal area beyond this point (in the absence of contractors) would necessitate buying either an additional machine, or a larger replacement. Such a possibility is ignored in gross margin planning.

Despite these criticisms, gross margin planning does impose a degree of economic logic on the selection of enterprises, and can be a useful starting point in planning from scratch. A particular virtue of the technique is that it is reasonably simple to use; the more precise forms of the procedure tend to be much more complex.

Programme planning

One such technique is *programme planning*. Like gross margin planning, it involves the progressive selection of enterprises by reference to normalized gross margins per unit of the most limiting resource. Here, though, the most crucial of the constraints are considered in an explicit, formal manner. The example from the previous section will help to illustrate the procedure. In Figure 16.2 the enterprises have been set out in a table which not only shows their normalized budgeted gross margins per hectare, but also quantifies three key constraints. The labour constraints are derived from tables of seasonal labour requirements discussed in Chapter 18.

Enterprise	Forecast gross margin/ha (£)	Rotation constraint (ha)	Spring labour constraint (hr/ha)	Autumn labour constraint (hr/ha)
Winter wheat	500	24[1]	2	8
Spring barley	350	72	8	0
Potatoes	800	15[2]	25	40
Sugar beet	600	15[2]	20	20
TOTAL AVAILABLE		72	900	800

[1] That is, each field can grow wheat two years in every six.
[2] Imposed by potato quota and sugar beet contract respectively.

Figure 16.2 *Programme planning example – table of enterprises and constraints*

The method proceeds as follows:

Step 1 The biggest gross margin is that for potatoes, which are thus introduced up to the maximum allowed by the rotation constraint: 15 ha. This leaves unused 525 hr of spring labour and 200 hr of autumn labour. Total gross margin so far is 15 × £800 = £12,000.

Step 2 The next biggest gross margin is that of sugar beet. This is introduced into the plan up to the limit imposed by the autumn labour constraint: 10 ha. This leaves unused 325 hr of spring labour, and no autumn labour. Total gross margin so far is £12,000 + (10 × £600) = £18,000.

Step 3 Spring barley uses no autumn labour (assuming that it is harvested before the end of August). Thus it can be introduced into the plan even though all the autumn labour is used up. It is introduced up to the limit imposed by spring labour: 41 ha. This leaves no spring or autumn labour, and gives a total gross margin of £18,000 + (41 × £350) = £32,350. *But* there are still 6 ha of the original limiting resource, the land, left unused.

Step 4 The gross margin of each of the enterprises is expressed per unit of one of the new limiting resources (say spring labour):

Winter wheat	500/2 = 250 £/hr
Spring barley	350/8 = 44 £/hr
Potatoes	800/25 = 32 £/hr
Sugar beet	600/29 = 30 £/hr

To maximize total gross margin, sugar beet, with the lowest gross margin per hour of spring labour, must be given up in favour of wheat, with the highest. Reducing the area of sugar beet releases 20 hr of spring labour (enough for 10 ha of wheat) and 20 hr autumn labour (enough for 2.5 ha of wheat) per ha.

To find how much sugar beet has to be lost, the 6 ha remaining to be filled are divided by (2.5 − 1). The '1' is deducted to allow for the fact that the replacement enterprise has to fill the space left by the outgoing enterprise, as well as the 'spare' 6 ha. The reduction in sugar beet is thus 6/1.5 = 4 ha, and the area of the new wheat enterprise is (6 + 4) = 10 ha.

Summary of the plan The above steps are summarized in Figure 16.3

Enterprise	Area (ha)	Gross margin (£/ha)	Total gross margin (£)
Wheat	10	500	5,000
Barley	41	350	14,350
Sugar beet	6	600	3,600
Potatoes	15	800	12,000
TOTALS	72		34,950

Figure 16.3 *Summary of the plan*

Since at the end of Step 3 in this example there were two most limiting resources, Step 4 should ideally be repeated with reference to autumn labour, in case the resulting plan gives a higher total gross margin than that above. (In this example it does not – try it.)

The method has most of the limitations of gross-margin planning with the additional drawback of being much more complex though little more precise. The example used above was a very simple one. Try using the technique for replanning a 200 ha mixed farm (or even the hypothetical Home Farm) where there are dozens of constraints and as many possible enterprises. You will rapidly be dazed by the seemingly endless progressions of calculations. Moreover the reliance on trial and error in some parts of the calculation casts doubt on the validity of the final results.

Programme planning is best regarded as an initial guide to the selection of enterprises, concentrating on a small selection of the most important constraints in order to keep the calculation simple. As long as the resulting solution is regarded as an intermediate step in the planning process, rather than the end-point, the technique can be valuable.

Linear programming

The advent of the computer has made possible the use of *linear programming* (LP). This can be thought of as a sophisticated extension of programme planning, although it uses a different method to arrive at a solution. Use of a computer enables a great many constraints and possible enterprises to be considered in a precise series of calculations. The form of these calculations need not concern us here; a useful explanation may be found in Chapter 15 of Barnard and Nix (1979).

In its basic form, LP shares many of the limitations of programme planning (such as the inability to cope with 'lumpy' inputs). Various modifications of the technique have been devised in attempts (with varying degrees of success) to eliminate these problems.

A further problem arises from the fact that LP is designed to produce the one plan that will maximize profits as long as the assumptions used in compiling the planning data are accurate. In one way this is a benefit – there is no ambiguity about the result. The plan chosen, however, could be the maximum-profit plan by only a small degree – perhaps a matter of pence. It is quite possible for the plan chosen to be one which is highly sensitive to the accuracy of the initial assumptions, i.e. is very risky, while the 'second-best' plan is a much safer option, and would probably be preferred by the farmer. Again, modifications to the basic LP have been devised to tackle this problem, but at the expense of simplicity and cheapness.

Cost has so far been a major problem, together with availability. A linear program capable of handling the replanning of a farm business needs a computer of considerable capacity, together with the services of an intermediary who can interpret the farmer's wishes to the computer, and the computer's response to the farmer. While the cost of computer time has fallen in real terms in recent years the cost of the intermediaries' time (often the largest expense) has escalated. This, coupled with the limitations mentioned above, has tended to restrict the popularity of the technique, and a farmer may find it difficult to obtain this service, even if he is prepared to pay a realistic price.

The best opportunities for linear programming of a farm are provided by the Agricultural Development and Advisory Service and big commercial firms which often use spare computer capacity by running such programs as part of their technical advisory services. As on-farm microcomputers become more sophisticated, however, small LP programs are becoming available for such machines.

Possibly the biggest drawback is the need for the farmer to take on trust the results produced by the technique. With the simple short-list and budget method, he can follow the reasoning through every stage. With LP (as far as he is concerned) figures are fed into a computer and a farm plan comes out at the other end; he has little idea what happens in between. For him to risk money in carrying out his plan requires either foolhardiness or great faith in the program and its operator.

For all its limitations, LP can be valuable in some circumstances, the most notable being where the range of possible enterprises is very great. It sifts and evaluates the various alternatives with a degree of objectivity which would otherwise be impossible. Its value is greatly enhanced if the farmer is able to test the effect on the plan of changing certain of his key assumptions, thus getting an impression of the riskiness of the first solution.

Systems simultation

An alternative approach to planning a business involves the building of a mathematical 'model' to represent the whole or part of the business. This is not a model in the sense of a balsa-wood or plastic miniature, but a collection interlocking equations which together approximate the actions and reactions of a particular system (such as an enterprise, or a business). Providing the model is a faithful representative of the system under study, various key assumptions can be changed in order to investigate the likely response of the system. This process is known as *systems simulation.*

Systems simulation is used primarily as a research tool, but the farmer may encounter one of its simpler manifestations, such as *automatic budgeting.* Here the computer program is designed to produce a set of budgets from a given set of assumptions concerning prices, yields, combination of enterprises, and so on (in other words a model of the business financial system). The speed of operation of the computer enables the farmer to test repeatedly the effects of varying his initial assumptions. The method is thus one of trial and error, lacking the formal, objective selection process incorporated in LP. On the other hand, it is more 'approachable', in that the methods used are those with which the farmer should be familiar, and though it might not produce the 'best' plan, it gives the farmer a chance to examine the consequences of a wide range of alternative possibilities. The humble computer spreadsheet can be very useful in this respect (see Appendices 4 and 5).

Moreover, such programs, needing less computer capacity than a full-blown LP, can easily be designed for on-farm microcomputers, thus allowing considerable flexibility.

Further reading

Barnard, C. S., and Nix, J. S., *Farm Planning and Control*, 2nd edition (London, Cambridge University Press, 1979), part III: 'The Combination of Enterprises'.

$$\boxed{17}$$

Planning for livestock enterprises

Introduction

Crop enterprises are fairly simple to budget for, and the basic principles have been covered in previous chapters. The biggest single difficulty is probably formulating appropriate rotations, and determining the value of including certain break crops in the cropping system; see Barnard and Nix (1979), Chapter 12.

Livestock enterprises are subject to various additional complicating factors, including the dependence of grazing livestock on crop enterprises, the continuous nature of some forms of livestock production, and the long production cycles of some types of animal. Factors such as these have implications for the choice of feeding policy, the allocation of forage costs, the estimation of potential production levels, and the choice of replacement policy for breeding livestock, among other matters.

Some of these topics (feeding, for instance) cannot be discussed in detail here; although they are vital to the planning process, they are more the province of a textbook on animal production. Where this is the case, the appropriate methods are described in outline, and references provided for further reading.

Feeding livestock

Selection of feeding policy

The aim in selecting a feeding policy for a given group of livestock is to find the lowest-cost combination of feedstuffs which will provide the nutrients required by the animals. In non-ruminant livestock it is possible to avoid this process by buying complete rations, or supplements for use with home-grown barley, from a feed manufacturer. In ruminant livestock enterprises, however, concentrate feeds, whether home-grown or purchased, must be carefully balanced with the bulk fodder which is available. Even in a non-ruminant livestock enterprise, the farmer may prefer to design his own rations.

Selection of rations has some similarity to the enterprise-selection problem discussed in the previous chapter. The difference is that here the objective is minimum cost rather than minimum profit, and the constraints tend to be minima, e.g. 'the ration must contain at least x per cent digestible crude protein', rather than the maxima of the enterprise-mix problem, e.g. 'no more than y ha of sugar beet may be grown in one year'.

201

One exception is the constraint of appetite; it is obviously no use selecting a ration which, though providing the necessary nutrients at the least cost, is so bulky that the animal cannot consume it all. A second is the quantity available of any ingredient which is in short supply, particularly forage. Other maximum constraints concern palatability, toxicity and similar factors.

The 'minimum' constraints are imposed by the nutrient needs of the animals concerned. Among these are protein, vitamins and minerals of various types, but the most critical is energy, needed not only to maintain the animal's bodily condition, but also to enable production of milk, wool, liveweight gain, and so on. This energy is measured in terms of *metabolizable energy* (ME) for ruminants, and *digestible energy* (DE) for non-ruminants, i.e. pigs and poultry. Tables of the nutrient requirements of different classes of livestock, and the nutrient content of various types of feed ingredient, are published in specialist publications such as MAFF (1984) and Whittemore (1980b) on pig production (Chapters 4 and 5).

The choices of selection method in planning a feeding policy are similar to those in planning overall farm policy. At the most sophisticated level, a version of linear programming can be used, requiring the use of a computer. No modern feed compounder would dream of formulating feeds without the aid of this technique (probably the most common application of LP).

The farmer who wishes to mix his own rations, and who does not have access to a suitable computer, has two alternatives. He can either use the technical advisory services of ADAS or the feed firm that sells him the feed supplement, or he can use a trial-and-error process. The latter is akin to the budgeting procedure described earlier in the book. The first task is to work out various rations which will give the required levels of nutrients wihtout exceeding the appetite limit. The cost of each ration is then calculated, and the cheapest alternative chosen.

This procedure does not have the precision and speed of the LP method, but as long as a number of alternatives are considered, the chances of finding a ration that comes near to the least cost are fairly high. Unfortunately, since lengthy calculations are involved, the busy farmer is likely to be tempted to take a short cut and limit his investigation to one or two possibilities only. Variants of 'automatic budgeting' (see page 199) are available, using on-farm microcomputers to simplify and speed up the process. This enables the farmer to examine a wide range of alternative rations in a short time, and provides a reasonable compromise between the extremes of linear programming and hand calculation.

A detailed, yet easily-followed guide to the selection of a feeding policy is provided by Nelson (1979).

The cost of feed ingredients

A key factor in the choice of feedstuffs is that of cost. Bought-in ingredients should be valued at their purchase price (historic or anticipated); home-grown, saleable crops at their net realizable value at the time of use (sale price less an allowance for marketing and transport costs).

Certain crops may be included in the farm system solely to provide feed for livestock. This applies to all forage crops, and often cash crops such as barley. The produce from these crops should be valued at a price which includes both the variable costs of production and the opportunity cost (see Appendix 1) incurred by giving up the chance of growing an alternative crop.

Growing grass for silage on a mixed farm may, for instance, limit the area available for winter wheat. In this case, the cost per hectare of growing silage is the variable cost of production plus the gross margin lost from a hectare of winter wheat. On a good arable farm, it might be worth cutting down on silage production, buying in barley and hay, and putting the saved land down to cash crops.

For a large proportion of farms, however, the area of cash crops is limited by husbandry considerations and by contracts, quotas, etc. On Home Farm, at least three-sevenths of the arable land must be in grass at any one time (as well as the permanent pasture land), and the area of wheat and root crops is limited (see Chapter 15). Thus grass is forced into the rotation; at the hectarage assumed in the budgets, it has a zero opportunity cost. The alternatives to barley are limited, and it is likely to have a low opportunity cost in these circumstances − thus it too can be justified as part of the rotation. In such circumstances, the barley should be valued at net realizable value, and the silage at the variable cost of production (making some allowance for the variable elements of labour and machinery costs − see Chapter 20).

Some farms will lie between the two above extremes − the grass area could be cut down by x ha, for instance, in order to make way for roots or a cereal crop. In such cases, the cost of the x ha of grass should include an opportunity cost element as described above. Only if this is done will the farmer realize the full marginal cost of growing his own feed.

Allocation of forage costs

The budgeting of forage costs for the first year of Adam Haynes' tenancy of Home Farm was straightforward. There was only one grazing livestock enterprise, so the forage costs could all be allocated to that enterprise, the dairy.

The majority of mixed farms have more than one grazing enterprise, however. The different types of livestock on these farms are not normally confined to separate areas of grassland, but share the total area. Sheep may follow the cows into a pasture to 'clean up', and beef animals may well eat hay from the same field as the dairy heifers. Since it is impossible to allocate the cost of individual fields to particular classes of livestock in such circumstances, an attempt must be made to apportion the total farm forage costs fairly between the grazing enterprises.

The most commonly used means of allocating forage costs is the *grazing livestock unit* (GLU) method. The forage needs of each type of livestock, averaged over the whole of the year, are expressed by reference to the forage needs of a Friesian dairy

Cattle		
Dairy cows	1.0	
Beef cows (excl. calf)	0.8	
Calf under 6 months	0.2	} 1.0
Other cattle, under 300 kg	0.4	
Other cattle, over 300 kg	0.6	
Sheep		
Lowland ewes plus lambs	0.2	
Hill ewes plus lambs	0.12	
Ewe replacements 18-month:		
Lowland	0.14	
Hill	0.1	
Store lambs, short-keep	0.02	
Store lambs, long-keep	0.04	
Other sheep	0.1	

Source: A.W. Speedy, *Sheep Production*, (London, Longman, 1980), Table 14.5.

Figure 17.1   *Grazing livestock units*

cow. Thus a Friesian cow is represented by 1.0 GLU, while an animal with one-fifth of a dairy cow's needs is represented by 0.2 GLU (see Figure 17.1).

Forage costs may then be allocated to the various grazing enterprises by simple proportion. Take the example of a farm with average annual numbers of 100 dairy cows, 20 dairy young stock over 300 kg, 20 dairy young stock under 300 kg, and 305 lowland ewes and rams. Total forage costs are estimated at £9000, including both winter and summer feeding, and home-grown and purchased fodder. These forage costs are apportioned as shown in Figure 17.2. Stocking rates of livestock can be expressed in terms of GLU per hectare (or vice versa), or the GLU used to calculate the stocking rate in terms of head per hectare (or vice versa). Thus if the

Livestock	Number of head	GLU per head	Total GLU	% of grand total	Share of forage costs (£)
Dairy cows	100	1.0	100	56*	5,000
Heifers, over 300 kg	20	0.6	12	7	600
Heifers, under 300 kg	20	0.4	8	4	400
Ewes plus lambs	295	0.2	59 }	33	3,000
Rams	10	0.1	1 }		
TOTAL			180		9,000

*That is (100/180) × 100%.

Figure 17.2   *Allocation of forage costs using GLU – example*

total forage area represented by the £9000 forage variable costs were 72 ha, the stocking rate would be 2.5 GLU/ha (0.4 ha/GLU). For the sheep flock, this can be expressed as 12.5 adult head/ha (or 0.08 ha/head).

This method has the enormous practical merit of being simple to use and easy to understand. It will be obvious, however, that the resulting allocation is only approximate. It ignores differences in types of forage, and the fact that better pastures may be reserved for the dairy herd, while the sheep and the heifers are exiled for most of the year to the poorer pastures. The units themselves are based on 'average' relativities, which make no allowance for the breed, condition or productivity of the animals on the farm in question. Moreover, there is disagreement between various authorities as to the GLU attributable to the various classes of livestock.

In most situations, the inaccuracies arising from the use of GLU are relatively small, and do not justify the use of a more complicated method. To a certain extent they can be reduced by adaptation of the units and/or the way in which they are used. As an example of the former, cows in a particularly high-yielding dairy herd could be given a value of more than 1.0. As an example of the latter, an area of forage might be allocated specifically for the use of the dairy herd, and GLU used only to allocate the remainder between the heifers, beef and sheep. Speedy (1980) recommends multiplying the area of poor pasture by 0.5, and of rough grazing by 0.25, to allow for their lower stocking rate potential.

When planning a new unit or contemplating a major change in farm policy, accurate budgeting of forage costs may be absolutely critical. In this case, GLU may be used in the early stages of planning the combination of enterprises. This will then provide the basis for more precise estimates, working from the nutritional needs of the livestock. Once decisions have been made concerning the composition of animal rations, the area, type and allocation of forage crops may be estimated with a reasonable degree of accuracy.

A third method, using *livestock unit grazing days* (LUGD) relates to historical data, and is thus of little direct use in planning the first year's allocation of grazing. It can, however, provide valuable information on which to base forage policy for future years. Records are kept of the number of days' grazing by each group of livestock, and the number and type (and thus forage consumption) of animals in each group. These records can be kept by the field or for the whole farm.

The LUGD attributable to each class of livestock is calculated by multiplying the number of animals in each group by the appropriate GLU, and multipying the product by the number of days spent by that group in grazing. The close recording of the number of grazing days allows the different stages in the life-cycles of livestock to be separated, and more precise GLUs can be used than the annual standards shown in Figure 17.1 (see Figure 17.3, overleaf).

The consumption by each group of home-grown conserved feed should also be recorded to allow accurate allocation. This can be converted to LUGD by multiplying by a factor of 20 per tonne of silage, and 70 per tonne of hay.

Type of stock	Specifications	Unit values
Dairy cows	Holstein, Friesian	1.0
	Ayrshire, Shorthorn	0.9
	Guernsey	0.8
	Jersey	0.75
Grazing cattle	Under 204 kg (0 – 11 months)	0.25
	204 – 340 kg (11 – 20 months)	0.5
	340 – 477 kg (21 – 30 months)	0.75
	Over 477 kg (over 30 months)	1.0
Suckler cows	Dry cow	1.0
	Spring-calving cow with calf	1.2
	Autumn-calving cow with calf	1.4
Weaned calves	Weaned calf, spring born	0.2
	Weaned calf, autumn born	0.4
Breeding ewes (dry)	18 – 36 kg	0.08
	36 – 55 kg	0.1
	55 – 68 kg	0.13
	68 – 77 kg	0.15
	77 – 91 kg	0.17
	Over 91 kg	0.2
Weaned lambs	Light lambs (27 – 36 kg)	0.08
	Heavy lambs (36 – 54 kg)	0.1
Breeding ewes (lactating)	Add 0.01 per ewe to the dry ewe standard for each 25% lambing %	

Source: W. Holmes, J. Craven, and J. B. Kilkenny, *in* W. Holmes, (ed.),
Grass: Its Production and Utilisation (British Grassland Society/Blackwells, 1980).

Figure 17.3   *GLU for use in LUGD calculations*

The total forage costs of the farm may then be apportioned by reference to the LUGD used by each class of livestock, in a similar manner to that used for GLU in Figure 17.2. Separate decisions must be made concerning the allocation of bought-in forage.

This method has the advantages over the simpler GLU method of allowing the division of costs between grazing and conservation, of being adaptable to situations where certain areas of grassland are reserved largely for particular classes of livestock, and of using more precise livestock units which can better allow for variations in size and type of livestock. On the other hand, it is largely restricted to grassland, is historical, can require a high level of recording skill (especially if used on a field basis) and still relies on units calculated for 'average' conditions.

It is used frequently where education or research requirements dictate a higher level of accuracy than that provided by the simple GLU method, but is not commonly found on commercial farms.

Estimating potential production

In preparing budgets for livestock enterprises, it is necessary to make an estimate of the likely physical performance of the animals concerned. For meat and wool production, this means estimating the final weight of the product sold. For breeding/suckling livestock it entails estimating numbers of offspring weaned per female parent, and for replacement livestock estimating the number of animals attaining the appropriate age and condition for transfer into the breeding herd/flock (or sale into somebody else's herd or flock).

In making such estimates the farmer will be guided by a combination of experience, advice from specialists and neighbours, and published standards.

Special difficulties arise when budgeting for continuous-production livestock, such as those producing milk or eggs. The production pattern of these items is not uniform over time; it is generally characterized by a low level of production at the beginning of the cycle (i.e. after calving in a dairy cow) rising rapidly to a peak production, which is then followed by a slow decline throughout the rest of the cycle. In the dairy cow, this is repeated after each calving, and is known as the *lactation curve*, while in egg production the pattern is repeated after an annual moulting period (although intensively housed poultry are usually replaced before moulting). Figures 17.4 and 17.5 illustrate these production patterns.

If cash-flow budgets are to be realistic, and profit budgets are to make the correct allocation of revenue between financial years, these production patterns must be taken into consideration. Since most egg production takes place under closely controlled conditions, predictions of performance can reliably be made by referring to standard curves of the type shown in Figure 17.5, which are usually provided by the breeder of the foundation stock.

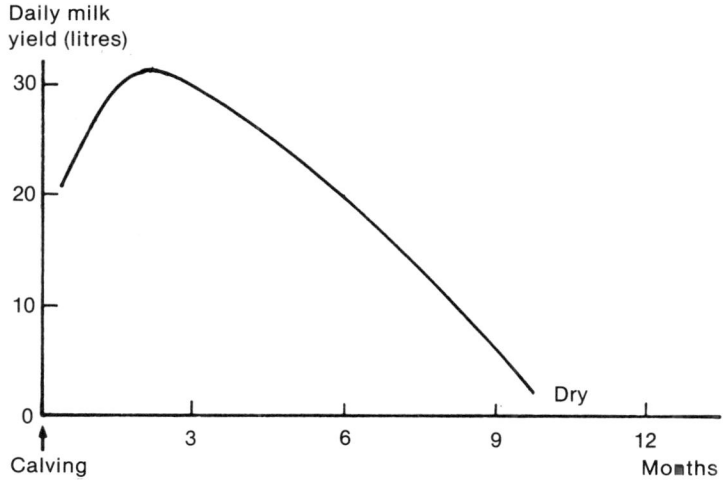

Figure 17.4 *Typical lactation curve for a dairy cow*

Figure 17.5 *Typical pattern of egg production*

The height and shape of a dairy cow's lactation curve will vary according to season of calving, condition of the cow, quality of forage, and other factors. For really precise budgeting, these factors should be taken into account; a valuable guide is Whittemore (1980a) on the dairy cow, especially Chapter 5.

A more simplistic approach is to use a standard lactation curve formula. One such is described by Russell (1985, p. 153). He identifies three phases:

1   A steady rise in milk yield up to a peak at 4 to 6 weeks after calving.
2   A peak daily yield of 1/200th of expected milk yield for the lactation (1/220 in the case of heifers).
3   A steady decline in yield thereafter at the rate of 10 per cent per month for the rest of the 10-month lactation.

This formula may be used in either of two ways. The first way is to estimate the likely average yield of milk per cow during the lactation (basing the estimate on experience, advice, or published standards), then applying the formula to give the monthly breakdown of milk sales. Thus if the herd average for cows is expected to be 6000 litres per lactation, the peak yield will be 6000/200 = 30 litres per day, declining by 3 litres each month until the end of the lactation. This result can be applied to the cows by monthly calving groups, and a similar operation performed for the heifers. Accumulation of the results of the various calculations will give an approximation of the pattern of milk production, and thus revenue, throughout the year.

The formula may also be used in reverse during the year, as a part of the control process. A check may be kept on peak yields, and an average peak yield calculated. This can then be inserted in the formula in order to work out how much the actual lactation yield is likely to differ from the target. If the average peak yield per cow works out at only 28 litres per day, say, the total lactation yield can be estimated in advance to be 28 × (200/1) = 5600 litres per cow. The effect of the difference on revenue can be calculated and appropriate remedial steps taken (see Part 4).

This somewhat crude formula must be used with care, since the peak yield will be affected by month of calving, short-lived feeding or disease problems, and so on. Nevertheless, it provides a useful rule-of-thumb guide for budgeting, and is used as the basis for the 'milkflow' spreadsheet shown in Figure A5.10 and A5.11, Appendix 5.

The farmer can obtain reliable and frequently-revised lactation predictions by using certain advisory services, such as those offered by Genus Management. The fees charged can be more than covered by the value of the time saved and the extra precision of control that is made possible.

Replacement of breeding livestock

Two questions arise under this heading: whether or not to rear one's own replacement livestock, and at what age to cull breeding livestock and replace with younger stock.

The home-rearing of replacement livestock is often justified on grounds other than those of simple cost. A livestock farmer may wish to guard against the importing of disease on bought-in animals; he may also be assuring himself of replacements of the required quality at the time he needs them, without having to pay the earth for them. He may wish to raise the standard of his herd or flock by genetic improvement. Where cash flow is particularly tight, home-rearing can ease the process of starting or expanding a breeding herd or flock, at the expense of time.

These are all very sound arguments for home-rearing. But it is important, as always, to test the financial effects of such a decision. The farmer must know how much it will cost him to be swayed by such arguments. It is particularly important for him to remember the principle of opportunity cost; rearing replacements will make demands on scarce resources, such as land and capital, and force the farmer to sacrifice other opportunities for making a return from those resources. Thus a partial budget should be drawn up, as in the Home Farm example in Figure 17.6 (overleaf).

Even if the partial budget gives a result which is financially unfavourable to home-rearing, the farmer may feel that the non-financial advantages justify the inclusion of home-rearing in the plan. At least he now knows how much that decision is costing him. Partial budgets may also be used to help determine the age at which old breeding stock should be culled and replaced. For a good many animals, replacement is dictated by death or incapacity rather than the farmer, so the most that can be done is to establish a general guideline.

The financial aspects most affected in this decision are the annual cost of buying or rearing livestock, the average annual level of production, and the cost of capital. The cost of replacement animals will increase with decreasing culling age; culling every two years will require twice as many replacements per year as culling every four years. The level of production will tend to decline after the first two or three production cycles. The older an animal is, the more likely it is to be culled or to die

Decision: Expand grass area of Home Farm by 12 ha at expense of barley in order to rear 20 two-year-old down-calving heifers per year.

Costs of change	£	Benefits of change	£
Revenue lost		*Extra revenue*	
Barley grain sales:		16 heifers transferred	
12 ha at 4 t/ha at £95	4,560	into breeding herd at	
Barley straw sales:		£600/head	9,600
12 ha at 2 t/ha at £15	360	4 heifers (in-calf)	
		sold at £550/head*	2,200
Extra costs			
Variable costs of		*Costs saved*	
rearing 20 heifers		Variable costs of	
(including forage and		12 ha barley at £130/ha	1,553
AI) at £260/head	5,200	Machine and labour	300
	10,120		
Balance (increase in net			
profit before interest)	3,535		
	13,655		13,655

*Surplus numbers allow some degree of selection before transfer into the breeding herd.

Figure 17.6 *Use of a partial budget in deciding whether or not to home-rear replacement breeding livestock*

in the middle of its production cycle; such events can have a marked effect on the average yields of older age-groups.

Figure 17.7 (opposite) shows the financial effects of a hypothetical replacement-rate decision. It assumes that the extra replacement heifers are purchased; were they home-reared their cost would be the variable cost of their production plus the opportunity cost of the extra land used. The example takes account of only one year's costs and benefits; for a more precise assessment, the net present values (see Chapter 19) arising from each of the alternative replacement policies over (say) a 10-year period, should be compared.

Livestock with long production cycles

Certain types of trading livestock, chiefly beef cattle and dairy heifers, take more than one year to reach the point of sale or transfer into another enterprise. In order to provide a regular annual output, a new batch of livestock is usually started each year. This results in an overlap of production cycles, with two, three or even four different age groups on the farm simultaneously.

A farm with an annual requirement of 20 replacement dairy heifers, calving at 2½ years, will for part of each year be supporting 20 + young calves, 20 + yearlings, and 20 + in-calf heifers. Further complications can develop in beef production if

Costs of change	£	Benefits of change	£

Revenue lost
5th lactation yield
  from 4 cows at 4600
  litres/cow (effective)*
  at £0.19/litre
	3,996	*Extra revenue*
		1st lactation yield
		  from 4 heifers at
		  4,800 litres/heifer
		  at £0.19/litre
			3,648

Extra costs
4 extra in-calf
  heifers per year
  at £600 per heifer
	2,400	*Costs saved*	

Cost of capital to
  pay for extra heifers
  at (say) 15% of £2,400
			3,648

for 1 year	360	*Balance* (decrease in	
	6,256	net profit)	2,608
	6,256		6,256

*That is, allowing for increased likelihood of mid-lactation mortality and obligatory culling in older cows

Figure 17.7 *Partial budget to test the effect of replacing Home Farm dairy cows at four years rather than five*

two batches, autumn and spring, are started each year, although in this case production conditions will differ sufficiently between the autumn and spring batches to allow them to be treated as two separate enterprises.

Two problems arise from this overlapping of production cycles. One is simply that of keeping track of the numbers of livestock, which can be eased by the use of a livestock movement chart (see Figure 12.2). Another possibility is the use of a flow diagram, such as that in Figure 17.8 (overleaf). The example used is that of a dairy herd with a replacement heifer herd. It could easily be extended to accommodate a beef enterprise.

The second problem is that of calculating gross margins in such a way as to give the detail required for precise control. This matter was discussed earlier in the context of historical accounts.

Further reading

Feeding policy

Barnard, C. S. and Nix, J. S., *Farm Planning and Control,* 2nd edition (London, Cambridge University Press, 1979), Chapter 9.

Ministry of Agriculture, Fisheries and Food, *Energy Allowances and Feeding Systems for Ruminants*, Reference Book 433, 2nd edition (London, HMSO, 1984).

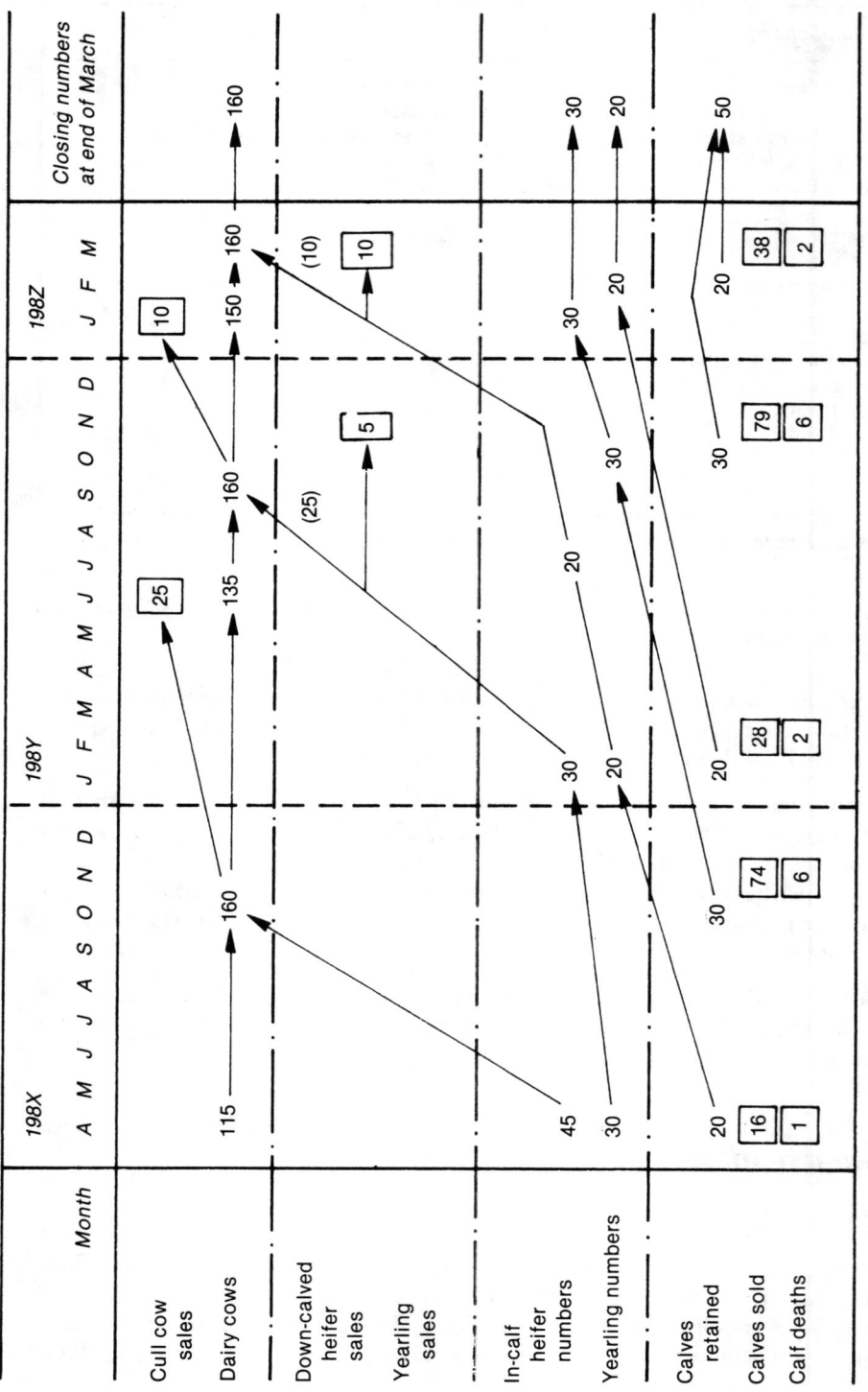

Note: The flow chart relates to a herd which is in the process of expanding from 115 to 160 cows. One cull is missed in 198Y due to a large inflow of young stock in the previous year.

Figure 17.8 *Livestock movement flow chart*

Nelson, R. H., *An Introduction to Feeding Farm Livestock*, 2nd edition (Oxford, Pergamon, 1979).

Whittemore, C. T. and Elsley, *Practical Pig Nutrition*, 2nd edition (Ipswich, Farming Press, 1977).

Wilson, P. W. and Brigstoke, T. D. A., *Improved Feeding of Cattle and Sheep* (St Albans, Granada, 1981).

General principles

Barnard, C. S. and Nix, J. S., *op. cit.,* part 2: 'The Organisation of Enterprises'.

Specific livestock studies

The following is a selection from the many texts available:

Goodwin, D. H., *Beef Management and Production* (London, Hutchinson, 1977).

Goodwin, D. H., *Sheep Management and Production* 2nd edition (London, Hutchinson, 1979).

Norman, L., Turner, R. A. E. and Wilson, K. R. S., *The Farm Business* (London, Longman, 1985), chapters 6 and 7.

Russell, K., *The Principles of Dairy Farming*, 10th edition (Ipswich, Farming Press, 1985).

Speedy, A. W., *Sheep Production* (London, Longman, 1980).

Whittemore, C. T., *Lactation of the Dairy Cow* (London, Longman, 1980).

Whittemore, C. T., *Pig Production* (London, Longman, 1980).

18

Labour and machinery planning

Introduction

Fixed cost control is crucial to the survival of a modern farm business. Of the fixed costs, labour and machinery are the most difficult, and the most important, to plan and control. Unlike such items as rent, mortgage interest, and accountant's fees, they are substantially under the farmer's influence. Since on most farms labour and power represent a major part of total fixed costs, economy in their use is essential.

Planning labour and machinery use is concerned largely with answering two questions. First, what is the optimum combination and level of use of men and machines? Second, what is the cost of implementing the chosen labour/machinery policy? These questions are inextricably linked; one cannot finally budget costs until the policy has been decided, while the choice of policy must reflect the cost of use.

There is thus no easy step-by-step recipe to follow. The simplest approach is probably to start by planning the labour requirements of a given farming system, and using this as a guide to labour and machinery needs. This will result in a basic plan, which can then be budgeted to show the likely costs involved. Alternative policies may then be evaluated by partial budgets showing the net financial effect of deviating from the original plan.

This approach may not be suitable for all situations, and the farmer may be forced into a repetitive trial-and-error process, planning and replanning until a suitable solution is found.

Estimating level of use

Simple guesswork

With experience, a farmer may feel confident enough to look at a proposed farm system and state that it will need a certain number of men, and a certain complement of machinery. In some situations this may be good enough as an initial rule-of-thumb measure. It allows too much room for error, though, to provide reliable estimates for planning and control, except where the labour and machinery force is dictated by the circumstances of the farm (on very small farms, for instance, or all-dairy farms).

Standard man-day and standard tractor-hour calculations

An alternative is to estimate the total amount of labour and machinery time required by the farm system in the space of one year, then divide by the annual contribution expected of each man or machine in order to determine the appropriate complement.

To calculate the number of men required, the area of each crop and type of livestock is multiplied by *standard man days* (SMD) required per hectare or per head (tables of SMD can be found in various regional Farm Business Survey publications, and in farm management handbooks such as Nix). The SMD for all the enterprises are totalled, and an addition (typically 15 per cent) is made to allow for the contingencies and maintenance work.

The grand total is adjusted for work performed by casual labour and contractors, and is then divided by 300 (the 'average' SMD contribution of a farm worker) to give the number of men required. Appropriate adjustments can be made for workers who are not likely to spend the whole of their working time in physical labour on the farm.

A similar calculation is used in estimating tractor numbers,* this time using standard tractor hours (again available in Nix and various Farm Business Survey results). The 'average' number of hours worked per tractor per year is generally taken to be 1000–1500, although there is some sense in using 800 for the first tractor, as suggested by Nix, in order to give greater flexibility.

Figure 18.1 (overleaf) shows the use of SMDs and standard tractor hours in determining the number of men and tractors required for a mixed farm system.

The results of the calculation suggest that the farmer could just manage with six men, plus himself. This leaves him no time for managing the business, which is likely to occupy at least a quarter of his time. The deficiency is relatively small, and could probably be taken up by the judicious use of casual labour and/or contractors.

This type of estimate suffers in precision, since the use of 'average' labour and machinery use per head or hectare, and of 'average' work output per man or tractor, assumes that all farms are alike with respect to methods, soils, topography, building layout, type and size of machinery, and so on. More important, the method makes no allowance for seasonal variation in daylight, fieldwork conditions, and labour demand. Adding to the complications is the fact that different authorities quote different figures; using data from Exeter University (*Farm Management Handbook 1991*) gives a requirement of 8 men.

Moreover, the actual farm on which Figure 18.1 is based is staffed by four men (including a working manager) and a woman, the latter having full responsibility for the pigs with alternate weekend relief. Actual labour cost in 1989/90 was £53,519; machinery cost was £17,995.

These drawbacks limit the technique to the role of an initial guide, which should always be followed up by more precise methods.

---

*Note that this and the subsequent methods concentrate on the number of tractors, with the assumption that this determines the number and type of the other machines.

Enterprise	Head or ha	SMD per head/ha*	Total SMD	Tractor hours per head/ha*	Total tractor hours
Winter wheat	8.0	2.25	18.0	15.00	120.00
Winter barley	25.8	2.25	57.9	15.00	386.25
Spring barley	10.4	2.25	23.4	15.00	155.70
Grass - grazing	48.7	1.00	48.7	2.50	121.73
Grass silage (2 cuts)	30.7	4.00	122.8	21.00	644.70
Grass silage (1 cut)	16.3	2.50	40.8	12.00	195.84
Maize (1 cut) - estimate	11.6	3.00	34.8	15.00	173.85
Dairy cows	108.0	5.00	540.0	6.00	648.00
Young stock (1-2yrs)	45.0	1.50	67.5	4.00	180.00
Y. stock (6-12 months)	45.0	0.75	33.8	2.25	101.25
Calves	45.0	1.50	67.5	2.25	101.25
Breeding sows	110.0	3.00	330.0	1.75	192.50
Boars	6.0	2.00	12.0	1.00	6.00
Other pigs over 1 month	721.0	0.30	216.3	1.00	721.00
Outdoor pigs	60.0	3.00	180.0	1.00	60.00
Ewes	226.0	0.50	113.0	1.25	282.50
Rams	6.0	0.50	3.0	1.25	7.50
Sub-total			1909.4		4098.07
+15% contingency			286.4		614.71
TOTAL HOURS			2195.8		4712.77
			(approx. 7 men)		(4 tractors)
		Cost per man:	10194	Cost per hour:	14.00
		Labour cost:	65240	Machy. cost:	57373

*Based on J.S. Nix , *Farm Management Pocketbook*, September 1990, pp. 90,120,122,188.

Figure 18.1   *Use of SMD and tractor hours*

The labour profile

One such method is the *labour profile*. The object is to calculate the labour requirement of each enterprise for each month of the year. Examination of the distribution of labour requirements will assist decisions concerning the number of men to employ, the extent to which casual labour and contractors are used, and the number and type of machines required. The clumsy standard man-day is abandoned in favour of the *man-hour*.

Tables published in Nix and similar handbooks give estimates for each enterprise of the man-hours required for each type of operation, and of the month(s) in which

Hours per hectare/head   (Average performance, Nix 1990)

Enterprise	ha/hd	Oct	Nov	Dec	Jan	Feb	Mar	Apr	May	Jun	Jul	Aug	Sep
Winter wheat	51.3	3.6	0.6				0.5	1.1	0.3	0.3		5.7	5.1
Winter barley	32.4	5.1	0.6				0.5	1.1	0.3	0.3	3.6	5.7	
Spring barley	27.2	0.7	1.1	0.7			3.7	0.6	1.1			6.0	2.6
Grass - leys	46.9						0.6	0.6	0.6	0.6	0.6	1.9	1.0
- perm. pasture	38.2						0.6	0.6	0.6	0.6	0.6	0.3	0.2
Silage	40								6.8	3.4			
Dairy cows	115	2.5	2.5	2.5	2.4	2.2	2.1	2.1	2.1	2.2	2.4	2.5	2.5
Followers (repl. units)	15	3.7	3.7	3.7	3.7	3.7	1.4	1.4	1.4	1.4	1.4	1.4	1.4
Ewes	190	0.3	0.2	0.2	0.3	0.3	1.0	0.4	0.3	0.4	0.2	0.2	0.3

Total hours

Enterprise	ha/hd	Oct	Nov	Dec	Jan	Feb	Mar	Apr	May	Jun	Jul	Aug	Sep
Winter wheat	51.3	184.7	30.8				25.7	56.4	15.4	15.4		292.4	261.6
Winter barley	32.4	165.2	19.4				16.2	35.6	9.7	9.7	116.6	184.7	
Spring barley	27.2	19.0	29.9	19.0			100.6	16.3	29.9			163.2	70.7
Grass - leys	46.9						28.1	28.1	28.1	28.1	28.1	89.1	46.9
- perm. pasture	38.2						22.9	22.9	22.9	22.9	22.9	11.5	7.6
Silage	40								272.0	136.0			
Dairy cows	115	287.5	287.5	287.5	276.0	253.0	241.5	241.5	241.5	253.0	276.0	287.5	287.5
Followers (repl. units)	15	55.5	55.5	55.5	55.5	55.5	21.0	21.0	21.0	21.0	21.0	21.0	21.0
Ewes	190	47.5	38.0	38.0	57.0	57.0	190.0	76.0	57.0	76.0	38.0	38.0	47.5
Total hours needed		**759.5**	**461.1**	**400.0**	**388.5**	**365.5**	**646.1**	**498.0**	**697.6**	**562.2**	**502.7**	**1087.4**	**742.9**
Hours available/man/month		182.0	131.0	132.0	135.0	122.0	171.0	176.0	216.0	224.0	231.0	216.0	195.0
Total available (3.5 men)		**637.0**	**458.5**	**462.0**	**472.5**	**427.0**	**598.5**	**616.0**	**756.0**	**784.0**	**808.5**	**756.0**	**682.5**

Figure 18.2 *Labour profile spreadsheet*

each operation is likely to occur. The man-hour requirements are then accumulated month by month, in the form of a table and/or a histogram. This is then compared to the theoretical availability of man-hours. Nix and others give typical monthly availability figures, which can be adjusted in the light of one's own experience to suit the situation of a particular farm. Allowance is made in these figures for poor weather, short days, illness and other contingencies, as well as the possibility of overtime working.

Figure 18.2 shows the application of the labour profile to another mixed farm. This data is shown in different ways in Figures 18.3 and 18.4. The technique may be used in two different ways. The farmer may use the labour profile to estimate how many regular workers he needs to cope with a given system. More usefully, perhaps, he can stipulate that no more than 3.5 workers are to be employed (leaving half of his own time for management) in which case the 3.5-worker availability line becomes an absolute boundary, and ways must be found of eliminating or redistributing excess labour at peak times. This is the approach illustrated in Figures 18.3 and 18.4.

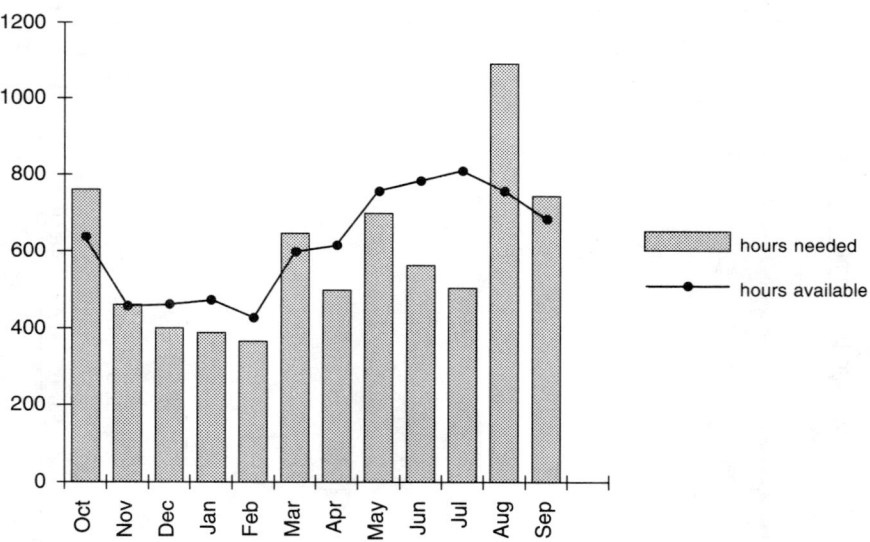

Figure 18.3   *Labour profile − labour need and availability compared*

Figure 18.3 indicates a potential deficit of labour in October, March, August and September, with no slack in November. Figure 18.4 shows how the various enterprises contribute to that deficit, with winter cereals having a significant effect in the late summer and autumn, and spring cereals and sheep contributing to the problems in March. Using this information, responses may be formulated which might include:

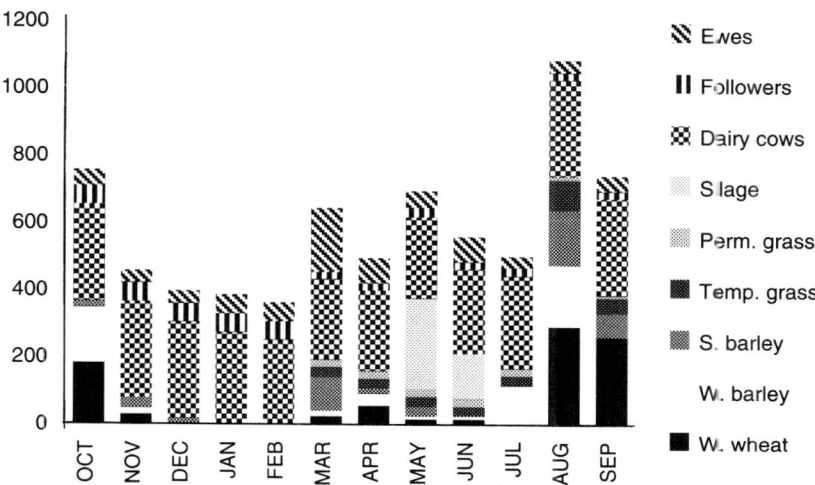

Figure 18.4 *Labour profile — pattern of labour use*

1   Changes in the farming system (such as switching some winter barley for spring barley, or eliminating the sheep flock);
2   Use of casual labour and/or contractors (for harvest and autumn cultivations, for instance);
3   Improving gang organization (such as using larger grain trailers to reduce manpower for transport);
4   Improving output per worker (by, for instance, putting some evening/weekend jobs, such as bale-carting, on a piece-work basis);
5   Substitution of machines for labour (such as using a fully mechanized big bale system instead of manhandling small bales).

Each of these possibilities has a cost, of course, but careful use of a labour profile and partial budgets can help in developing a system which balances labour use with other financial considerations.

Where machinery is concerned, the labour profile cannot serve as anything more than a rough guide.

The gang-work day chart

Apart from the difficulty of determining machinery requirements, the labour profile has the major limitation of ignoring the fact that men and machines are frequently used in teams. One example is that of silage-making, where the team may consist of four tractor/man units; one harvesting, two carting, and one filling the clamp.

Enterprise and operations	Timing of operations	Area (ha)	Work rate (ha/GWD)	GWD needed	Gang size (men)	Machinery
Winter wheat						
Seed-bed cults.	Up to mid-Oct	50	8.00	6.25	1	2 tractors
Combine drilling	Oct	24	12.00	2.0	1	2 tractors
Spring barley						
Plough	Oct – Feb	30	3.50	8.6	1	1 tractor
Sugar beet						
Plough	Sep – Dec	12	2.00	6.0	1	1 tractor
Harvest	Up to end Dec	12	0.90	13.3	3	3 tractors harvester 2 trailers
Maincrop potatoes						
Harvest	Up to early Nov	10	0.70	14.3	3	3 tractors harvester 2 trailers
Riddling	Oct – May	10	0.40	25.0	3	riddle

Notes: Work rates and gang sizes based on J. S. Nix, *Farm Management Pocketbook*, 11th edition. No allowance made for dairy (treated as an independent unit) or for casual labour for potato picking.

Figure 18.5 *Gang-work day data for October to December*

For many farms, particularly small farms and those whose workforces are composed of relatively independent, specialist workers (such as stockmen), this is not a significant problem. In such cases, the labour profile or simpler methods are adequate. Where team-working *is* common, the *gang-work day chart* should be used.

The gang-work day (GWD) chart works on a similar principle to that of the labour profile, with one axis measuring the number of men required and the other showing the number of working days available in each month. The time requirements for each operation are measured in hectares per day, rather than per man-hour, and are considered for gangs of men rather than for individuals. The time required for an operation is shown in the GWD chart as a block, with the height determined by the number of men in the gang, and the breadth by the number of days required to complete the operation. It is usually necessary to show only those parts of the year where the labour profile indicates a labour problem.

The blocks representing the various operations are pieced together, rather like a jigsaw puzzle. The resulting picture can be interpreted in a fashion similar to the labour profile, with the aim of smoothing out the most dramatic peaks in labour requirement. There may be some overlaps (as when a combining team carts bales in the evenings), and there will certainly be gaps between blocks. The latter, in moderation, may be regarded as opportunities for general maintenance, and as a contingency allowance for poor weather and other mishaps. If, in a peak season, the gaps appear excessive, thought must be given to the possibilities of changing gang sizes, and/or the way they work, and/or the cropping system.

Figures 18.5 and 18.6 demonstrate the application of the technique to an arable farm for the autumn period. The chart (Figure 18.6) shows that it is possible for the operations to be completed, given 'typical' conditions. There is little room for error, though, and the farmer will clearly be doing little management during the period, being needed for physical work. Like the labour profile, the chart can be used as a basis for identifying ways of ameliorating the situation, including the use of contractors, or the introduction of a less ambitious farming system.

As well as being more realistic with regard to labour planning, the gang-work day chart eases decisions concerning the size and type of the machinery complement. Thinking of labour in terms of gangs inevitably involves consideration of the machinery used by the gangs, and the emphasis on type of operation rather than enterprise further clarifies the issues.

Other techniques for the planning and control of work

Even with the help of labour profiles and gang-work day charts, the job of planning and controlling work progress can be one of the most difficult and time-consuming aspects of the farmer's job. In the long term it means ensuring that operations are carried out at the optimum point in the production cycle of the crops or livestock concerned. In day-to-day management it entails making sure that jobs are given the appropriate priority, and that each member of the team is

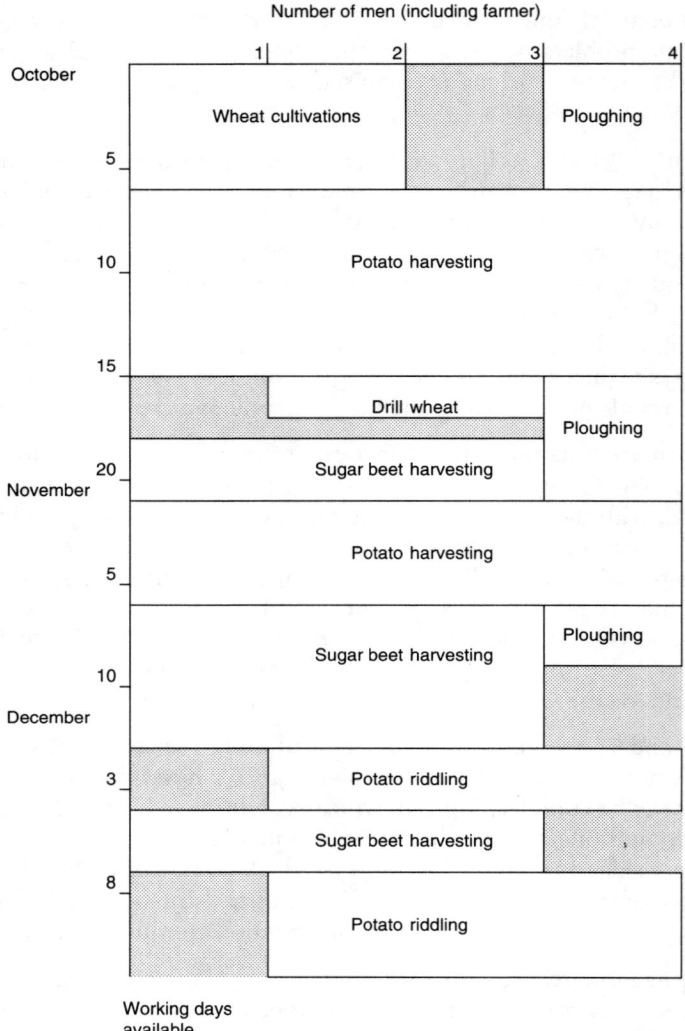

Figure 18.6   *Gang-work day chart*

in the right place, at the right time, with the right equipment, and knows what is expected of him.

A combination of simple techniques has been suggested by Errington and Hastings (1981) to help the farmer in planning and controlling work progress. For long-term planning, the use of a *year planner* is suggested, on which the farmer can indicate the likely pattern of work in the months ahead. This enables him to monitor his actual progress, and to anticipate the effect of delays on the completion of future operations. It also acts as a valuable aid in the compilation of labour profiles and gang-work day charts for future years.

With the aid of the year planner, a *job list* may be compiled for each week as it arrives, with the order or priority of the jobs clearly marked, as well as deadlines for their completion. This in turn can be used to draw up a *work schedule* for the farm, showing who is expected to do what, and when. Naturally weather and other unpredictable events will interfere with the planned schedule, but the value of the procedure lies in the facility for weighing up the week's activities quickly and accurately, and reallocating work according to the new priorities.

Some types of work, particularly those which consist of a large number of interdependent elements, can be scheduled by use of *network analysis (critical path analysis)*. The number of agricultural operations to which this technique is appropriate is small, with the greatest potential being in the intensive livestock and horticultural areas. Modern computer programs are beginning to extend the application of the technique Further information may be found in Lockyer and Gordon (1991).

A farmer may well feel that certain operations could be 'streamlined' in order to speed their progress or to reduce the effort required. A variety of techniques are available for the investigation of the way in which work is performed; these techniques are known collectively as *work study*. Some apply to the work of individuals, some to the work of gangs of men, others to combinations of men and machines. Some are concerned primarily with reducing distance travelled, while others are concerned mainly with the time taken to perform the operation.

Many of these techniques can be of value in farming, but to describe them in the detail that they deserve is beyond the aim of this book. Useful references are Fields (1969), Currie (1972) and International Labour Organization (1979).

Estimating labour and machinery costs

Estimating labour costs

The cost of labour on a farm comprises a fixed element and a variable element (these terms are used in their strict sense, and not in the compromise sense of the agricultual gross margin).

Fixed	*Variable*
Basic wage	Overtime
Benefits in kind*	Bonuses
Employer's National Insurance contribution	Casual labour*
Employer's liability insurance	
Community Charge (where paid by employer)	

*If the calculation is intended to provide figures for a whole-farm profit budget, care should be taken to ensure that these items are not double counted in both fixed and variable costs.

The fixed element is relatively easy to estimate for a given labour force, since (subject to inflation and the minimum requirements of the law) it is largely determined by the farmer. The basic wage will be the minimum laid down by the current Agricultural Wages Order, plus increments for craftsmen and supervisory grades, and whatever extra that the farmer feels is necessary to attract and retain good workers.

Benefits in kind (such as cottages, milk, potatoes, and payment of phone rental) should be priced at the opportunity cost to the farm business (for produce, the normal farm sale price; for cottages, the rent, less expenses, which could be otherwise obtained or, if higher, the return which could be expected if the cottage were sold and the money safely invested). Employer's National Insurance contributions and employer's insurance are dictated by the wages paid. These are both calculated as percentages of the gross earnings, including overtime and bonuses, and thus contain a variable element.

The variable elements of labour costs are more difficult to forecast, since the amounts used of overtime, bonus work and casual labour are likely to be affected by external factors such as weather. Use of labour profiles and gang-work day charts will help in estimating the hours required, after which the appropriate rates of pay can be applied to find the total cost.

Estimating machinery costs

Machinery costs may similarly be classified into fixed and variable elements:

Fixed	*Variable*
Depreciation	Fuel and oil
Tax and insurance	Spares and repairs
Lease payments	Contract hire*
Cost of capital	

Depreciation has already been discussed (Chapter 5), and road tax is a set amount. Quotations for insurance are obtainable by phoning insurance agents or brokers, and for leasing terms by contacting the relevant companies. Use of contractors may be estimated with the help of the gang-work day chart, while phone calls to local contractors will help in pricing. Fuel and oil, and repairs and maintenance, are the most difficult costs to estimate: Nix gives some help here (Section III, Table 4), but one usually has to rely on a combination of experience and inspired guesswork.

Whether or not the cost of capital is included, and at what rate, depends on the intended use of the costing. If the costs are for inclusion in a whole-farm budget, the cost of capital will be calculated on a whole-farm basis, by reference to the cash-flow budget, and need not be included in the machinery costing. If the costs are intended for comparison between alternative machinery policies (as in the next section) the cost of capital should be calculated by multiplying the average value of the machine (purchase price minus anticipated resale price divided by 2) by the percentage rate of opportunity cost of capital (see Chapter 19).

*See footnote on previous page.

An alternative to the detailed costing of machinery is to take the total number of tractor hours (as calculated earlier in this chapter) and multiply by the cost per standard tractor hour for the type of farm concerned. The latter may be obtained from regional Farm Business Survey handbooks, but will need updating for use in budgets.

This approach suffers from all the problems of using standard tractor hours, plus those associated with the use of standard costs, which cannot allow for differences between individual holdings in a particular farming type. It can in many situations give a reasonable approximation, however, while needing much less time and effort than the more precise method described above.

Investigating alternatives

Introduction

Once a 'basic' plan has been formulated and costed, various alternatives to that plan may be investigated. This investigation is largely a matter of using partial budgets, although *breakeven charts* can be useful. The latter are used to plot the cost of each of the alternatives under consideration against a measure of scale, such as the number of hectares on which a machine is used during the year, or the number of tonnes of a given product processed per annum.

An example of a breakeven chart is given in Figure 18.7, comparing the use of a

Figure 18.7 *Breakeven chart*

contractor with the purchase of a new 3.6 m cut combine harvester. It is assumed that the use of a contractor will not, in this instance, affect the regular labour cost beyond reducing overtime payments slightly.

The implication of Figure 18.7 is that, for the particular farm and machine under consideration, it would be worth the farmer using contractors if he is planning to harvest less than about 80 ha per year. This is not to say that it would not be worth using a smaller and/or second-hand machine for smaller areas, nor does the chart take into account factors such as timeliness (see below).

The following subsections list the principal financial and non-financial considerations in a selection of common labour/machinery decisions. The lists are intended to be indicative rather than exhaustive.

Increase regular work-force by one man

*Possible benefits**
Reduction in overtime, casual labour, use of contractors.
Change in farm system (if labour previously limiting) to give greater profits.
Opportunity to reduce some machinery costs by use of more labour-intensive methods.
Improvement in quality of output.
'Spare' labour acts as contingency allowance for emergencies.
Farmer can spend less time on manual work and more on management and/or leisure.
Maintenance and appearance of farm can be improved.

*Possible costs**
Extra wages, National Insurance, employer's liability insurance, benefits in kind.
Need for extra machinery (especially for field work).
Demands on farmer's organizing ability increased.

Replace some regular labour and machinery by use of contractors and/or casual labour

Possible benefits
Reduction in *number* of men and/or machines, saving basic costs of employment and ownership.
Reduction in *use* of men and/or machines, saving overtime and bonus payments, and machinery running costs.
Change in farm system (if specialist labour skills and machinery previously limiting) to produce higher profits.
Improvement in quality of output, e.g. if contractor uses more modern, sophisticated machinery.
Reduction in capital requirements.

---

*The emphasis here is on the work 'possible' – not every one of these aspects will apply to every decision, and some are mutually incompatible.

Possible costs

Direct cost of employing contractors and/or casual labour.

Reduction in quality of output, e.g. contractors in a hurry may be less careful than our drivers.

Risk of contractor not coming exactly when required, with resulting loss of output.

Increased worry and demands on organizational ability (outside influences involved; difficult to control).

Reaction of existing employees to reduction in workforce, and/or loss of overtime and bonus payments.

Replace two small machines by one large machine

Possible benefits

Probably only one operator required; save overtime and bonus payments; possibly reduce workforce by one man.

Lower initial price: one machine of a given capacity usually costs less than two smaller machines with an identical combined capacity.

Lower running costs (ditto).

Change in farm system (if labour previously limiting) to earn higher profits.

Improvement in timeliness of operations (key tasks performed faster).

Favourable reaction of employees (especially the potential driver).

Possible costs

Loss of flexibility in use.

Consequences of breakdown, operator illness, etc. are greater.

Reaction of employees to reduction in workforce and/or loss of overtime.

Buy secondhand rather than new

Possible benefits

Lower purchase price; eases cash flow and may make the difference between having and not having.

Lower interest costs in consequence.

Possible costs

Higher maintenance and repair costs.

Reduction in quantity and quality of output, due to age and obsolescence.

More frequent breakdowns may affect timeliness of operations.

Lower operator comfort and safety.

Extra worry generated by unreliability.

Replace a machine next year rather than this

Possible benefits

Initial expense delayed; eases cash flow and reduces depreciation expense.

Possible costs

Higher annual repair costs.

Initial capital allowances delayed.

Remainder as above for secondhand machine.

Lease rather than buy

Possible benefits

Lower initial payments; eases cash flow and money can be put to good use elsewhere.

Lower overall costs if profits too low to allow initial capital allowances to be taken.

Greater security than borrowing on overdraft (though not loan).

Fixed rental rates (valuable if interest rates rise).

Possible costs

Loss of capital allowances if profits are high enough to allow these to be taken.

Fixed rental rates (disadvantage if interest rates fall).

Further reading

General

Barnard, C. S. and Nix, J. S., *Farm Planning and Control*, 2nd edition (London, Cambridge University Press, 1979), chapters 4 and 5.

Machinery costs

Butterworth, W. and Nix, J. S., *Farm Mechanisation for Profit* (St Albans, Granada, 1983).

Morris, J., 'Tractor repair costs', *Farm Management*, vol. 5, no. 10, 1988.

Planning and control of work progress

Errington, A. and Hastings, M. R., 'Work planning in agriculture', *Farm Management*, vol. 4, no. 5, 1981.

Gladwell, G., 'Labour and machinery analysis and planning', *Farm Management*, vol. 5, no. 9, 1985.

Lockyer, K. and Gordon, J., *Critical Path Analysis*, 5th edition (London, Pitman, 1991).

Work study

Currie, R. M. (revised J. E. Faraday), *Work Study*, 3rd edition (London, British Institute of Managment and Pitman, 1972).

Fields, A., *Method Study* (London, Cassell, 1969).

International Labour Organization, *Introduction to Work Study*, 3rd edition (Geneva, ILO, 1979).

19

Capital planning

Introduction

For the majority of businesses, capital is the most limiting resource in the long term. Given enough capital, other resources such as land, labour or management skills may be bought, although it may take time for the right plot of land to come on the market or the right worker or manager to offer himself for employment. Since capital plays such a key role, it is vital that the farmer should be able to calculate its cost, measure the efficiency of its use, and know where to seek additional capital needed for survival and/or expansion of his business.

Discussion of the effects of inflation has been postponed to Chapter 21, in order to simplify the discussion of techniques.

Sources of capital

A prime consideration in any plan which involves the investment of capital is that of where the money is to come from. The most profitable of schemes is as nothing if insuffecient cash is available for its implementation. Possible sources of capital may be divided into internal sources and external sources.

Sources of capital internal to the business include personal savings of the owner(s), and profits retained from former years. They also include various forms of capital release: sale of land (and possible lease-back); sale of surplus cottages; hire of machinery, buildings and other assets instead of purchase; change from a system with high working-capital requirements to one with low working-capital requirements; and so on. The advantages of obtaining capital from internal sources are that it does not incur a continuous interest charge, and that the farmer is not indebted to an outsider to the business as a direct result of the use of the capital. On the other hand, it can often incur a heavy opportunity cost (such as sale of land at a heavy discount for lease-back, or lost profitability as a result of a change in system). There is also a limit to its availability.

External sources include gifts, grants, widening of the ownership of the business, and credit. If you have friends or relations who are sufficiently rich and enlightened to make you substantial gifts, all well and good, but in most circumstances it is necessary to look further afield. Grants are available from the Ministry of Agriculture, Fisheries and Food (MAFF) to promote environmental improvement, diversification into non-agricultural enterprises, agricultural co-operation and horticultural and orchard improvement. Details of these schemes are available from local offices of the Agricultural Development and Advisory Service and summaries are found in many farm management handbooks (e.g. Nix, section IV, part 7).

For non-agricultural developments, grants or low-interest loans may be available from other sources, such as the English Tourist Board, the Rural Development Commission, and the Countryside Commission. Assistance for schemes involving amenity tree-planting, conservation of certain types of natural environment, and similar activities, are often available through bodies such as the Countryside Commission and local authorities.

Bringing other people into the ownership of the business by the formation of a partnership or a limited liability company will also bring money in, but it may not be possible to find someone at the appropriate time who is prepared to risk his money, is trustworthy and with whom one can happily work (see Appendix 2).

The above sources are unlikely to prove sufficient to maintain the pace of development required by most farmers, unless the farmer is well-established, rich, or lucky. Thus many farmers, particularly the younger ones, are forced to resort to credit. To borrow money exposes the business to extra risk, and means that the owner of the business has to be 'beholden' to someone outside the business. If one is sensible about the level and type of borrowing, however, the risk need not be large.

The main (but certainly not only) sources of credit, listed in approximate order of term, are as follows:

Short-term	Trade credit
	Credit cards
	Overdraft
	Hire purchase (lease hire)
	Leasing (finance lease)
	Short- and medium-term loans
Long-term	Mortgage, i.e. loan secured on land or property

Most farmers make use of *trade credit* to some degree. It is commonplace for businesses to buy and sell on credit, and thus at any one time a business is likely to owe money to a supplier. For a certain period after the invoice date, this credit is free (usually three or four weeks). The cost of extending credit beyond this period can be expensive, however, both in terms of lost goodwill and in terms of cash. A typical credit charge is '2 ½ per cent cash discount if payment is made within 28 days of invoice date'. If the bill is settled two weeks late and the discount is lost, the marginal cost of the delay is equivalent to an annual interest rate of 67 per cent.

Credit cards work on a similar system to trade credit, and their cost is high unless the balance outstanding is cleared each month. Their cost may be outweighed by their convenience in the purchase of relatively small items.

The largest single source of credit for farms in the UK is the clearing bank network. The credit supplied by a bank may be in the form of an overdraft and/or loans. An *overdraft* is a negative balance in a bank current account. It fluctuates from day to day as money flows into and out of the account. Interest is calculated on the daily balance outstanding, and is thus payable only on money that is in use. An overdraft is technically repayable on demand and as a result is usually the cheapest source of credit available.

A *loan* is borrowed from the bank on a contractual basis. The bank gives the borrower a sum of money, on the condition that it is repaid in an agreed pattern, and that interest is paid at specified times during the period of the loan (see next section in this chapter). A loan is more expensive than an overdraft, since interest rates tend to be higher in reflection of the longer call of the money, and since, unlike an overdraft, interest has to be paid whether or not the money is fully used. It is rather safer than an overdraft, however, due to the existence of a contract and a clearly specified term. A banker will usually prefer to finance major asset purchases by means of loans, using the overdraft to finance seasonal fluctuations in working capital.

Loans are also available from other institutions, often for specific purposes. The Agricultural Mortgage Corporation lends primarily for land purchase, but will also help to finance other capital improvements, diversification, horticulture and woodlands, providing it is granted a first mortgage on agricultural property as security. The Lands Improvement Company also finances land purchase, but on larger properties, and will take other forms of security. Building societies and various merchant banks will provide finance for the purchase of non-agricultural property.

A major source of loans for farming is private finance, supplied by family or friends. This usually has the advantage of being relatively cheap, and does not lead to the same worries about being responsible to a commercial organization (an uncle or aunt is often more tolerant over the timing of repayments than a bank manager would be). This is not always the case, however, and there may be other, non-financial costs involved.

There remains a number of other sources of farm credit, including hire purchase (or 'lease purchase') and leasing of machinery and livestock. Generally speaking, these are more expensive than bank finance. From time to time, however, it is possible to find credit bargains in this field, especially when the machinery trade is slow and dealers are anxious to keep their stock moving.

When seeking borrowed money, the farmer should first be sure to use a source of credit which is appropriate to the type of investment. The adage, 'never borrow short to invest long' is ancient, but still as true as ever. It is also important for him to remember that he is asking the lender to risk money in the farm business. The lender may take a lot of persuading, especially if the farmer is young and/or inexperienced, and the presentation of the proposal can make all the difference between it being accepted or rejected. Budgets will normally be required, especially monthly cash-flow budgets, and honesty and accuracy in these budgets helps to boost the confidence of the lender in the proposal.

It is likely that the lender will require some form of *security*, or *collateral*, in case things go wrong. A mortgage for land purchase, for instance, will usually be secured on the title deeds of the land, meaning that if the borrower fails to service the loan, the lender can sell the land in order to recoup his investment. Where the assets are insufficient, or of the wrong type to provide adequate security, it may be possible to secure the credit by guarantee. In other words a third party pledges to pay the amount guaranteed to the lender if the borrower defaults. The role of guarantor is often played by a friend or relative of the borrower. Guarantees may also be obtained from the government through the Loan Guarantee Scheme: details are available from banks.

A good 'track record', combined with a healthy balance sheet and the confidence of the lender, may be sufficient security for overdrafts and short-term loans. By definition this is likely to apply to the well-established farmer rather than the young incomer.

Finally, most lenders pride themselves on their judgement of character. Thus personal presentation, in the form of appearance, confidence and enthusiasm, deserves attention.

Estimating the cost of capital

Estimating interest costs

Borrowing money from a source outside the business will incur interest charges. The annual interest charge is calculated by applying a percentage rate to the capital borrowed. The exact way in which this is done depends on the form of borrowing, i.e. whether it is in the form of an overdraft, a reducing balance loan, an annuity loan, or some other variant.

The interest on an *overdraft* is calculated on the daily balance outstanding, and is paid quarterly in arrears. Estimation of likely interest charges is relatively easy as long as a cash-flow budget is available (see Chapter 7).

A *reducing-balance loan* is one where the principal, i.e. the capital borrowed, is repaid in equal instalments, and the interest charge is calculated by applying the appropriate percentage interest rate to the amount of capital still unpaid. For example, a three-year loan of £3000 might be paid off in equal instalments of £500 per half year. Assuming that interest is paid six-monthly in arrears at 10 % per cent per annum, the payment for the first half-year will be £150 [£3000 × (10%/2)]; for the second half-year £125 [£2500 × (10%/2)]; for the third half-year £100 [£2000 × (10%/2)]; and so on (see Figure 19.1).

Although the reducing-balance type of loan makes interest calculations easy, it has the disadvantage of high interest payments at the beginning of its life (often the time at which an investment project most needs cash). This is so even after

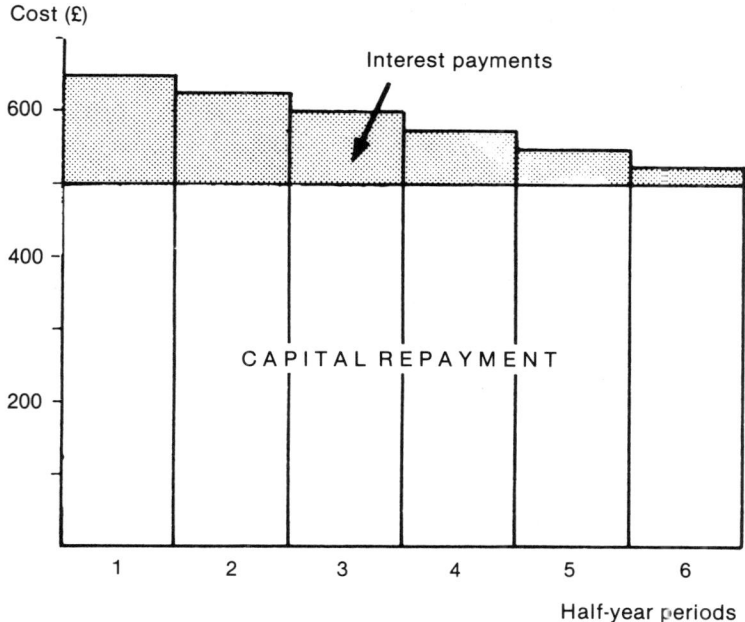

Figure 19.1 *Reducing-balance loan illustration (10% interest)*

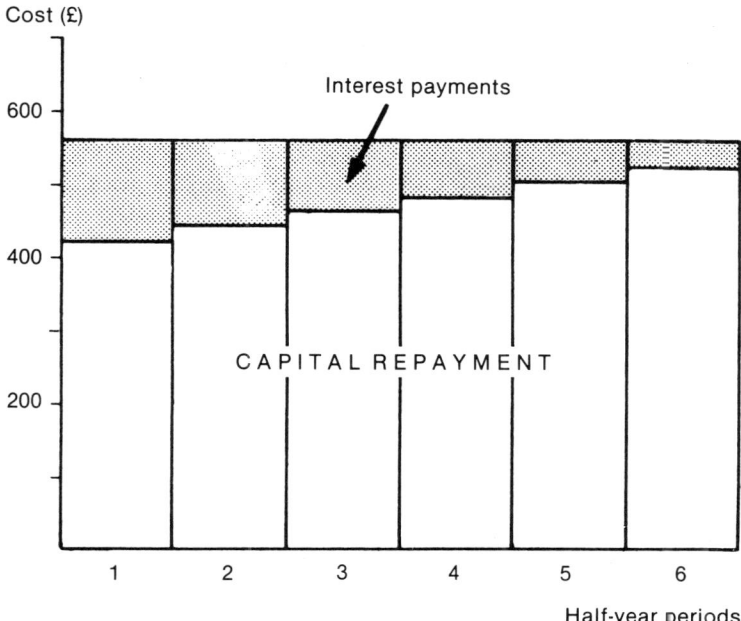

Figure 19.2 *Annuity loan — illustration (10% interest)*

allowance has been made for the fact that interest payments can be set against income tax. A commonly-used alternative, which does not suffer from this problem, is the *annuity* form of loan.

The aim in using an annuity loan is to arrange payments of capital and interest so that the gross payment for each period is the same. In order to do this and yet keep capital and interest payments in step with each other, a mathematical formula is used which results in smaller payments of capital, and larger payments of interest in the early stages of the loan than in the later stages (see Figure 19.2).

Since interest payments are an allowance expense against income tax, the net effect is one of relatively small net payments at the beginning of the loan, rising as the life of the loan progresses. To calculate annual interest charges for a given loan, it is not necessary to use the mathematical formula, since tables are available which show interest and capital payments due for loans of various terms and interest rates. Such a table for a 5-year loan is shown in Figure 19.3. More comprehensive tables are to be found in various publications, including farm management handbooks by Nix, Agro-Business Consultants, and others.

To determine interest payments due in a given year of a loan, the point is found where the year intersects with the appropriate interest rate. The interest due is calculated by multiplying the amount of the loan (in £000s) by the factor in the 'interest' column. The repayment of principal is calculated in the same way, using the factor in the 'principal' column. Thus in year 3 of a 5-year loan of £10,000, at 15 per cent interest, the interest charge is £102 × 10 = £1020 and the repayment of principal is £196 × 10 = 1960.

A third type of loan is where the capital is repaid in full at the end of the term, with interest charged on the full amount throughout the term. It is usual to secure the capital payment with an endowment life assurance policy, designed to mature at the end of the term; hence the term *endowment loan*. The interest may be set against profit as an expense, and tax relief at half the current basic rate is deducted from the policy premiums by the assurance company.

Year	Interest rate													
	10%		11%		12%		13%		14%		15%		16%	
	I	P	I	P	I	P	I	P	I	P	I	P	I	P
1	100	164	110	161	120	157	130	154	140	151	150	149	160	145
2	84	180	92	178	101	176	110	174	119	172	128	171	137	169
3	66	198	73	198	80	197	87	197	95	197	102	196	110	196
4	46	218	51	220	56	222	62	223	67	224	73	225	78	227
5	24	240	27	243	30	248	33	252	36	256	39	259	42	263

Notes: I = interest payment; P = repayment of capital. Assumes payment in arrears at the end of each year. In practice more frequent payment is likely, giving slightly lower interest costs. Payment half-yearly in arrears gives interest per £1000 in the first year of £96 at 10% and £154 at 16%.

Figure 19.3 *Amortization table for five-year loan (£ payment per £1000 borrowed)*

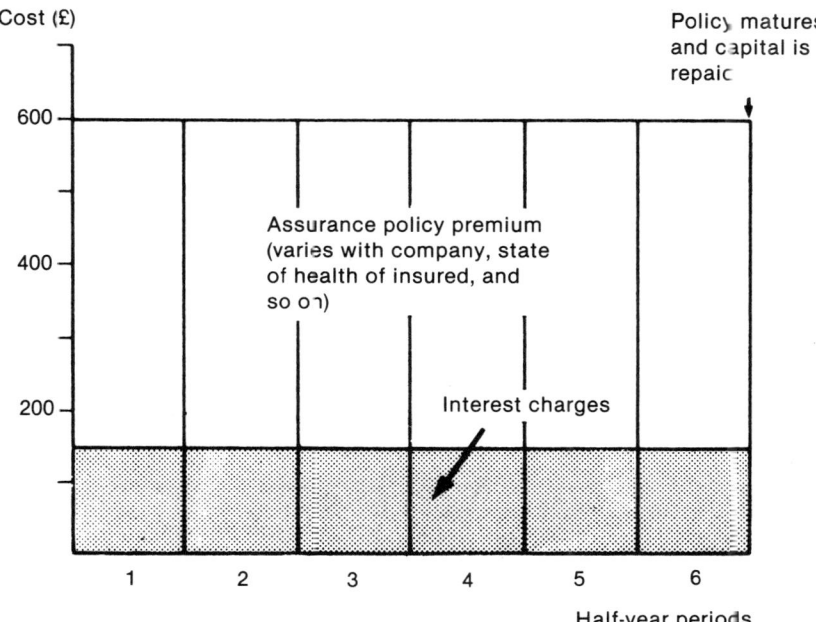

Figure 19.4 *Endowment loan – illustration (10% interest)*

The overall cost of such a loan can be lower than either of the types described above, but the initial cost is higher than an equivalent annuity loan – see Figure 19.4.

In budgets prepared for a normalized year, an alternative (cruder) method of estimating interest costs is by applying the appropriate percentage rate to the average capital borrowed. If it is assumed that the borrowed capital is paid off at a more-or-less constant rate, the average capital can be estimated as ½(initial capital). Initial capital includes the working capital needed to finance the running costs of the proposed system up to the point at which it becomes self-financing. Note that the definition of average capital used in this context is slightly different from that used in the context of return on capital later in this chapter.

Estimating the opportunity cost of capital

Any capital invested in the business, whether borrowed or owned, has an opportunity cost; by using it in one particular fashion, the farmer is sacrificing the opportunity to use it in other ways. This opportunity cost is represented by the potential return from the best of these other uses, expressed as a percentage of the amount invested. The concept of opportunity cost is particularly useful when making decisions between alternative investments,* each alternative being assessed by reference to the earning power of all the capital involved. This should provide a stiffer test than a comparison with interest rates on borrowed capital.

---

*In whole-farm budgets it is more appropriate to use the actual interest paid, if any.

Estimating the opportunity cost of capital can be difficult in practice. If the farmer is considering only one possible use of the capital within his business, he can take the opportunity cost to be the return that he could obtain by investing the money in, say, gilt-edged securities or a bank deposit account, plus an allowance for the difference in riskiness of the two types of investment.

Where two or more uses of capital within the business are possible, the opportunity cost of any one of those uses is given by comparison with not only the gilt-edged security/deposit account option, but also the potential returns from the other within-business uses. The easiest way of doing this is by comparing marginal rates of return on capital, discussed in the following sections.

Comparing alternative uses of capital 1: simple measures

Whole-business measures of return on capital

The effectiveness of use of capital is generally measured in terms of return on capital. In other words, the annual income generated by the employment of a given quantity of capital is expressed as a percentage of that quantity. If an investment of £1000 generates an income of £200 per year, the return on capital is $(200/1000) \times 100 = 20$ per cent. At first sight this looks a simple task, but it can be far from easy to decide what figures to take for the income generated and the capital employed.

One possibility is to refer to statements of profit and capital which relate to the business as a whole. These statements may concern periods in the past or in the future. The most common measures of return on capital arising from these statements are:

1   Return on net capital.
2   Return on net assets.
3   Return on tenant's capital.

The *return on net capital* measures the earning power of the farmer's personal stake in the business. It is calculated by using the formula:

$$\frac{\text{Net profit for the year in question}}{\text{Net capital}} \times 100$$

and is expressed as an annual percentage rate. Net profit is taken from the profit and loss account (or budget), and net capital from the closing balance sheet (historic or budgeted). Where opening and closing net capital differ markedly, there is some justification for using the average of the two instead of just the closing figure.

Return on net assets measures the return on all the capital employed in the business, after reducing the influence of fluctuations in short-term assets and liabilities. It is calculated by use of the formula:

$$\frac{\text{Net profit for the year before}}{\text{Net assets}} \times 100$$

where net assets equals total assets minus current liabilities. Profit is used before interest since the interest charge represents part of the return on the assets employed, and to use a profit after interest would be to double-count this part of the return.

Return on tenant's capital measures the income generated by those assets which are specific to the businessman's role as a farmer, rather than any role he might have as an owner of land. It is calculated by the formula:

$$\frac{\text{Management and investment income}}{\text{Tenant's capital}} \times 100$$

This is specifically an agricultural measure, and is only meaningful in comparisons between farms (see Chapter 14).

All of the measures described above can be valuable in giving a general impression of the efficiency of capital use in the business, through comparisons between years, between farms, and with budgets. But consider the case of a farmer who wishes to investigate the potential return from a specific use of capital; an investment 'project'. His main concern will be not the effect on the overall return on capital of the whole business, but whether that extra investment will be worthwhile in its own right. He will need to relate the *extra* income generated to the extra *capital employed;* in other words to estimate the marginal return on capital.

Simple marginal return on capital

Simple marginal return on capital is also known as 'accounting rate or return' or just 'rate of return'. It is calculated by using this formula:

$$\frac{\text{Average annual extra profit}}{\text{Initial or average extra capital invested}} \times 100$$

and is expressed as an annual percentage rate.

The *average annual extra profit* is derived usually from normalized partial budgets. It should be before interest charges, since the latter represent part of the return on capital, and double-counting must be avoided. The profit may be before or after tax. Ideally the after-tax figure should be used, since the various uses of capital under investigation may have different tax implications. In practice, it is usually too difficult to estimate the likely tax effects when using average annual figures.

The *initial capital* is represented by the initial cost of any assets purchased (net of grants and discounts), plus the extra working capital required, less any capital released by the change (such as sale of replaced equipment, or working capital set free). Working capital is the cash required to finance the extra running costs up to the point at which the extra revenue begins to exceed the extra expense. In the example of the expansion of a dairy herd, extra working capital would include the cost of extra feed and other materials consumed during the weeks before the milk cheque reflected the increased production. Estimation of the extra working capital required is made easier by the availability of a full or partial cash-flow budget.

Average capital may be used as an alternative to initial capital. It reflects the decline in value of wasting assets over the life of the project and can be estimated by using the formula:

$$\text{NIC(ND)} + \tfrac{1}{2}[\text{NIC(D)} - \text{WDV}] + \text{WDV}$$

where NIC(ND) is the net initial cost of non-depreciating assets (including working capital), NIC(D) is net initial cost of depreciating assets and WDV the anticipated written-down value of depreciating assets at the end of the project life. This assumes a straight-line decline in value of depreciating assets.

Return on initial capital is the more stringent of the two tests, since average capital will never be greater than initial capital. When compared with the more precise discounted cash-flow techniques, return on initial capital tends to give a pessimistic result, and return on average capital an optimistic one. For this reason alone it is usually best to use initial capital.

Once a simple marginal rate of return has been calculated, it may be compared with the cost of capital in order to determine whether or not the investment is likely to be worthwhile. The first such comparison must always be with the cost of interest payable on borrowed money, since if the project cannot even cover the cash costs of using the capital, it would be financially foolish to consider it further. The other comparison must be with the opportunity cost of the capital employed, i.e. with the marginal return which could be obtained from other investments of the capital concerned.

Despite its relative ease of calculation, simple marginal return has several limitations. The most important of these is illustrated by the example shown in Figure 19.5. The two projects each give a simple marginal return on capital of 25 per cent. This implies that the decision-maker will be indifferent between the two projects, and yet in practice he may have a strong preference for one or the other. He may, for instance, prefer project 1 because he only has £500 to spend, or project 2 because it has a longer life, and will go on producing 25 per cent for three years more than project 1. He is certainly likely to be influenced by the fact that by investing in project 1 he is likely to recover his initial investment more quickly than by investing in project 2.

Of these three problems, the first two are common to all percentage rates of return and are, in any case, reasonably easy to overcome when interpreting the results of the calculations. The third, the inability to discriminate between projects on the basis of the timing of their income flow, is a major fault of this particular method. It is in the nature of humans to prefer the receipt of £1 now to the receipt of £1 in the future, even in the absence of inflation. A method of investment appraisal which ignores this 'time preference' characteristic is of dubious value, except as an initial rule-of-thumb screening device.

	Project 1 (£)	Project 2 (£)
Initial investment	500	1,000
Extra profit:		
Year 1	250	250
2	150	250
3	125	250
4	70	250
5	30	250
6		250
7		250
8		250
Average annual extra profit	125	250
Marginal return on capital	25%	25%

Figure 19.5 *Comparison of two projects by simple marginal return on initial capital*

Payback

One method of judging investment projects in a way that allows for time preference is to calculate their *payback period*. The payback period of a project is simply the time that it takes to recoup the initial investment from the net cash flow generated by that investment. As an example, consider the project shown in Figure 19.6. The payback time is three years, since by the end of the third year enough cash has been generated to recover the initial investment with £100 to spare.

The initial investment is calculated net of grants, discounts, and any capital released by superseded projects. Annual cash flow should include interest payments (but not repayments of borrowed capital) and any fixed or working capital that is likely to be set free at the end of the project's life. It should ideally also include an allowance for changes in tax liability arising from the project. In practice it is rarely worth making anything more than a rough guess at the tax implications, given the crudity of the technique.

Although it is not expressed as a percentage rate of return, payback may still be used to compare the income generated by an investment with the cash and

	£
Initial investment	*1,000*
Net cash flows	
Year 1	600
2	300
3	200
4	200
5	100

Figure 19.6 *Payback – example*

opportunity costs of the capital employed. Comparison with the cost of borrowed money is effected by the inclusion of interest charges in the annual net cash flows; if the project does not pay back, it cannot support the interest charges. Comparison with other opportunities is via comparison of the payback period with those of other potential uses of the capital. The use with the lowest payback is, by implication, the most worthwhile.

Payback takes account of time preference, and is quick and simple to calculate. It is in common use as a rule-of-thumb measure for the initial screening of investment possibilities, and is especially useful when liquidity is a problem. Its simplicity makes it a rather crude measure, however. In particular, it ignores cash flows after the payback period. In the example in Figure 19.7, project 1 comes out as 'best' by the payback method, even though project 2 is likely to produce a steady stream of cash for the next 20 years.

The only way of allowing for time preference in comparisons between investment projects, while at the same time incorporating a reasonable degree of precision, is to use discounted cash-flow techniques.

	Project 1 (£)	Project 2 (£)
Initial investment	1,000	1,000
Net cash flows:		
Year 1	600	200
2	300	200
3	200	200
4	200	200
5	100	200
.		
.		
.		
20		200
Payback (years)	3	5

Figure 19.7 *Payback comparison of projects with widely differing lives*

Comparing alternative uses of capital 2: discounted cash-flow techniques

The discounting principle

An earlier section of this chapter discussed a device which implicitly takes time preference into account – interest. An interest charge reflects the time preference of the lender, since he will not part with his money unless the fee he is offered is sufficient to compensate him for his sacrifice of present consumption. Similarly it reflects the time preference of the borrower, since he will be prepared to borrow the money only if the benefit he expects to gain from its use is greater than the interest charge.

The formula for calculating compound interest states that a sum of money X placed in an interest-bearing investment will, if left untouched, grow to a value of $X(I + r)^n$ over n years at a compound interest rate of r (expressed as a decimal). Thus a sum of £100, if invested at 15 per cent interest, will grow to £100 $(1 + 0.15)^5$, or approximately £200, by the end of five years. Reversing the calculation, a sum of £200 which is likely to be received in five years' time is equivalent to £200$/(1 + 0.15)^5$, or approximately £100 in the present.

It is possible to think of the time preference of a farmer in terms of a percentage compound rate. Assume for the moment that the time preference rate of a given farmer is 15 per cent (we will worry about how this is determined at a later stage). If he expects to receive £200 in five years' time, we can refer to the formula above and deduce that he is likely to be indifferent between £100 now and £200 in five years' time. Put another way, the *present value* of £200 in five years' time is £100.

The net present value method

The idea of expressing future receipts in terms of 'present values' may be applied to an investment project such as project 1 in Figure 19.7. Given a certain time preference rate, each year's net cash flow can be reduced to a present value by multiplying it by $1/(1 + r)^n$. This process is known as 'discounting'. Luckily tables such as that shown in Figure 19.8 (overleaf) are available, giving the value of $1/(1 + r)^n$ for a wide range of values of r and n^*. The value of $1/(1 + r)^n$ at a discount rate of 15 per cent is thus 0.497.

The present values of all the annual net cash flows may then be summed to give the total present value. An example of this calculation is shown in Figure 19.9 (page 241), using project 1 from Figure 19.7.

The next stage of the calculation is to deduct the capital cost of the investment from the total present value of the net cash flows. If the resulting *net present value* (NPV) is positive, the rate of return on the capital invested is greater than the discount rate used in the calculation. The reverse applies if the NPV is negative. In the case of project 1, the NPV is positive, so the investment is worthwhile even after the time preference effect has been taken into account.

Although this calculation does not result in a percentage rate of return, it can still be used in comparisons with the cost of capital. For comparisons outside the business the discount rate can be set to reflect interest rates. Thus if all the money for the project were being borrowed at a rate of 10 per cent, the discount rate would need to be at least 10 per cent, and possibly as much as 15 per cent to give a safety margin in view of the risk involved. This can be thought of as the 'hurdle' rate which any project has to exceed to be considered. For comparisons *within* the

*This example is from the Scottish Agricultural College's *Farm Management Handbook* – others can be found in Nix and ABC.

Years	Percentage										
	1	4	5	6	7	8	9	10	11	12	13
1	0.990	0.961	0.952	0.943	0.934	0.925	0.917	0.909	0.900	0.892	0.884
2	0.980	0.924	0.907	0.889	0.873	0.857	0.841	0.826	0.811	0.797	0.783
3	0.970	0.888	0.863	0.839	0.816	0.793	0.772	0.751	0.731	0.711	0.693
4	0.960	0.854	0.822	0.792	0.762	0.735	0.708	0.683	0.658	0.635	0.613
5	0.951	0.821	0.783	0.747	0.712	0.680	0.649	0.620	0.593	0.567	0.542
6	0.942	0.790	0.746	0.704	0.666	0.630	0.596	0.564	0.534	0.506	0.480
7	0.932	0.759	0.710	0.665	0.622	0.583	0.547	0.513	0.481	0.452	0.425
8	0.923	0.730	0.676	0.627	0.582	0.540	0.501	0.466	0.433	0.403	0.376
9	0.914	0.702	0.644	0.591	0.543	0.500	0.460	0.424	0.390	0.360	0.332
10	0.905	0.675	0.613	0.558	0.508	0.463	0.422	0.385	0.352	0.321	0.294
11	0.896	0.649	0.584	0.526	0.475	0.428	0.387	0.350	0.317	0.287	0.260
12	0.887	0.624	0.556	0.496	0.444	0.397	0.355	0.318	0.285	0.256	0.230
13	0.873	0.600	0.530	0.468	0.414	0.367	0.326	0.289	0.257	0.229	0.204
14	0.869	0.577	0.505	0.442	0.387	0.340	0.299	0.263	0.231	0.204	0.180
15	0.861	0.555	0.481	0.417	0.362	0.315	0.274	0.239	0.209	0.182	0.159

Years	Percentage										
	14	15	16	17	18	19	20	25	30	35	40
1	0.887	0.869	0.862	0.854	0.847	0.840	0.833	0.800	0.769	0.740	0.714
2	0.769	0.756	0.743	0.730	0.718	0.706	0.694	0.640	0.591	0.548	0.510
3	0.674	0.657	0.640	0.624	0.608	0.593	0.578	0.512	0.455	0.406	0.364
4	0.592	0.571	0.552	0.533	0.515	0.498	0.482	0.409	0.350	0.301	0.260
5	0.519	0.497	0.476	0.456	0.437	0.419	0.401	0.327	0.269	0.223	0.185
6	0.455	0.432	0.410	0.389	0.370	0.352	0.334	0.262	0.207	0.165	0.132
7	0.399	0.375	0.353	0.333	0.313	0.295	0.279	0.209	0.159	0.122	0.094
8	0.350	0.326	0.305	0.284	0.266	0.248	0.232	0.167	0.122	0.090	0.067
9	0.307	0.284	0.262	0.243	0.225	0.208	0.193	0.134	0.094	0.067	0.048
10	0.269	0.247	0.226	0.208	0.191	0.175	0.161	0.107	0.72	0.049	0.034
11	0.236	0.214	0.195	0.177	0.161	0.147	0.134	0.085	0.055	0.036	0.024
12	0.207	0.186	0.168	0.151	0.137	0.124	0.112	0.068	0.042	0.027	0.017
13	0.182	0.162	0.145	0.129	0.116	0.104	0.093	0.054	0.033	0.020	0.012
14	0.159	0.141	0.125	0.111	0.098	0.087	0.077	0.043	0.025	0.014	0.008
15	0.140	0.122	0.107	0.094	0.083	0.073	0.064	0.035	0.019	0.011	0.006

Figure 19.8 *Table of discount factors*

business, all projects under consideration should be ranked in order of magnitude of their NPVs. The 'best' investment is indicated by the project within the highest NPV.

We have in the net present value technique a method of investment appraisal which enables implicit comparison of return on captial with the cost of that capital, while allowing for the pattern of cash flow over time. It reflects growth in wealth brought to the business by the investment, and thus consistently ranks projects in order of the size of that growth.

The technique has various limitations, however. One of these is that the size of the NPV is affected by the size of the investment. Take two projects, one of which gives a NPV of £100 and the other a NPV of £150. According to the procedure described above, the second of the two should be chosen. If it is then revealed that

Project 1: Initial investment £1000			
'Hurdle' discount rate (%): 15			
Year	Annual net cash flow	Factors for 'hurdle' discount rate	Present values at 'hurdle' rate
0	−1,000	1.000	−1,000
1	600	0.870	522
2	300	0.756	227
3	200	0.658	132
4	200	0.572	114
5	100	0.497	50
Net present value:			44

Figure 19.9   *Calculation of net present value – example*

the first involves an investment of £500 and the second an investment of £1000, however, common sense suggests that the first gives the higher rate of return.

This drawback can be overcome to some extent by use of the *profitability index* (PI). The profitability index is calculated by dividing the total present value of the cash flows by the total present value of the investment required; the higher the PI the better. Thus in the example above, the PI of the first investment is £600/£500 = 1.20, while that of the second is £1150/£1000 = 1.15. This measure helps to overcome one of the problems of the NPV method, in relating the NPV to the size of the initial investment. It can be particularly valuable in ranking projects when capital is rationed (see Mott, 1989, chapter 5), but being a relatively crude device is best used in conjuction with, rather than instead of NPV.

A more central problem is that the concept of a NPV is awkward for a layman to understand. Most farmers have a good idea of what is meant by 'return on capital', but few will have a grasp of the implications of a net present value. This is no reflection on the education of the farming community; it is just that NPV is not a convenient yardstick. Ideally, we need an investment appraisal technique which will incorporate the discounting principle and yet give a percentage rate of return on capital. Such a technique is the internal rate of return method.

The internal rate of return method

In Figure 19.9 the NPV of the project 1 was calculated to be + £45. The fact that the NPV is positive implies that the actual rate of return is greater than the rate of discount (15 per cent) used in the calculation. If a discount rate of 20 per cent is

year	annual net cash flow	factors for 20% discount rate	present values at 20% discount rate	factors for 18% discount rate	present values at 18% discount rate
Project 1: Initial investment £1000					
0	−1000	1.000	−1000	1.000	−1000
1	600	0.833	500	0.847	508
2	300	0.694	208	0.718	215
3	200	0.579	116	0.609	122
4	200	0.482	96	0.516	103
5	100	0.402	40	0.437	44
	Net Present Values:		−39		−7

Figure 19.10 *Calculation of internal rate of return*

used, the resulting NPV is negative − see Figure 19.10. From this we can deduce that the actual rate of return lies somewhere between 15 and 20 per cent. This actual rate of return is known as the *internal rate of return* (IRR) or *discounted yield*. To determine the IRR with more precision, this trial and error process is continued until a discount rate is found which results in a NPV of zero. In this case, a discount rate of 18 per cent gives a NPV of − £8; this is near enough in most circumstances for us to state that the IRR is about 18 per cent.

Where tables of sufficient detail are not available, or where greater precision is required, it is necessary to use *interpolation*. This is a simple proportions sum which assumes that the relationship between discount rate and NPV is linear. The process is illustrated by Figure 19.11.

We know that, for project 1, the IRR lies somewhere between 15 and 18 per cent. This point is represented by x in the diagram, and corresponds, by definition, to a net present value of 0. By simple proportion, the ratio of a to b is the same as that of c to d. Distance a is thus given by $(c/d) \times b$, i.e.

$$(44/51) \times 3 \text{ per cent} = 2.6 \text{ per cent}$$

and the IRR is given by adding this result to the lower of the two discounted rates used:

$$15 \text{ per cent} + 2.6 \text{ per cent} = 17.6 \text{ per cent}$$

The formal expression of this calculation is:

$$\frac{\text{NPV at 'hurdle' rate}}{\text{NPV at hurdle rate} - \text{NPV at second rate}}$$

times   Difference between discount rates (per cent)
plus   Lower of the two discount rates
equals   Internal rate of return

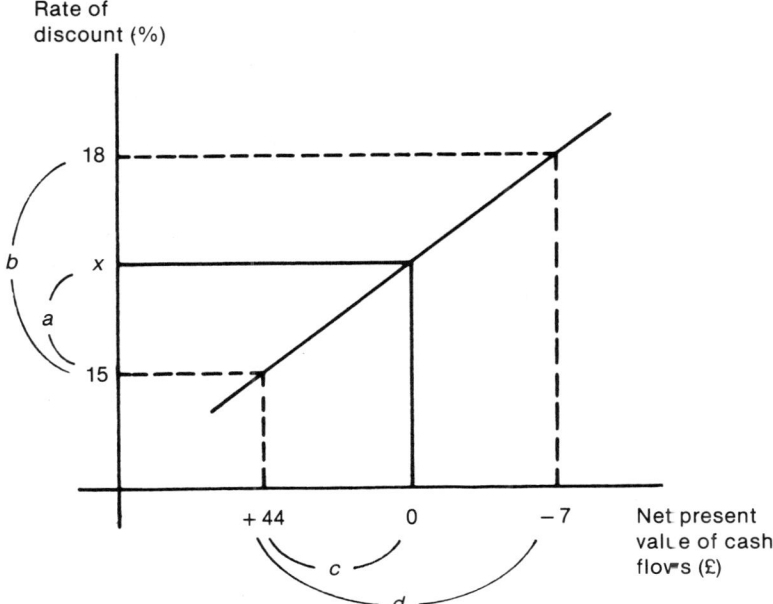

Figure 19.11 *Interpolation*

Once the IRR has been calculated, it can be compared with the cost of capital in the manner described in relation to the simple marginal rate of return earlier in this chapter.

Like NPV, the internal rate of return technique has its limitations. In particular, when the cash flow of a project changes from positive to negative during the project life, IRR can give more than one solution (see Lumby, 1991, pp. 102–6). In most cases the effect will not be significant, but it nevertheless casts doubts on the reliability of the method. Furthermore, the rate of return does not reflect the size of a project, a characteristic which becomes especially limiting when capital is rationed (see Mott, 1989, chapter 5). Nevertheless, it provides a way of expressing the outcome of DCF calculations which is easy to understand and to communicate, and allows easy allowance for risk (see Chapter 20).

In general, NPV (ideally supported by the profitability index) is preferable on grounds of consistency, with IRR having values of convenience and ease of communication.

Discounting techniques – the pros and cons

As a whole, discounting techniques are time-consuming and are based on a concept which is initially difficult to grasp. Because it is possible to manipulate cash flow data in a precise manner, there is a huge danger of being carried away with the technique, forgetting that the results must be considered in the light of the farmer's objectives, and that the data itself, being forecast for many years ahead, is far from precise. The risk that events may not turn out as forecast should be incorporated in the calculations, using the techniques described in Chapter 20. Nor should the ramifications of the project for the *monthly* cash flow be ignored; it is easy to be lured into overtrading by an apparently profitable, but cash-hungry project.

Despite these drawbacks, the fact remains that the only reliable way of assessing the worthwhileness of an investment, taking account of time preference, is by the use of discounted cash-flow techniques. The methods force the farmer to consider investment projects thoroughly, looking at annual net cash flow rather than vague measures of annual profitability, and making allowance for the implications of such aspects of taxation and increases in asset values.

To describe fully every aspect of the use of NPV and IRR would require far more space than is available here. The reader who wishes to use the techniques on 'real-life' examples is recommended to make use of the references listed below.

Further reading

Bright, G., 'The current economics of machinery leasing', *Farm Management*, vol. 6, no. 6, 1987.
Camm, B. M., 'The choice in borrowing', *Farm Management*, vol. 5, no. 10, 1985. A useful review of the credit sources open to farmers.
Checkley, K., *Finance for Farming* (London, Institute of Bankers, 1982).
Dyer, L. S., *A Practical Approach to Bank Lending* (London, Institute of Bankers, 1977). Written by bankers for bankers, albeit at a time when banker/farmer relations were easier than at present.
Mitchell, W., 'Essential information for bank borrowing', *Farm Management*, vol. 5, no. 12, 1986. A guide to approaching the bank manager for funds.
Poole, A. H., 'Farm indebtedness: stimulus or millstone', *Farm Management*, vol. 6, no. 2, 1986.
Soffe, R. J., 'How much does an overdraft really cost?', *Farm Management*, vol. 6, no. 6, 1987. The effects of bank charges on the cost of credit.

Examples of the use of DCF techniques

Bateman, I., 'The financial potential for farm-based forestry in the UK following recent government policy developments', *Farm Management*, vol. 6, no. 11, 1988.
Hayton, R., 'Business strategy and the apple business', *Farm Management*, vol. 7, no. 6, 1990.
Lingard, J., 'Investing in irrigation', *Farm Management*, vol. 4, no. 1, 1980.
Meikle, S. M., 'A management approach for orchard evaluation', *Farm Management*, vol. 7, no. 10, 1991.
Savill, P. S., Crockford, K. J. and Spilsbury, M. J., 'Economic returns from farm woodlands, *Farm Management*, vol. 6, no. 9, 1988.
Sells, J. E., 'A financial assessment of a long-term project: coppicing', *Farm Management*, vol. 7, no. 10, 1991.

Investment appraisal

Barnard, C. S. and Nix, J. S., *Farm Planning and Control,* 2nd edition (London, Cambridge University Press, 1979), pp. 50–79.

Kerr, H. W. T., Farm Management Notes (Nottingham University). Although dated, these papers are well worth the trouble that might be needed to obtain them:

An Introduction to the Technique of Discounting Cash Flows to Assess Investment Projects (No. 36, 1968).

An Example of Discounting Cash Flows to Assess the After-tax Return on an Agriculatural Investment (No. 38, 1968).

Handling Working Capital in Discounted Cash Flow Calculations (No. 41, 1970).

Lumby, S., *Investment Appraisal and Financing Decisions,* 4th edition (London, Chapman & Hall). Excellent on theory and practice.

Mott, G., *Investment Appraisal 1989* (London, Pitman Publishing 1989). Excellent practical handbook for the manager. Concise and cheap.

Allowing for risk and uncertainty

Introduction

Any attempt to plan ahead is subject to risk and/or uncertainty;* in other words there is a strong possibility that the predictions will not be realized. The budgets for Home Farm used earlier in this book, for instance, rely heavily on assumptions relating to yields, prices, numbers of livestock, etc. The budgets indicate that if these assumptions are justified, the prospects for the business in the short term are good. But what if feed costs per cow turn out to be 20 per cent higher than expected and wheat yields are 10 per cent down? Naturally some account of such possibilities has to be taken in the planning process.

Before examining ways of allowing for risk and uncertainty in the planning process, it is worth taking a brief look at the causes of risk, and ways in which the business might be adapted in order to minimize its impact. The environment of a business has several components. One way of classifying these components is to group them into physical, economic, political/social, and human aspects. The risk attached to the running of a business derives from variation in all these categories.

The physical environment is the first one thinks of in this respect when considering a farm business; weather, disease and pests can have enormous impact on the outcome of even the best-laid farm plans. Almost as great are the influences of economic, political and social factors, such as changes in consumption patterns, introduction of new agricultural policy, and resistance to intensive livestock on the grounds of smell and/or animal welfare. The aspect more often taken for granted is the human factor, yet this can contribute at least as much to the risk level in a business as any of the others. A business is owned and staffed by people, any one of whom may unexpectedly fall ill, have an accident, have his judgement affected by personal worries, or just make an uncharacteristic error.

The impact of risk on the business may be reduced in various ways. Some risks, such as fire, crop failure or personal injury, may easily be covered by normal commercial insurance. Other risks can be spread by diversification; in other words, running a variety of enterprises so that a poor year for one product does not cripple the whole business. The farmer can avoid enterprises which are known to be particularly risky, and can safeguard prices by buying futures or selling produce

*Risk is the effect of variations in the business and its environment whose occurrence can be predicted with some degree of probability. Uncertainty is the effect of variations whose likelihood of occurrence is entirely unknown. In practice it is difficult (and usually pointless) to distinguish between the two, and the terms are here treated as interchangeable.

forward on contract. He can adopt a policy of maintaining reserves of various forms, such as a larger labour force, machinery complement, or bank balance than he would normally need, or a higher equity percentage than strictly necessary. A common feature of agriculture is the farmer who is never happy unless he has one or two years' supply of hay in the barn, ready for the bad year to end all bad years.

The common factor in all of these strategies is that each has a price, in terms of either lost potential or of increased costs. The price limits the freedom of the owner of a business to reduce the adverse effects of risk upon his business. A certain level of risk is therefore something a businessman has to live with. This does not mean that he should be fatalistic about it; he should be able to adapt his financial management so as to cope with most eventualities.

Allowing for risk and uncertainty in planning

The role of careful budgeting and control

The first line of defence against risk when planning should be a meticulous attention to detail in the budgeting process. This applies in particular to forecasting; the more informed are one's guesses about the future, the less risk is attached to those guesses. It is always wise to be slightly conservative in forecasting, to counteract the inevitable tendency towards over-optimism in budgeting. Things *will* go wrong; costs *will* be higher than expected; yields *will* be lower than hoped.

Just as important as informed forecasting is the operation of a system of budgetary control, so that as soon as it begins to look as if the original assumptions of the plan are likely to be proved wrong, alternative courses of action may be formulated (see Part Four of this book).

These devices help to minimize the degree to which risk affects the outcome of a particular plan, but they give the farmer no impression of the risk that may be inherent in that plan, and no means of comparing alternative plans with respect to the risk levels involved. Techniques which do tackle these problems are the breakeven budget, flexible budgeting and sensitivity analysis.

The breakeven budget

A *breakeven budget* is used to determine the amount of variation that can be tolerated in one of the key elements of a profit budget before the anticipated margin is eliminated, i.e. the breakeven point is reached. Although it is possible to use this technique in conjunction with a whole-business profit budget, it is most suitable for use with a partial budget.

The first step in the process is to express the anticipated margin (i.e. the increase or reduction in profit in the case of a partial budget; net profit or loss in the case of a whole-farm budget), in terms of the variable under consideration. This variable could be a price, a unit quantity, or a number of head or hectares. Deducting this expression of the anticipated margin from the original level of the variable gives the breakeven level of that variable.

A example will help to clarify the process. In the normalized partial budget used to investigate the introduction of a caravan site to Home Farm (Figure 9.3) it was assumed that the average occupancy rate would be 60 per cent. The resulting increase in profit after interest (Figure 9.4) was expected to be £2646. A 1 per cent change in occupancy rate is worth £240 (£14,400/60) and so £2646 represents £2646/£240 = 11 per cent. This is the amount by which the occupancy rate would have to fall before the change resulted in a decrease, rather than an increase in profits. The breakeven occupancy rate is thus 60 per cent − 11 per cent, or 49 per cent.

The same technique can be used to investigate the variability in prices, as well as quantities. The nightly charge originally assumed for the caravan site was £4. Each £1 change in the charge is worth £3600 (14,400/4). The change needed to merely break even is thus a fall of £2646/£3600 = £0.74 per night. The breakeven charge would thus be £4 − 0.74 = £3.27 per night.

The breakeven point gives the farmer a reference against which to measure risk. Adam Haynes can, for instance, look at the breakeven occupancy rate of 49 per cent and ask himself how likely it is that actual yields will drop that far. He may decide that such an event is unlikely, and so be reassured that the risk arising from variation in occupancy rates is small. Similarly, he may look at the breakeven nightly charge and ask himself how likely it is that the price will have to drop that far. The way in which he reacts will depend to some extent on his character, since some people are more nervous of taking risks than others.

The breakeven budget has a valuable role as a quick rule-of-thumb measure of the risk involved in a given plan. It also has the advantage that its implications can be readily understood. It has a major flaw, however, in that it can only be used to investigate variability in one element of a budget at a time; all the other possible varieties are assumed to stay constant. In the Home Farm example, for instance, we can look at the effect of changes in the occupancy rate *or* the nightly charge, but not the effect of both changing at the same time.

Flexible budgeting

Flexible budgeting takes all variables into account by the preparation of more than one budget for a particular plan. Budgets such as those for the Home Farm in Part Two are based upon the farmer's expectation of the most likely occurrences. Flexible budgeting would involve preparation of at least one other version, based upon his feelings of what the worst possible outcome would be (the 'downside risk').

This again gives the farmer a set of reference points, enabling him to see the possible range of financial results arising from his plans. It can be used with partial and whole-business budgets, for profit, cash flow and capital. Its particular value is that it forces the farmer to consider explicitly the effects of a bad year or years, and thus brings home the financial consequences of risk. It may discourage him from pursuing some of his wilder schemes, or at least encourage him to prepare contingency plans in case the worst happens.

The biggest limitation of this approach is the amount of work involved, although it need not be used on every budget, and the use of partial budgets around a 'central' budget can reduce the effort (see Chapter 9). Use of computerized budgeting techniques, particularly spreadsheets, virtually eliminates this limitation, and makes this a powerful planning tool (see Appendices 4 and 5).

Sensitivity analysis

Sensitivity analysis measures the responsiveness, or 'sensitivity', of a margin to changes in one or more of the elements comprising that margin. It can be characterized as a question: 'What changes in x will result from a given change in the level of y?', where x is a measure of profit, cash flow or capital and y is one of the components of that measure, such as fertilizer price, labour use, crop yield, interest rate, and so on. The technique is illustrated in Figure 20.1, using the normalized partial budget for the Home Farm caravan site (Figure 9.3). The most significant elements of the budget are identified, and estimates made of their likely levels under the best and worst assumptions. The figures in the right-hand column show which of the elements cause the most variation in the balance of the budget.*

Variable		Level	Effect on extra profit after interest	Range (£)
Occupancy rate (%)	B	70	+ 2,400	
	ML	60	–	9,600
	W	30	– 7,200	
Site charges (£/night)	B	4.50	+ 1,800	
	ML	4.00	–	5,400
	W	3.00	– 3,600	
Running costs (£)	B	3,000	+ 300	
	ML	3,300	–	1,500
	W	4,500	– 1,200	
Fixed investment costs (£)	B	25,000	– 1,250	
	ML	30,000	–	2,500
	W	35,000	– 1,250	
Barley Output (£/ha)	B	360	+ 50	
	ML	410	–	100
	W	460	– 50	

B = Best likely   ML = Most likely   W = Worst likely

Figure 20.1 *Sensitivity analysis*

*Figure 20.1 and 20.3 allow for changes in interest arising from changes in fixed capital but, in the interests of clarity, not working capital.

The analysis will give an impression of the riskiness of the plan but, perhaps more important, will also show the elements to which the balance is most sensitive. In the example, these are occupancy rate and nightly charge. This is useful in two ways. First, the farmer can see clearly which items need closest monitoring during the course of the plan, to ensure that the hoped-for results materialize. Second, the most variable items can be combined into two-way and three-way analyses in order to show the likely effect of simultaneous variations in more than one variable.

The two-way analysis in Figure 20.2 shows the effect of simultaneous variation in occupancy rate and nightly charge, using the same data as for Figure 20.1. The farmer can immediately see the potential outcome of his worst fears, and his best hopes, being realized.

Extra profit after interest (£)				
Occupancy rates (%):	30	40	50	60
Site charges (per night)				
£ 4.50	−954	1746	4446	7146
£ 4.00	−2154	−246	2646	5046
£ 3.00	−4554	−2754	−954	846

Figure 20.2   *Two-way variance analysis*

It is possible to take the process further, and build up tables showing three-way or even four-way analysis. Such tables tend to be cumbersome and difficult to interpret, and thus much of the benefit is lost. Use of *a tree diagram* can overcome some of the problems by showing the analysis in an easily assimilable, pictorial form. An example of a tree diagram is shown in Figure 20.3 (overleaf). This shows a three-way sensitivity analysis, incorporating variation in initial investment.

Like all management techniques, sensitivity analysis has its limitations. It gives an impression of the effects of risk, without attempting to quantify those effects. It is limited to the investigation of simultaneous variation in three or four assumptions only, if the results are to be comprehensible. It does not include the effect of alternative decisions which could be made by the manager of a business, but examines the outcome of only one decision at a time. Problems can arise in a two-way or three-way analysis in cases where the variables are independent.

On the other hand, it is a technique which allows the farmer to examine the likely effects of his worst, best, and most likely assumptions on the outcome of a budget. It is a highly flexible device, and can be used in relation to any financial measure, including gross margins, profit, cash flow, bank balance, net capital, and rate of return on capital.

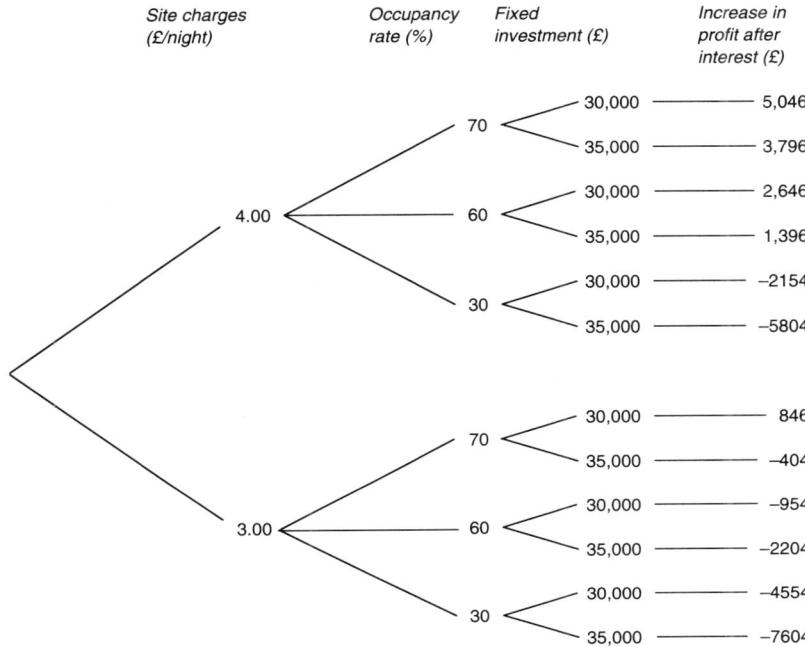

Site charges (£/night)	Occupancy rate (%)	Fixed investment (£)	Increase in profit after interest (£)
		30,000	5,046
	70	35,000	3,796
		30,000	2,646
4.00	60	35,000	1,396
		30,000	−2154
	30	35,000	−5804
		30,000	846
	70	35,000	−404
		30,000	−954
3.00	60	35,000	−2204
		30,000	−4554
	30	35,000	−7604

Figure 20.3 *Tree diagram*

Techniques are available which either extend the capability of sensitivity analysis or provide a more sophisticated alternative. These techniques include probability analysis, decision trees, game theory, and various types of computer-based simulation models. Further information can be found in the references at the end of the chapter.

The development of cheap computerized budgeting techniques – particularly spreadsheets – has radically transformed the ease and effectiveness of use of sensitivity analysis during the last decade. Once a budget is compiled on the computer, key figures can be changed at the press of a button, and outcomes calculated within seconds. Variance tables and tree diagrams have their place even here in allowing the clear presentation of the results to the decision-maker.

Risk and investment appraisal

All the above methods can be incorporated into the investment appraisal procedures described in the previous chapter. Sensitivity analysis, for instance, can be applied to net cash flows, marginal tax rates, initial investment, cost of capital, and so on. Conservative budgeting can be applied to financial forecasts, as well to the length of the project life.

An additional means of allowing for risk is to add a margin to the cost of capital. If, for instance, the only comparison for an investment project were with the return from a safe investment (in, say, a building society) at 10 per cent per annum, several extra percentage points should be added to this rate before its use as a comparison. Otherwise there is danger of a highly risky project with an expected rate of return of 11 per cent being accepted, even though the safe 10 per cent is likely to be more acceptable to the owner in the long term. The comparison might rate thus be 15 per cent, or even 20 per cent to compensate for the differences in riskiness.

The size of the risk margin varies with the riskiness of the project, and with the attitude to risk of the investor. It is subjectively determined, and is thus prone to error. While more precise methods of allowing for risk are normally to be preferred (particularly if a computer is being used for calculations), this is nevertheless a convenient and neat means of incorporating an allowance for risk into investment appraisal.

Further reading

Anderson, J. R., Dillon, J. L. and Hardaker, B., *Agricultural Decision Analysis* (Iowa State University Press, 1977).

Barnard, C. S. and Nix, J. S., *Farm Planning and Control*, 2nd edition (London, Cambridge University Press, 1979), chapter 16 (2nd edition only).

Carsberg, B., *Economics of Business Decisions* (Harmondsworth, Penguin, 1975).

Griffiths, R. F. (ed.), *Dealing with Risk* (Manchester University Press, 1981).

McCrimmon, K. R. and Wehrung, D. A., *Taking Risks* (London, Collier MacMillan, 1986). Fat but approachable: a comprehensive guide.

Moore, P. G. and Thomas, H., *The Anatomy of Decisions* (Harmondsworth, Penguin, 1976). Particularly good on decision trees.

Risk and investment appraisal

Bull, R. J., *Accounting in Business*, 6th edition (London, Butterworths, 1990), chapter 16.

Hull, J. C., *The Evaluation of Risk in Business Investment* (Oxford, Pergamon, 1980).

Lumby, S., *Investment Appraisal and Financing Decisions*, 4th edition (London, Chapman & Hall, 1991), chapters 8 and 11.

Mott, G., *Investment Appraisal* (London, Pitman, 1989), chapter 9.

21

Allowing for inflation

Introduction

The term 'inflation' refers to a rise in the level of prices in *general*. It may alternatively be considered as a fall in the purchasing power of the currency of an economy. The usual measure of inflation in the United Kingdom is the rise in the Retail Price Index, which shows the change in cost of a 'typical' household's purchases.

Ideally, this general rise in prices should be distinguished from *specific* price movements; changes in relative prices of individual types of goods and services in response to changes in supply and demand, government policy, and so on. In practice, it is often difficult to make this distinction.

The aim of this chapter is to outline the main effects of inflation on the financial management of a business, and to suggest ways in which allowances may be made for these effects.

Inflation and financial accounts

Financial accounts are those which are required by law from every business. They are prepared, usually by a professional accountant, in accordance with various conventions. One of these is the 'historic cost' convention; in general, assets are valued on the basis of their cost when originally purchased. In times of inflation, the use of this convention inevitably creates distortions in the 'message' imparted by the accounts. Among these distortions are that the values of physical assets are understated; the decline in purchasing power of financial assets (mainly cash and debtors) and liabilities is ignored; and depreciation allowances, being calculated on the basis of understated asset values, are insufficient to finance the replacement of wasting assets.

When inflation is high, these distortions can affect the usefulness of the financial accounts in decision-making. The principal danger is that 'paper' profit increases, caused by inflation, encourage corresponding increases in cash withdrawals, whether for taxation, personal drawings or new investments. The consequence is likely to be a decline in liquidity (and possibly an increase in gearing) since the inflationary increase in profit is needed to pay for increases in input prices over the next year. If it has been spent elsewhere, cash will have to be obtained from

255

another source in order to maintain production. This 'other source' is likely to be some form of borrowing.

Where inflation is sufficiently high to cause significant problems of this sort, the most sensible approach for the typical farm business is to rely on management accounts for decision-making, and use financial accounts solely for taxation purposes.

In the late 1970s and early 1980s, when the inflation rate in the UK was always in the teens, and at times over 20 per cent, much consideration was given to establishing a form of accounting which would correct the resulting distortions in financial accounts, giving a more 'accurate' picture of financial performance (see Further Reading). The convention adopted, *current cost accounting* (CCA), was imposed on public companies for a three-year trial period from 1981. CCA seeks to eliminate the effects of inflation-induced increases in stock values, to adjust depreciation calculations so that the annual charge is based on the cost of replacing assets, and to make corresponding adjustments to the value of physical assets in the balance sheet. It also attempts to take account of the reduction in the value of liabilities and of financial assets.

For various reasons, including falling inflation rates, difficulty of comprehension by shareholders, and distortions created by CCA in trying to correct those of inflation, companies were allowed to revert to reliance on the historic cost convention at the end of the trial period. CCA has quietly fallen out of use in the UK, but it or its main rival, the *current purchasing power* (CPP) method may still be found in other countries with high inflation rates.

Inflation and management accounts

Alternative approaches

The difficulties caused by high inflation for the use of management accounts are the same as those noted in respect of financial accounts; profit become an unreliable guide to the availability of cash, and the accuracy of both profit and capital statements as measures of performance is reduced.

The first problem is overcome easily by recognizing the inherent limitations of profit as an indicator of disposable income at the best of times, let alone in an inflationary period. The obvious alternative is to rely on scrupulous attention to cash-flow budgeting. Ideally a five-year rolling cash-flow budget should be used with, for instance, the first year budgeted on a monthly basis, the second quarterly, and the remainder in outline only.

Being more detailed and, in many respects, more accurate than financial accounts, management accounts allow the effects of inflation to be more easily seen and, therefore, to be distinguished from the effects of changes in the performance of the business. In using management accounts in times of inflation, two alternative courses of action are open – allow for inflation only in the *interpretation* of the accounts, or adjust for inflation in their *calculation*.

For convenience of analysis, the latter may be preferable, with CCA being the best documented of the various methods (see Further Reading). On the other hand, the majority of farmers find the preparation of management accounts in historic form a sufficient burden, without adding the complexity of inflation accounting. Even if a computer is available to perform the calculations, there is a risk of error in the interpretation of the adjusted accounts, due to insufficient understanding on the farmer's part of the operations that have been performed on the data.

For these reasons this section concentrates on the first of the two alternatives, which involves preparation of accounts in historic cost form, i.e. as described throughout this book, and allowing for the effects of inflation within the interpretation process. Thus depreciation is based on the historic cost of the asset concerned, and the values of stocks reflect their market value at the time of their valuation.

The balance sheet

In interpretation of opening and closing balance sheets, a 'common sense' revaluation of physical assets will allow ratio analysis to proceed in the usual way. This revaluation could rely entirely on the farmer's own knowledge of current market values, but reference to journals, or the making of a few phone calls, e.g. to a local estate agent for an indication of land values, may be necessary. Where a machinery complement is large and varied, it will probably be sufficient to determine the approximate percentage difference between written-down value and sale value of a few representative machines, and apply this percentage to the WDV of the complement as a whole.

This may seem a crude technique, but it is similar to the procedure used by a bank manager when assessing the credit-worthiness of a farming client. All the clearing banks use forms called 'farmers' balance sheets' or 'confidential statements' on which the manager enters the current market value of assets and liabilities. These values are determined in discussion with the farmer.

If this method is good enough for the critical gaze of a bank manager, it should be sufficient for the farmer's needs. It is an *impression* of stability that is sought, after all – measures such as the current, solvency and gearing ratios are, in most farm businesses, relatively insensitive to small errors in valuation.

To avoid confusion, these adjustments should normally be made after the balance sheet has been reconciled with the profit and loss account. If assets are revalued *before* reconciliation, a *holding gain* equivalent to the amount by which the asset has been upvalued should be credited to the capital account. This enables reconciliation of the revalued account, and at the same time allows the capital account to indicate the source of that part of the increase in net capital.

In flow of funds analysis, inflationary increases in asset values should be balanced by an extra 'use' category labelled 'holding gain'. As well as ensuring that the calculation works out, this provides an indication of the impact of inflation on the business. If desired, it can be subdivided to show separately the gains due to revaluation of stocks, machinery, and property.

Enterprise accounts

Analysis of full cost or gross margin accounts relies on three types of comparison; with previous years' accounts for the same farm; with published standard or survey data; and with budgets for the current year (see Chapter 14). Of these, the first is the worst affected by inflation, since discrepancies in costs and returns between years reflect not only differences in management, climate, specific price levels, etc., but also the general upward movement of prices. The most sophisticated of inflation accounting methods cannot avoid this problem. Some value may be derived from a comparison of physical performance between the years, but financial comparisons are of dubious worth.

Comparisons with survey or standard data are less afflicted in this respect, since, in theory, the comparison figures should be exactly contemporary with the original account. In practice this is difficult, if not impossible, to achieve, but any resulting errors are likely to be relatively small. It is important that both account and comparison are calculated on the same basis; some FBS regions make adjustments for inflation in their publications, especially with respect to machinery depreciation and breeding livestock. Where this is the case, similar adjustments must be made in the account to be analysed if the comparison is to have any meaning.

The third form of comparison, that with the original budgets, is at any time the most useful of the three. It is the least affected by the presence of inflation, since general price rises may be built into the budget in the first place. It may turn out that the actual inflation rate is different from that expected, but such differences will usually be small, and their impact can be minimized by frequent monitoring and rebudgeting where necessary. As long as the account is calculated on the same basis as the budget, no adjustments are necessary.

The methods outlined above lack the precision of inflation accounting methods such as CCA, but will be sufficient for all normal purposes. Since the onus for allowing for inflation is thrown on to the farmer's judgement, he must be sure to incorporate adequate detail in enterprise accounts, and to study their make-up with particular care. It is not enough, for instance, for him to register that the dairy gross margin is £600; he must be aware that £100 of that gross margin arose from an inflation-induced increase in breeding stock values. Moreover, distortion of the financial values renders physical data all the more important, and every effort is needed to ensure that details of quantities and qualities of inputs and outputs are recorded with precision.

The use of variance analysis with account comparisons (Chapter 14) enables isolation of the influence of price changes, as opposed to physical variations. The farmer may then use his judgement as to how much of the price difference is due to specific price changes rather than inflation.

Inflation and farm planning

The comments made with respect to management accounting also apply to the preparation of budgets. In most circumstances the sensible course is to avoid specific adjustments for inflation, letting closing stock values reflect their forecast net realizable value at the time of valuation. Planning techniques other than budgeting, such as gross margin planning and linear programming, tend to rely on normalized data, and are thus largely unaffected by problems of increases in stock valuation, understated depreciation charges, etc.

A problem which is peculiar to planning techniques is the increased difficulty of forecasting prices. Having to predict specific price changes is bad enough, but in times of inflation it is necessary to forecast general price rises as well. An associated difficulty is the uncertainty of timing of price increases. The prices of many goods and services move in an irregular fashion; suppliers will hold prices constant for several months and then increase them by an amount that reflects both past and expected levels of inflation. With the majority of sales and purchases, the effects are relatively insignificant, and tend to balance each other out. With large purchases, such as machinery, the accuracy with which the timing of price rises is predicted can be critical.

The consequence of both effects is that precision in planning becomes even more difficult to achieve. Cash reserves are particularly susceptible to this loss of precision. Take the example of a farmer who, in a given year, buys store cattle at £350 per head, and sells them six months later for £450 per head. If, the next year, he has to pay £420 per head, and receives £540 at sale, he will probably feel that the higher sale price is adequate compensation for the higher purchase price.

To finance this operation, however, he will need another £70 cash per head over six months (and this is ignoring increases in other costs, such as feed). If his budgets are based on last year's prices, he may find himself very short of cash before the six months are up. It is even possible that he will have to sell some of the cattle before they are finished, at little or no profit, in order to raise cash for essentials such as rent or living expenses.

To avoid such eventualities, even more energy than usual should be devoted to forecasting prices for the year ahead. In addition, flexible budgeting and sensitivity analysis can be used to test the effect of different inflation rates and timings of price rises. Budgetary control measures should be reviewed, with the possibility of increasing the frequency of budget/actual checks. In this way, the effects of any unforeseen fluctuations in the inflation rate may be spotted at the earliest possible stage, and remedial action taken.

Inflation and investment appraisal

The presence of inflation can distort the message given by the calculation of return on capital of investment projects. As an example, take the farmer who calculates that a certain safe investment is likely to give him a return on capital of 15 per cent per annum. In an inflation-free economy, such a return would indicate a very worthwhile project. If, on the other hand, this calculation relates to a period with an inflation rate of 20 per cent per annum, the project looks less attractive. The returns from the project are not sufficient to keep pace with inflation; in fact the project will lose money in 'real' terms.

The *real rate of return* is an 'inflation-free' rate; it can be estimated by deducting the annual inflation rate from the nominal rate of return that we have used up to now.* The real rate of return corresponding to a nominal rate of 15 per cent and an inflation rate of 20 per cent is thus about − 5 per cent.

The estimate of annual inflation rate is based usually on expectations of changes in the retail price index, although this may be an imperfect guide to the decline in purchasing power of money owned by someone whose spending pattern differs markedly from the 'typical' pattern assumed by the index.

When an investment project is tested by the techniques described in Chapter 19, its annual percentage rate of return is compared to the cost of the capital invested. It matters little whether this comparison is in real or nominal terms, as long as both parts of the comparison are expressed in the same currency. The most common error in investment appraisal is to calculate the rate of return in real terms, i.e. building no inflation into cash flow or profit estimates, testing against a cost of capital expressed in nominal terms. The result is the rejection of many projects which would in fact have been well worthwhile.

Thus if no inflation is built into the basic calculation, the result should be compared with the cost of capital in real terms. In many ways this is the simplest solution to the inflation problem, as long as it can be assumed that the values of all inputs and outputs will rise in price at the same constant rate over the project life, and that the rate is identical to the investor's 'personal' inflation rate. If these conditions do not apply (for instance if costs are likely to rise faster than prices of outputs − a common story in agriculture), the simplicity is totally lost in attempts to adjust cash flows for differential price movements in real terms. In such cases it is more appropriate to use nominal values throughout, building anticipated price increases into cash flows, and discounting by the nominal (i.e. inflation-boosted) cost of capital. This has the further advantage of making the result easier to understand: if the appraisal is carried out on behalf of, rather than by a farmer, the use of a real rate of return complicates a communication process which is already fraught with problems, especially if discounted cash-flow techniques are being used.

A more detailed, but readable discussion of inflation and investment appraisal can be found in Chapter 7 of Mott (1989).

---

*More precisely, real rate of return is $1 - [(1 - r)/(1 - I)]$, where r is the monetary rate of return and I the inflation rate, both expressed as fractions.

Further reading

General

Bull, R. J., *Accounting in Business*, 6th edition (London, Butterworths, 1990), chapter 12.
Kirkman, P. R. A., *Accounting under Inflationary Conditions* (London, Allen & Unwin, 1974).
Scapens, R. W., *Accounting in an Inflationary Environment* (London, Macmillan, 1977).

Agricultural

Lewis, R. W. and Jones, W. D., 'Current cost accounting and farm businesses', *Journal of Agricultural Economics*, vol. 31, no. 1, 1980. Theoretical examination of implications of CCA for farm businesses.

Investment appraisal

Lumby, S., *Investment Appraisal and Financing Decisions*, 4th edition (London, Chapman & Hall, 1991), chapter 6.
Mott, G., *Investment Appraisal* (London, Pitman, 1989), chapter 7.

Appendices

Basic economic concepts

This appendix gives only the briefest outline of those economic concepts mentioned in the text of the book. For a more detailed exposition, see a general agricultural economics text, such as B. Hill and D. Ray, *Economics for Agriculture:* Food, Farming and the Rural Economy (Basingstoke, Macmillan, 1987).

Scarce resources

A scarce resource is one that is not freely obtainable by everyone who wants it. As a result, people are prepared to pay for it. Scarce resources are normally classified for convenience into land, capital (including stocks of materials), labour (including various levels of labour skill) and management expertise.

Opportunity cost

The cost of using a scarce resource in a particular activity is the benefit that is lost by using the resource in this activity rather than in the next most beneficial activity. This lost benefit is known as the 'opportunity cost', since it results from the sacrifice of the opportunity to employ the resource in the alternative activity.

This principle is of particular value when one is choosing between alternative courses of action, and is thus encountered several times in the course of this book (see, for instance, Chapters 9 and 19). As an example of its use, take a farmer who is intending to introduce field-scale vegetables on a farm which has hitherto grown only cereals and grass for beef. The cost of land used for the enterprise is not the rent paid, but the opportunity cost – in this case probably the profit lost from a displaced barley crop, although it could be the potential profit from a crop which has not been grown on the farm, such as sugar beet.

In some cases, the direct financial cost of employing a resource may be higher than the profit from alternative uses. In such situations, the opportunity cost is equal to the financial cost, the lost opportunity being that of selling, or not purchasing, the resource in question.

Diminishing returns

The theory of diminishing returns relates the intensity of use of a given resource to the resulting output. Suppose that, in production of a certain good, all inputs except one are kept constant. If this one input is increased by equal amounts, there will come a point where each successive increment in the variable input begins to produce a smaller increase in output than the one before. If the process is continued long enough, a point will be reached where extra units of the input produce no further increase in output, and may even *depress* the output (an example of this can be found in the application of fertilizer to a crop – excessive rates will lead to depression of growth through scorching and other effects).

The theory has two lessons for management. The first is that a farmer cannot keep pumping in inputs and hope for unlimited increases in production, since the point will eventually be reached where the output resource will be zero or even negative.

The second lesson concerns the relationship between the *values* of inputs and outputs. Figure A1.1 shows the same production process as that shown in Figure A1.2 with two differences. The first is that the latter has been adapted to show the economic relationships, by multiplying the units of outputs by their unit price. The second is that diagram shows the *extra*, or marginal value of the output compared to the *extra* value of the inputs employed, i.e. the marginal cost.

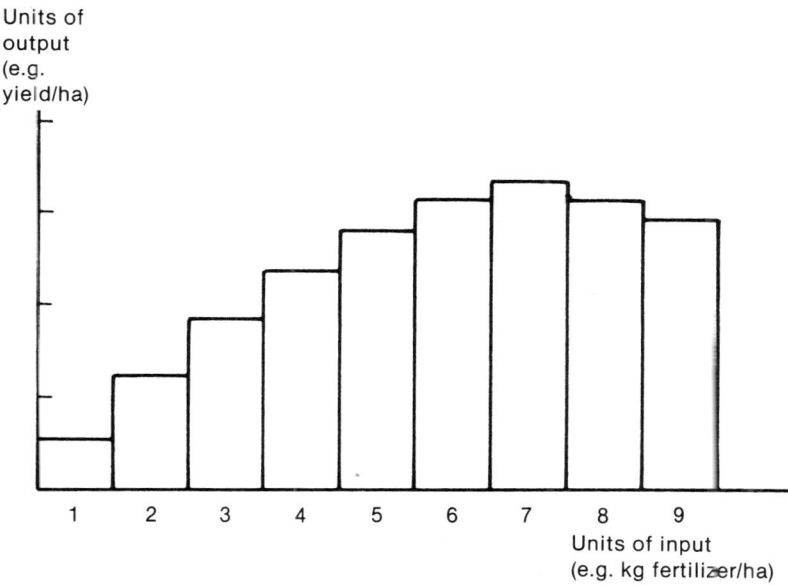

Figure A1.1 *Diminishing returns*

Thus diminishing returns is reflected in a declining marginal value of ouput, while marginal cost stays constant. Early in the progression the marginal value of the output is greater than the marginal cost of the input producing it (e.g. point A). As long as this is the case, it is worth committing more input and thus producing more. The point will eventually be reached, however, where the marginal value of the output is exactly equal to the marginal cost (point B). This is the maximum-profit point of production; to use any more of the input gives rise to greater extra costs than is recouped by the extra revenue generated.

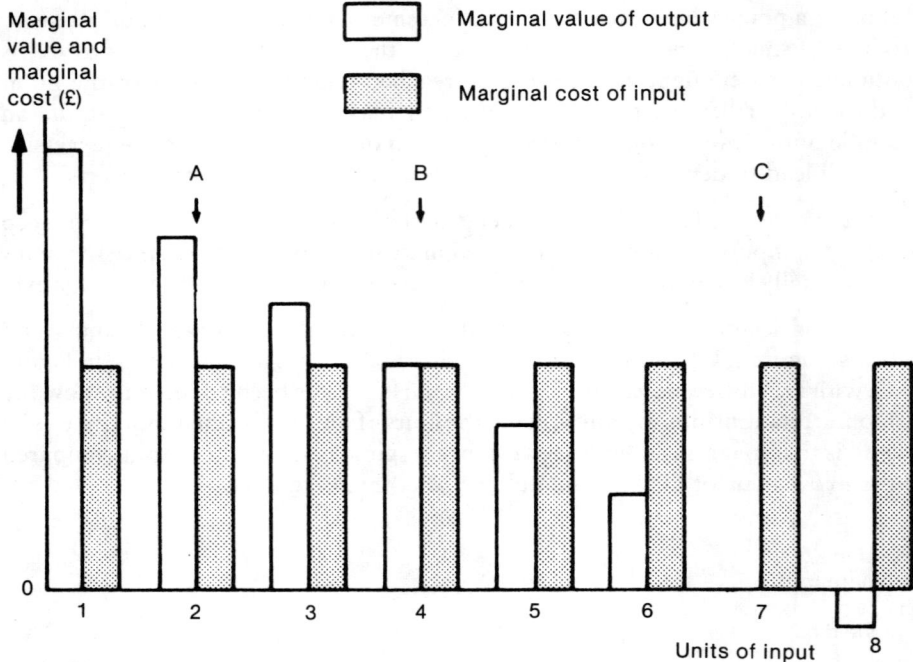

Figure A1.2 *Diminishing returns – marginal values and costs*

This point is reached *before* the point of maximum physical production discussed above (point C). Put crudely but simply, maximum yield does not necessarily mean maximum profit.

The theory of equi-marginal returns

This theory states that, in order to derive maximum profits from the use of a given resource, it should be allocated among its various uses in such a way that if a further unit of that resource were employed in any one of those uses, the effect on profit would be identical, whichever use was concerned.

As an example, take a farm which consists of only two enterprises, A and B, each using the scarce resource X. Suppose that an extra unit of X became available, and that if that unit is used in enterprise A it will generate twice as much extra profit as if it were used in B (see Figure A1.3, page 264). It makes sense to employ the extra unit of X in A, if one is aiming for maximum profit. It would also make sense to make successive transfers of units of X from their current use in B to more profitable use in A. This transfer should continue until, due to the effect of diminishing returns to X, the extra profit from the marginal unit of X is the same in both enterprises.

This principle underlies techniques described in Chapter 16 in particular.

	Product A	Product B	
Units of X required per unit of output	5	1	200 units possible
Units of X required per unit of output	2	4	1,000 units possible
Profit per unit of output	£10	£5	
Profit per unit of X	£2	£5	
Maximum possible profit	£400 (200 × £2)	£1,000 (200 × £5)	

Figure A1.3 *Maximizing profit tc the most limiting resource*

Maximizing returns to the most limiting resource

This concept is a corollary of the theory of equi-marginal returns One is more often dealing with the allocation of a mixture of resources than with a single variable resource. In this situation, profits will be maximized by taking the course of action which maximizes the profit per unit of the most limiting resource. Take the example of a choice between the production of two products, A and B, each of which employ two scarce resources, X and Y (Figure A1.3). At first sight, product A looks attractive, due to its high profit margin per unit output. The outputs of both A and B are limited, however, by the availability of X and Y, of which X is the most limiting (it restricts production of A to 40 units and B to 200 units, while Y restricts A to 500 units and B to 250 units). The product which gives the most profile per unit of X is B. Therefore the farmer should concentrate on production of B.

This concept is applied particularly in Chapters 16 and 19.

Economies of scale

It is often the case that increasing the size of a business or an enterprise results in a less-than-proportionate increase in costs. The larger scale of operation allows greater efficiency in the use of 'lumpy' inputs in particular.

The capital and running costs per tonne harvested of a small combine harvester are almost certain to be greater than those of a machine of double the capacity, especially considering that the labour requirement is the same. Similarly, the cost of a cattle yard capable of holding 200 animals will be less than double that of a yard of similar design with a capacity of 100, all other things being equal.

The degree to which a business can benefit from such *economies of scale* is limited by various countervailing influences, such as those caused by increasing organization and communication difficulties, loss of flexibility, monotony of

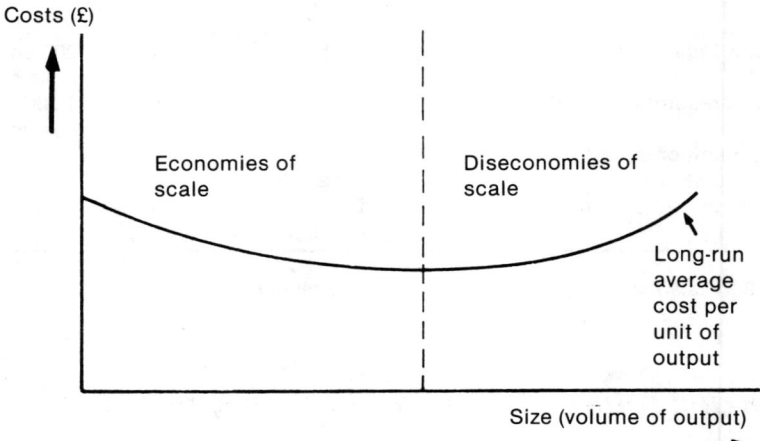

Figure A1.4   *Economics and diseconomics of scale*

work, and so on. When the scale of operation reaches a certain point, these *diseconomies of scale* will more than offset the economies (see Figure A1.4).

These characteristics must be borne in mind throughout the planning process, particularly when using the techniques described in Chapter 16. They are also of special relevance to Chapter 18 (estimating labour and machinery costs).

Partnerships and companies

Throughout this book the sole proprietor form of business ownership has been assumed. Other forms of ownership are subject to the same general financial management principles, but differ in detail. The purpose of this appendix is to give a brief introduction to the two most common forms of ownership and their influence on financial accounts.

Partnerships

In its most basic form, a partnership consists of two or more people working together in order to make a profit for themselves. Ideally, their association will be formally constituted by means of a legally binding partnership agreement which will set out the way in which profits will be shared, voting procedures, and so on. Each partner is jointly and severally liable for the debts of the partnership, which means that if the business gets into financial difficulties, each of the partners has to participate in paying off the debts to the full extent of their personal assets. The actions of one partner could bankrupt another. As long as there is at least one fully liable partner, one or more partners may elect to be 'sleeping' partners, with their liability limited to the amount they have invested in the partnership. In doing so, however, they sacrifice the formal right to vote on decisions.

There are two main motives for forming a partnership. The first is to enable individuals to pool their resources – usually capital (including machinery and property) but also physical labour and specific abilities. The second is to reduce the collective tax liability of the partners – usually important only in the context of a family business, since the tax savings arise through the principal of the business sharing income with other members of the partnership. Other motives for forming a partnership include spreading risk, sharing responsibility, gaining reflected 'respectability' by taking a well-known and credible partner and providing a means whereby younger members of a family may gradually build up investment in, and control of the family business.

The accounts of a partnership are identical to those of an equivalent sole proprietorship, except that additional information has to be provided concerning the division of profits and capital between the partners. An extra account called the *profit and loss appropriation account* shows how profits are shared: the division will depend on what is written in the partnership agreement. This may allow for interest on the capital injected by the partners (allowing for different levels of investment by the partners); for a 'salary' to allow for the fact that the partners may put different amounts of work into the business, and for a split of the remaining profits in agreed proportions.

	£		£
Interest on initial capital			
J. Haynes (12% of £60,000)	7,200.00	Net profit brought down:	17,279.00
A. Haynes (12% of £39,034)	4,684.08		
Salary: A. Haynes	5,000.00		
Share of remaining profits (50% each):			
J. Haynes	197.46		
A. Haynes	197.46		
	17,279.00		17,279.00

Figure A2.1 *Example of profit and loss appropriation account*

If, for instance, Adam Haynes' uncle had formed a partnership with Adam, rather than just letting the farm to him, their profit and loss appropriation account for the end of the first year (based on Figure 11.7) might be as shown in Figure A2.1. This assumes that John Haynes contributed £60,000 of the initial net capital, with Adam supplying the remainder, and also injecting a futher £4,500 during the year. The partnership agreement specifies that the profit should first reward the capital

CAPITAL ACCOUNTS				
J. Haynes		60,000	Initial capital	94,534
A. Haynes: initial	34,534		Capital injections	4,500
plus capital injection	4,500	39,034		
		99,034		99,034

CURRENT ACCOUNTS			
J. Haynes:			
Private drawings	3,400	Balance brought down	0
Tax	1,512	Interest on capital	7,200
Benefits in kind	2,000	Share of profits	197
Closing balance	485		
	7,397		7,397
A. Haynes:			
Private drawings	7,000	Balance brought down	0
Tax	1,000	Interest on capital	4,684
Benefits in kind	2,435	Salary	5,000
Closing balance	-554	Share of profits	197
	9,881		9,881

Figure A2.2 *Example of joint capital and current accounts*

contributions of the pair by an interest charge of 12 per cent, then Adam's work with a nominal salary of £5000, with the remainder divided fifty-fifty. Note that if Adam's 'salary' had been higher (say £8000), the final item would be sharing a residual loss, rather than profits.

The other account to be affected is the capital account, which must show how the capital stakes of the partners are affected by the profitability of the business, and the various external demands on it. This is often divided to show a joint capital account, showing initial and subsequent injections of capital, and a joint current account showing the accumulation of profits. Figure A2.2 shows joint capital and current accounts for the Home Farm situation described above. The separate accounts show clearly the fact that, without the capital injection during the year, net capital would have declined. The current account also indicates that, because of the higher demands he is putting on his share of the profits, Adam's stake in the business has declined, while John's has increased (albeit by relatively small amounts).

Limited liability companies

The fact that partners are jointly and severally liable for debts is often a significant deterrent to their formation, and an alternative is the limited liability company. Here the investors each make a contribution to the capital of the company at its inception, and profits are subsequently allocated in proportion to those shares. Profits that are not distributed to shareholders are retained as 'reserves', helping to finance the company in much the same fashion as does the current account in the partnership.

In the typical company, each shareholder's liability is limited to that money he or she has invested, i.e. original investment plus the appropriate share of accumulated reserves. This reduces the risk to the shareholder, but at the potential expense to creditors, who, if the business fails, will only be able to recover what is left in the company, irrespective of the wealth of the individual shareholders. For this reason small companies often find it difficult to obtain credit, or directors are asked to provide personal security such as the title deeds of a house, or a personal guarantee.

Companies can take many forms, but the most common in agriculture is the private company, usually owned by the members of a family. The shareholders can be as few as two. All or some of the shareholders will be elected as directors, giving them the right to participate in decision-making between general meetings (otherwise the only way in which shareholders can formally influence matters). The formation of a company requires formal registration with Companies House, involving registration and legal fees (although see Roberts, 1983, for a do-it-yourself guide) and some loss of privacy, in that accounts and other information must be filed annually with the Registrar of Companies and are open to public scrutiny.

Apart from limited liability, the attractions of forming a company are much the same as those identified above for a partnership. Income tax is levied on the company, rather than the individual shareholders, in the form of Corporation Tax, giving some potential tax savings for the more profitable farm businesses (see Appendix 3). A valuable benefit is the aspect of continuity: while a partnership is automatically dissolved by the death of one of the partners, a company, providing that at least two shareholders are left, can live on. On the other hand, the company structure can reduce the freedom of action of the business and/or incur considerable costs when significant change is required.

In the accounts, the most noticeable difference is likely to be that in place of 'net capital' in the balance sheet is a statement of share capital and reserves (usually just 'profit and loss account' indicating accumulated surpluses over the business' life, but possibly others such as a general reserve. Figure A2.3 shows an example. Share capital plus reserves are equivalent to the net capital of a sole trader or partnership and can be used as such in ratio analysis.

It is likely that the profit and loss account will include 'directors' salaries' as an expense. Since sole traders and partnerships are not allowed to include salaries of owners in their financial accounts, profit comparisons between farms of various forms of ownership (and between company farms and survey data) must be made with care. These salaries, together with 'dividends' or payouts to the shareholders (shown in an appropriation account) are roughly equivalent to the private drawings of a non-company business.

```
Financed by:
        SHARE CAPITAL
        (authorised and issued)          1,000
        RESERVES
        Provision for future taxation    2,500
        General reserve                  9,034
        Profit and loss account         86,431

                                        98,965
```

Figure A2.3 *Capital account for company*

Further Reading

This has been a selective introduction to two forms of ownership, omitting many others such as co-operative associations, co-operative companies, machinery rings, share farming, contract farming and voluntary non-profit organizations. The texts listed here will provide a starting point for those who wish to learn more.

Bull, R. J., *Accounting in Business*, 6th edition (London, Butterworth, 1990), chapters 9, 10 and 11.

Blume, H. and Norton, M., *Accounting and Financial Management for Charities* (London, Directory for Social Change, 1980).

Centre of Management in Agriculture, *Practical Share Farming* Corby, British Institute of Management, 1986).

Evans, M., 'The benefits and problems of machinery sharing', *Farm Management*, vol. 6 no. 5. Useful article on machinery rings, groups and syndicates.

Furlong, L. A. C., 'Farming as a limited company', *Farm Management*, vol. 6, no. 5, 1987.

Garbutt, D., *Accounting Foundations* (London, Pitman, 1980), chapter 20: 'Not-for-Profit Organization'.

Panes, C., 'Farm partnerships', *Farm Management*, vol. 4, no. 3, 1980.

Roberts, D., *How to Form a Company: A Practical Guide to the Formation of Private Companies* (Cambridge, ICSA Publishing, 1983).

Sinclair, W. I. and McMullen, J., *Business Tax and Law Guide* (London, Longman, 1990), chapter 5: 'Company and Partnership Law'.

Watkins, D., *Be Your Own Boss: Starter Kit* (Cambridge, National Extension College, 1986), chapter 10: 'Working in a Cooperative'.

Wright, D., 'Contract farming agreements', *Farm Management*, vol. 7. no. 4, 1989.

Information about agricultural co-operatives can be obtained from the Co-operative Development Division of Food from Britain, New Covent Garden, London SW8 5NQ.

Budgeting for tax

This is not the place for a detailed discussion of taxation. It is too complex, too specific to the UK, and subject to such frequent change that any discussion is out of date by the time it gets into print. Advice is given at the end of this section for the reader who wants to study the issues in greater depth, or who needs to establish the tax liability arising from a major business decision in detail.

Nevertheless, since tax payments can have a significant effect on cash flow, it is worth knowing the basics of the tax system, particularly income taxation, as they apply to business. All rates, allowances and other values quoted below are for the 1991/92 tax year.

Personal income tax

Residents in the UK are liable to pay Income Tax on income received, at the rate of 25 per cent of taxable income up to £23,700, and 40 per cent of taxable income in excess of that amount. These are marginal rates, so that if a person earns £25,700 taxable income, he or she will pay only 40 per cent on that amount which exceeds £23,700, £2000, making a total tax liability of (£23,700 × 25 per cent) + (£2000 × 40 per cent) = £6725.

In calculating a person's taxable income various allowances are deducted from the gross income. By far the most common allowances are the *Personal Allowance* (£3295) and the *Married Couple's Allowance* (£1720). Anyone in receipt of income is allowed to claim a Personal Allowance against that income. Thus if Adam Haynes were single and had no other sources of income, his taxable income could be estimated by deducting his Personal Allowance from the farm profit of £17,379, giving £13,984, which will in turn give rise to a tax liability of £3496.

If he were married, and his wife had no independent source of income, the family's income tax liability can be reduced further by Adam's claiming the Married Couple's Allowance of £1720. Total allowances will now be £5015, taxable income £12,264 and tax liability £3066. If Adam's wife has a source of income of her own (say £20,000 per year salary) she will be able to claim her own Personal Allowance. Total allowances for the family are now £8310, giving rise to a taxable income of £28,969 (£17,279 + £20,000 − £8310) and a tax liability of £8033 (note that since at this income level the allowances are reducing that part of the income which is taxed at 40 per cent, they are significantly more valuable than in the previous examples).

Even if Adam's wife has no external source of income, she can nevertheless benefit from her own Personal Allowance if Adam pays her a regular salary in recognition of her contribution to the business or, better still, makes her a partner in the business. If they formed a fifty-fifty partnership, for instance, each would receive a share of profit of £17,279/2 = £8640. Against Adam's share can be set a Personal Allowance and the Married Couples Allowance, giving a taxable income of £3625, and against his wife's can be set a Personal Allowance of £3295, giving a taxable income of £5345. The total tax liability is thus reduced to £8970 × 25 per cent = £2243.

Income tax and businesses

If Adam were an employee, the income tax on his wages or salary would be deducted from his salary by his employer on the Inland Revenue's behalf under the *Pay As You Earn* (PAYE) scheme. As a sole proprietor of or partner in a business, however, he will be taxed under a different system (Schedule D) on an annual basis. His accounts will be submitted annually to the local Inspector of Taxes, who will assess the taxable income from this and other information supplied (the annual tax return, for instance). Once the assessment is finalized, it is passed to the Collector of Taxes who will normally request payment of the tax due in two equal half-yearly instalments.

Once a business is established, its owners are assessed for income tax on the profits from that financial year of the business which ended in the previous tax assessment years (6 April to 5 April). Thus in any tax assessment year, Adam will be assessed on profits arising during the Home Farm financial year ending in the previous September. Since the first instalment of tax will not be payable until the January of the assessment year, there will be a delay of 15 months between the end of a financial year and the first payment of tax on the profits arising therein. For a business with a financial year ending between 6 April and the end of September, the delay will be even greater. This is obviously a useful cash-flow benefit, although the 'previous year' system may be phased out during the 1990s.

The 'net profit' used in determining income tax liability may not be identical to that produced in management accounts. Various adjustments are allowed (and some enforced) in calculation of taxable income from the business. Some of these, such as arrangements for recently established businesses (to get them on to the 'previous year' system), for recently liquidated businesses (to get them off it), for averaging farm profits between years and for bad and doubtful debts are too specific for this discussion.

On the other hand, it is important to be aware that depreciation has to be recalculated using standard rates (25 per cent diminishing balance for machinery and plant; 4 per cent straight-line for buildings and fixtures), the result being termed *capital allowances*. Losses can be set against income from other sources arising in the same year (if such income exists) and otherwise set against profits in subsequent years: special arrangements exist at the commencement and cessation of a business. Stocks of farm livestock and crops can be valued at cost of production or current market value, whichever is the lower: where the cost of production of livestock is not accurately known, it can be estimated at 60 per cent of market value for home-bred cattle, and 75 per cent of market value for sheep and pigs (unless this gives an obviously incorrect estimate, such as in the case of pedigree stock).

Perhaps most valuable to the livestock farmer (and potentially most confusing when it comes to interpreting farmers' accounts) is the *Herd Basis* of valuing breeding livestock. This allows the value of the herd or flock to be kept at a constant levels for tax purposes until the herd or flock is dispersed, and thus changes in price level of stock do not affect the taxable profits as long as the number of animals is maintained. On election by the farmer (within two years of the end of the tax assessment year in which the herd or flock was established) the value of the herd or flock is removed from the profit statement, thus reflecting its fixed asset nature. Purchase of replacements and sale of culls still appear in the profit statement, acting as a form of depreciation charge. Increases in the size of the herd or flock are shown in the closing valuation at cost. The proceeds from substantial and permanent reductions in the size of the herd or flock (i.e. more than about 20 per cent) are subject to neither income tax nor capital gains tax.

Woodlands are not subject to Income (or Corporation) Tax.

National Insurance (NI)

National Insurance is a tax on gross income. For an employee ('Class 1 contributions') the rate is 2 per cent on earnings below £52 per week, and 9 per cent on earnings above that level up to a maximum of £390 per week. Where the employer operates an approved pension scheme which is contracted out of the state system, the upper rate is reduced to 7 per cent. In addition, the employer must make a contribution ranging from 4.6 per cent (on earnings between £52 and £84.99 per week) to 10.4 per cent (on all earnings above £185 per week): lower rates again apply for 'contracted out' employees.

A self-employed person, such as a sole trader or a partner, is liable to pay a flat-rate NI contribution ('Class 2') of £5.15 per week if annual earnings are above £2900 per annum, plus an earnings-related contribution ('Class 4') of 6.3 per cent on profits or gains between £5900 and £20,280 per annum. 'Class 3' contributions are voluntary payments of a flat-rate £5.05 per week for those who do not meet the £2900 minimum for class 1 contributions, but who wish to preserve state pension rights.

Corporation Tax

Corporation Tax (CT) is levied on profits of limited liability companies, whether those profits are distributed or not. Unlike Income Tax, the period for assessment is the company's accounting year, not the tax assessment year, and tax is assessed on a current-year, not a previous-year basis. Tax is payable within 9 months of the end of the company's financial year – rather sooner than non-corporate businesses, and creating potential cash-flow problems in the business planning to switch from a partnership or sole proprietorship to a company.

The current rate of tax is 33 per cent on all profits, but this only applies to profits exceeding £1,250,000 in a year. Most agricultural companies in the UK will be subject to the small companies' rate of 25 per cent, applying to profits up to £250,000 per annum (a sliding scale applies between £250,000 and £1,250,000). The tax is payable in stages: if any distributions are made during the year (e.g. the shareholders of a small company withdraw money for living expenses), *Advance Corporation Tax* (ACT) is payable on those distributions at the rate of one-third, and paid to the Inland Revenue in the quarter in which it arises. If the directors consider withdrawing the money as salaries rather than distributions of profit, they have to face the fact that income tax will have to be deducted by the company by PAYE before payment is made: moreover those salaries will be subject to Class 1 NI contributions, both employees' and employers'. When the final assessment of Corporation Tax is made at the end of the year, any ACT payments made will be taken into account.

For companies where the individual annual incomes of the owners are likely to be significantly more than the 40 per cent Income Tax threshold, and where the owners leave part of their annual profits in the company, the lower CT rates can be attractive. In other circumstances, however, the earlier payment requirements and harsher treatment of benefits in kind such as houses and company cars are likely to discourage small businesses not having other motives, such as acquiring limited liability (see Appendix 2), from acquiring company status purely on tax-saving grounds (see Furlong, 1987).

Capital Gains Tax (CGT)

This is a tax on gains arising through the disposal assets. It is chargeable even where the disposal is wholly or partly a gift, although tax liability on gifts can be 'held over' until the recipient sells the assets. Some assets are exempt, including a person's main private dwelling, private car and depreciating business assets such as machinery (and livestock on the Herd Basis). The taxable gain is measured by the difference between the market value at disposal, and the cost of acquisition. Where the asset was bought before 31 March 1982, the gain is taken as the difference between market value at disposal and that at 6 April 1982. All gains are subject to *Indexation Relief*. In other words that part of the gain which arose through general inflation is removed from the tax calculation.

Capital gains are effectively added to the top of the taxable income assessed for Income Tax purposes and are thus subject to tax at either 25 per cent or 40 per cent. Unused Personal Allowances and other IT reliefs are not allowable against gains, but the first £5500 of each person's capital gain in any one year is exempt from CGT. For companies, capital gains are taxed as part of Corporation Tax, and thus subject to tax at rates of 25 per cent to 33 per cent: there is no £5500 annual exemption in this case.

Capital losses can be set against other capital gains in the same year, or carried forward (never back) to subsequent years. Capital losses may not be set against profits except in the case of a company.

Apart from those already mentioned, two major reliefs can substantially reduce the impact of CGT on a business. The first is *Retirement Relief*: if a sole trader, partner or full-time working director of a company disposes of all or a substantial part of his or her interest in the business at or after the age of 60, the first £150,000 of the gain realized, and 50 per cent of the gain between £150,000 and £600,000 is exempt from CGT. The assets must have been in the owner's hands for ten years to justify the full relief. Retirement due to ill-health before the age of 60 can also attract relief.

Roll-over Relief on the disposal of business assets applies when the proceeds of the disposal are reinvested in qualifying business assets within a period from one year before, to three years after the disposal. Thus if a farm is sold, giving rise to a taxable gain, reinvestment of the proceeds into a new farm (or into qualifying assets in a totally different form of business) will 'roll over' the gain into the new assets and the tax deferred until those assets are in turn sold or given away. If only part of the proceeds of the sale are reinvested (if, for instance, some money is retained for that once-in-a-lifetime world cruise), only partial relief will be available.

Inheritance Tax (IHT)

Inheritance Tax is a tax on all transfers of wealth from an individual. It is charged at 40 per cent on cumulative transfers of over £140,000 made within three years of the donor's death: the rate is progressively reduced for transfers made between three and seven years of the donor's death, and transfers made more than seven years before the donor's death are exempt from tax.

From the time of transfer, a gift becomes a *Potentially Exempt Transfer* (PET) until the donor's death or the elapse of seven years, whichever is the sooner. If the gift is not a complete gift – in other words the donor reserves the right to enjoy benefits arising out of the assets of the house (e.g. profits, or rent-free accommodation) – the gift is considered to be a 'gift with reservation' and does not become a PET until a donor relinquishes the benefits.

Transfers between spouses are free of IHT, and various other exemptions are available, including the first £3000 of gifts in any tax year; outright gifts to each of any number of persons up to £250 in a tax year; wedding gifts (up to £5000 per donor if a parent of one of the couple, £2500 if a grandparent or great-grandparent, £1000 otherwise); and gifts to charities, political parties and for the benefit of the national heritage.

Donors of farmland who meet certain qualifications relating to their active involvement in farming, and the period of occupation of the land, can obtain *Agricultural Property Relief*, reducing the value of the property for tax purposes by 50 per cent (30 per cent if the land is let rather than farmed by the owner). Other business assets may also attract *Business Property Relief* which, subject to similar conditions, reduces the value by 50 per cent (30 per cent for minority shareholders in unquoted companies or where assets used in the business are owned personally by a controlling partner or shareholder).

Tax estimation in practice

The above is merely a selection of the most common and basic considerations relating to taxation in the UK, and is designed to assist you in making a rough estimate of tax for planning purposes. All information should be checked against up-to-date references before use.

Where tax is likely to have a significant effect on plans for the business, the references below will provide some guidance. There is no substitute for the advice of a qualified accountant *with experience in agricultural taxation*: the ranks of farmers are littered with those who have needlessly paid thousands of pounds in tax for the sake of saving a few hundreds in professional fees. Finally, though this might seem perverse advice in an industry where the tax inspector is traditionally viewed as an arch-enemy, do consider asking the local Inland Revenue office for help. The staff will not assist you in devising tax-avoidance schemes, but they will explain your entitlements and help you understand the official procedures.

Further reading

Furlong, L. A. C., 'Farming as a limited company', *Farm Management*, vol. 6, no. 5, 1987.
Mitchell, W., 'Passing on assets to the next generation', *Farm Management*, vol. 7, no. 6, 1990.
Nix, J. S., Hill, G. P. and Williams, N., *Land and Estate Management*, 2nd edition (Chichester, Packard Publishing, 1989), chapters 14 and 15.
Scottish Agricultural Colleges, *Guide to Income Tax of Farm Businesses*, latest edition (Aberdeen, Scottish Agricultural Colleges).
Sinclair, W. I., *Allied Dunbar Tax Guide*, latest edition (London, Longman).

See also the journals *Farm Tax and Finance* and *Farm Tax Briefing*: various free advisory leaflets from the Inland Revenue; and leaflets published by most accounting firms of reasonable size. Certain national newspapers publish 'layman's guides' to tax, available in large newspapers, and *Which?* magazine publishes a detailed *Tax-Saving Guide* shortly before the start of each tax year.

Personal computers in farm management

The ten years since the publication of the first edition of this book have seen enormous advances in business computing, and what was then regarded as a luxury justified only on the largest farms is now well within the reach of all but the smallest. Microcomputers (now often referred to as *personal computers* or PCs) have increased dramatically in computing power while becoming cheaper in real terms, and it is now possible to buy a computer system suitable for most small businesses in virtually any high street electrical store. Software (the programs that make the computer equipment (hardware) do its stuff) has in turn become much more sophisticated and, best of all, much more 'user-friendly', so that an intelligent novice can tap the power of a computer without being daunted by programming languages, codes, and so on.

While in the early days of micro-computers each make of machine had its own operating system, making transfer of software between machines difficult (if not impossible), there are now just two main types of operating system: the IBM-compatible system (such as MS-DOS) and the Apple Macintosh system. The latter is an extremely easy-to-use system, very good for producing high-quality print and graphics as well as performing all the basic computer functions. It has been slower to catch on in business circles than the IBM standard, however, with the result that IBM-compatible machines tend to dominate this market. Moreover the large volume and more open marketing approach of IBM have ensured that costs are lower for IBM-type machines and software. All the major UK farm business software is designed for use with IBM-compatible computers.

Computers and farming

Any person involved in financial management to the extent implied by this book should seriously consider enlisting the aid of a computer in one form or another. Not to do so is to risk spending valuable time that could be better used for thinking in performing mechanical calculations, or worse still, being ill-informed for want of time to do those calculations. The competitive position of the non-computer-using business will be steadily eroded in the increasingly competitive 1990s.

Computers can be used in various ways by a farm business. A *computer bureau* service can be used (offered by an accountant or specialist consultant): the farmer sends information on request to the bureau, where it is processed by the bureau's computer and the results sent back to the farmer. In this way management accounts for enterprises and complete businesses can be provided with little effort on the farmer's part, without the cost of ownership of a computer and without the need for anyone in the farm business having to come to terms with computer operation.

On the other hand, the fees are likely to be costly, and the business loses the flexibility of being able to process information when needed, and in the specific form it requires. An alternative is to purchase a complete business management 'package', including computer, software and a certain amount of introductory training and support. Several firms offer specialized farm accounting and management packages in the UK, typically based round a financial recording process (either cash analysis or double-entry). Once the income and expenditure has been entered for the period in question, reports can quickly be produced to show financial accounts (profit and loss accounts, balance sheet, flow of funds), gross margins, cash flows and detailed analysis of overhead costs. It is usually possible to produce budgets for the coming year, and it may be possible to link this directly with the accounts to enable the computer to perform comparisons of actual and budgeted performance, including variance analysis. Additional facilities may include specialist physical recording and management programs, such as records of a pig fattening herd, records of dairy herds, breeding and productive efficiency and arable crop recording. The computer will also be able to cope with the standard office tasks such as word-processing, described below.

Modern business packages are easy to use and once set up can save an enormous amount of repetitive work while producing a precision of management reporting that would otherwise be impossible. One deterrent for the smaller farm is likely to be the cost of the package, though. At the time of writing, a very basic specialist farm system is likely to cost at least £3000. Not much compared to a tractor but still, even after tax relief (it is a business asset) enough to make the owner of a family farm think twice. Costs can be substantially reduced by using standard business (i.e. non-agricultural) software, for accounts and payroll calculations, for instance, though such software may need to be adapted to the peculiarities of a farm business.

A related problem is that the likely financial benefit can be difficult to assess and farmers are understandably reluctant to take the advantages on trust. Another, often stronger deterrent is the unjustified mystique that has built up around computers: many potential users are frightened of approaching a computer in case its 'cleverness' will show up their 'ignorance'. Help is available to counter both problems. The excellent article by Annette Morley listed below gives very clear guidance to a prospective user: the Agricultural Development and Advisory Service has specialists who advise and publish useful booklets; and the Agricultural Training Board and local agricultural colleges run courses in most areas on using computers on the farm.

Do-it-yourself farm computing

One way of reducing the cost, and thus the risk, of buying a computer is to start with a cheap, standard office machine combined with off-the-shelf software applications. These will typically include a *word processor*, a program that allows the computer to act as a superior sort of typewriter, able to store the typing in its memory so that it can be recalled for alteration and re-use at a later date. Automatic spelling checkers, and the facility to correct typing on the computer screen before printing, make it possible for even the most ham-fisted of typists to produce a professional result.

More relevant to this book, perhaps, is the *spreadsheet* software, allowing calculations to be set out on the computer screen in such a way that the figures are recalculated automatically when any element of the calculation is changed. In a cash-flow budget, for instance, changing the interest rate or one of the revenue items would result in the whole of the budget being recalculated in an instant. A graph can be produced of the final bank balance (see Figure 7.7, for instance) which will be redrawn every time an alteration is made in the budget.

Every table in this book was produced using such a spreadsheet program. The management accounting system of one of the largest farming companies in south-west England was built up from small beginnings using a standard spreadsheet package. The modern spreadsheet is a most powerful and flexible management tool. Moreover, because it works in a very obvious manner, it is extremely easy for even a novice to use. Appendix 5 contains a number of sample spreadsheets intended to provide a starting-point for the farm-based user.

Another standard type of software application is the *database*, available at many levels of sophistication but basically a way of storing records in a form that enables them to be easily retrieved and the information sorted. For instance, if a database is used to store information about the cows in a dairy herd, the program can then be subsequently used to identify all the cows giving less than 5000 litres of milk per year, all those put to a certain bull, all those with a history of mastitis and so on. Databases can be used for field records, accounting records and machinery records, and they can also be used in combination with a word processor to produce a whole series of identical letters, personally addressed to, say, potential customers for the new organic beef enterprise.

Programs are available which combine word processor, spreadsheet and database in one *integrated software* package. Examples at the time of writing include Microsoft 'Works' and Lotus 'Symphony'. Such packages allow easy transfer of information between the component parts, and allow the acquisition of all three functions (and often a few others besides) for a relatively low cost. This is an ideal place for a low-budget user to start, allowing progression on to more specialized applications as he or she grows in confidence, and possibly eventually making the transition to a full-blown agricultural management package.

Further reading

Harrison, S. R. and Course, C. P., 'Wordprocessing in the farm office', *Farm Management*, vol. 5, no. 9, 1985.

Houseman, I., 'Communications in agriculture: the role of information technology', *Farm Management*, vol. 7, no. 7, 1990.

Morley, A., 'Practicalities of farm computing', *Farm Management*, vol. 7, no. 1, 1989.

Moverley, J., *Microcomputers in Agriculture* (London, Collins). Dated, but still a useful overview.

Scudamore, P., 'The development of on-farm computer systems', *Farm Management*, vol. 5, no. 9, 1985.

Temple, M., 'Spreadsheet programs for farm management advisory work', *Farm Management*, vol. 5, no. 12, 1986.

Williams, N. T., 'Using database management systems in farm management', *Farm Management*, vol. 6, no. 4, 1986.

Sample spreadsheets for financial calculations

On the following pages you will find various computer spreadsheets arranged to display the formulas which provide the instructions to the spreadsheet to perform the calculations. All but the milk production calculator and the second of the discounted cash-flow worksheets are based on figures elsewhere in the book – and indeed were used to generate those figures.

These examples do not display everything that a spreadsheet can do: they are intended to help you get started on designing spreadsheets for your own use, and thus most of the ideas and functions are quite simple. You should investigate ways of developing the examples, for instance:

Figure A5.1	Try linking several gross margin worksheets to a financial summary worksheet to give you an instantly updatable profit calculation. Further development could include depreciation calculations, and linking to a balance sheet and cash-flow budget. The Home Farm budget were produced on just such a set of linked worksheets, allowing changes to be made rapidly and comprehensively.
Figure A5.2	Most modern spreadsheets have charting facilities. Try getting yours to produce a chart of closing bank balance from the cash-flow budget (as in Figure 7.7).
Figures A5.3 to 5.5	These are actually part of the same worksheet, as you will see from the row and column references. You could build 'alarm' formulas into the ratio section, so that whenever a particular ratio falls below your idea of the danger level, a warning message appears in a worksheet cell.
Figure A5.6	As with the cash-flow budget, you could use the table as a base for charts such as those in Figures 18.3 and 18.4.
Figures A5.8 and 5.9	There is great scope for adding to the sophistication of this worksheet. Columns could be added to show the payback of the initial investment from the annual net cash flow, which in turn would allow the incorporation of an overdraft type of borrowing rather than just a loan.

The annual net cash-flow column could be linked to a cash-flow budget (like Figure 7.4 but using the columns for years rather than months).

Figures A5.10 to 5.11   The formulas in this spreadsheet are based on a very crude approximation of a lactation curve, which makes no allowance for season of the year or for different patterns between cows and heifers. If you are of a scientific inclination, you could generate new, more accurate formulas. Another possibility is the incorporation of a quota monitor which will warn you if you are in danger of over (or under) producing.

The spreadsheets were produced using Microsoft Excel 3, on an Apple Macintosh computer. Other spreadsheets use slightly different conventions: Lotus 1-2-3, for instance, uses '@' rather than '=' to denote a formula, and describes a range of cells with two periods (e.g. A1..A12) rather than Excel's colon (e.g. A1:A12). Any initial confusion should, however, be capable of resolution with the help of the software manual and a dose of common sense.

	A	B	C	D	E	F	G	H	I	J
1	ENTERPRISE	dairy			ha or head?	80	YEAR	9x-9y		
2							VERSION	2		
3	products>>	milk		calves		culls				
4		qty.	£	qty.	£	qty.	£	qty.	£	
5	cash received	400500	76095	74	7400	20	11000			
6	closing debtors	11000	1980	7	700					
7	'-opening debtors	-12000	-2280	-5	-500					
8	sales	=SUM(B5:B7)	=SUM(C5:C7)	=SUM(D5:D7)	=SUM(E5:E7)	=SUM(F5:F7)	=SUM(G5:G7)	=SUM(H5:H7)	=SUM(I5:I7)	
9	transfers out									
10	benefits in kind	700	133							
11	closing valuation			10	800					
12	-opening valuation			-10	-800					
13	OUTPUT	=SUM(B8:B12)	=SUM(C8:C12)	=SUM(D8:D12)	=SUM(E8:E12)	=SUM(F8:F12)	=SUM(G8:G12)	=SUM(H8:H12)	=SUM(I8:I12)	
14										
15	inputs>>	purch. livestock		conc. feed		straw		vet/med		
16		qty.	£	qty.	£	qty.	£	qty.	£	
17	cash paid	25	17500	86	12900			1	2500	
18	closing creditors			20	3000					
19	'-opening creditors'			-25	-4000					
20	purchases	=SUM(B17:B19)	=SUM(C17:C19)	=SUM(D17:D19)	=SUM(E17:E19)	=SUM(F17:F19)	=SUM(G17:G19)	=SUM(H17:H19)	=SUM(I17:I19)	
21	transfers in			42	3780	26	390			
22	'-benefits in kind'									
23	opening valuation			20	2800					
24	-closing valuation			-20	-2800					
25	VARIABLE COST	=SUM(B20:B24)	=SUM(C20:C24)	=SUM(D20:D24)	=SUM(E20:E24)	=SUM(F20:F24)	=SUM(G20:G24)	=SUM(H20:H24)	=SUM(I20:I24)	
26										
27	MISCELLANEOUS	VALUATION	CHANGES		breeding	livestock		crops in gd.		total
28						no.	£		£	£
29	closing valuation					82	53300			=G29+I29
30	-opening valuation					-77	-50050			=G30+I30
31	valuation change					=SUM(F29:F30)	=SUM(G29:G30)	=SUM(H29:H30)	=SUM(I29:I30)	=SUM(J29:J30)
32										

	A	B	C	D	E	F	G	H	I	J
			GROSS	MARGIN					£	£/hd
33	=B1				Qty/hd	£/UNIT QTY			TOTAL	
34	head	TOTAL								
35	=F1	QUANTITY								
36		=B13			=C36/(A35)		=IF(C36=0,0,I36/C36)		=C13	=I36/A35
37		=D13			=C37/(A35)		=IF(C37=0,0,I37/C37)		=E13	=I37/A35
38		=F13			=C38/(A35)		=IF(C38=0,0,I38/C38)		=G13	=I38/A35
39		=H13			=C39/(A35)		=IF(C39=0,0,I39/C39)			=I39/A35
40	misc. valn. changes	xxxxxxxx		xxxxxxxx	xxxxxxxx	xxxxxxxx	xxxxxxxx		=G31+I31	=I40/A35
41	OUTPUT								=SUM(I36:I40)	=SUM(J36:J40)
42										
43	VARIABLE	TOTAL			Qty/hd				£	£/hd
44	COSTS	QUANTITY							TOTAL	
45		=B15			=C45/A35		=IF(C45=0,0,I45/C45)		=C25	=I45/A35
46		=D15			=C46/A35		=IF(C46=0,0,I46/C46)		=E25	=I46/A35
47		=F15			=C47/A35		=IF(C47=0,0,I47/C47)			=I47/A35
48		=H15			=C48/A35		=IF(C48=0,0,I48/C48)			=I48/A35
49		=J15			=C49/A35		=IF(C49=0,0,I49/C49)			=I49/A35
50		=K15			=C50/A35		=IF(C50=0,0,I50/C50)			=I50/A35
51		=L15			=C51/A35		=IF(C51=0,0,I51/C51)		=#REF!	=I51/A35
52									=#REF!	=I52/A35
53	VARIABLE COST		GROSS	MARGIN					=SUM(I45:I52)	=SUM(J45:J52)
54									=I41-I53	=J41-J53

Annotation (pointing to G38): This formula means 'if C38 is 0, then enter 0 here – otherwise enter I38/C38'. It stops the program trying to divide by 0 (a logical impossibility)

Figure A5.1   *Spreadsheet formulas for gross margin worksheet (Figure 6.11)*

	A	B	C	D	E
1	CASH FLOW BUDGET		YEAR	199x/9y	
2					
3	% interest rate	15	TOTAL	Oct	Nov
4					
5	*RECEIPTS*				
6	Milk	1	=SUM(D6:O6)	2280	3800
7	Calves	2	=SUM(D7:O7)	500	3500
8	Cull cows	3	=SUM(D8:O8)		
9		4	=SUM(D9:O9)		
10	Sheep	5	=SUM(D10:O10)		
11		6	=SUM(D11:O11)		
12	Pigs	7	=SUM(D12:O12)	6300	6300
13		8	=SUM(D13:O13)		
14	Poultry	9	=SUM(D14:O14)		
15		10	=SUM(D15:O15)		
16	Wheat	11	=SUM(D16:O16)		
17	Wheat straw	12	=SUM(D17:O17)		
18	Oats	13	=SUM(D18:O18)		
19	Apples	14	=SUM(D19:O19)		
20	Potatoes	15	=SUM(D20:O20)		
21		16	=SUM(D21:O21)		
22		17	=SUM(D22:O22)		
23	Sundries	18	=SUM(D23:O23)		
24	VAT charged	19	=SUM(D24:O24)		
25	VAT refunds	20	=SUM(D25:O25)		
26	Capital - grants	21	=SUM(D26:O26)		
27	machinery sales	22	=SUM(D27:O27)		4000
28		23	=SUM(D28:O28)		
29	Personal receipts	24	=SUM(D29:O29)		
30	TOTAL RECEIPTS		=SUM(D30:O30)	=SUM(D6:D29)	=SUM(E6:E29)
31					
32				=D3	=E3
33	*PAYMENTS*				
34	Feed: cows	25	=SUM(D34:O34)	3750	
35	young stock	26	=SUM(D35:O35)		
36	pigs	27	=SUM(D36:O36)	2800	14000
37		28	=SUM(D37:O37)		
38	Vet and Med: cows	29	=SUM(D38:O38)	212	208
39	Vet and Med: pigs	30	=SUM(D39:O39)	100	100
40	L/stock purch: cows	31	=SUM(D40:O40)		
41	pigs	32	=SUM(D41:O41)	2500	2500
53					
54					
55	Overdraft interest	46	=SUM(D55:O55)		
56	Loan interest	47	=SUM(D56:O56)		
57	Hire purchase	48	=SUM(		
58	Leasing charges	49	=SUM(		525
59	Overhead sundries	50	=SUM(		1725
60		51	=SUM(		
61	Capital - orchard	52	=SUM(		
62	machinery	53	=SUM(		7000
63	capital repayment	54	=SUM(D		
64	Personal - drawings	56	=SUM(D64:O64)	960	980
65	tax	57	=SUM(D65:O65)		
66	VAT paid	58	=SUM(D66:O66)		
67	TOTAL PAYMENTS		=SUM(D67:O67)	=SUM(D34:D66)	=SUM(E34:E66)
68	N. CASH FLOW	59	=C30-C67	=D30-D67	=E30-E67
69	OPENING BALANCE	60	-21000	=C69	=D70
70	CLOSING BALANCE	61	=C68+C69	=D68+D69	=E68+E69
71	monthly interest		=IF(C69<0,-C69*B3/1200,0)	=IF(D70<0,-D70*B3/1200,0)	=IF(E70<0,-E70*B3/1200,0)
72					
73					
74					

Callout note (pointing to cell E71): This means: "If the number in cell E70 is negative, the interest charge is -E70 multiplied by the interest rate (i.e. cell B3 divided by 100 to convert it to a decimal, and divided again by 12 to bring it to a monthly rate). If it is not negative, the interest charge is 0"

Figure A5.2 *Spreadsheet formulas for cash-flow budget (Figure 7.4)*

	A	B	C/D	E	G	H	I	J	K
1									
2		29/9/9X		Projected balance sheet at:					
3									
4									
5				*Fixed assets:*					
6		10000		Orchard		13572			
7		39000		Machinery and plant		37998			
8		10000		Vehicles		8000			
9		50050		Dairy herd		55000			
10		=SUM(B6:B9)		Fixed assets				=SUM(H6:H9)	
11									
12				*Current assets:*					
13				Stocks					
14		800		Trading livestock: calves	700				
15		24750		Trading livestock: pigs	24050				
16		3780		Crops in store: barley grain	4231				
17		390		Crops in store: barley straw	480				
18		8484		Miscellaneous stores	13202	=SUM(G14:G⁻8)			
19		9080		Trade debtors		8010			
20		0		Cash in bank		0			
21		0		Cash in hand		0			
22		=SUM(B14:B21)		Current assets		=SUM(H18:H21)			
23									
24				*Current liabilities (due within one year):*					
25		6800		Trade creditors		9889			
26		21000		Bank overdraft		30588			
27		=SUM(B25:B26)		Current liabilities		=SUM(H25:H23)			
28									
29		=B22-B27		Net current assets				=H22-H27	
30									
31		=B10+B29		Total assets less current liabilities				=J10+J29	
33									
34				*Creditors due after one year:*					
35		34000		Mortgage				25800	
36									
37				*Capital account:*					
38				Opening net capital	=B44				
39				="+net profit"	17279				
40				="+capital injections"	4500				
41				="–private drawings"	-10400				
42				="–income and capital tax"	-2512				
43				="–benefits in kind"	-4435				
44		94534		Closing net capital	=SUM(G38:G43)			=G44	
45		=B44+B35						=J44+J35	
47									

Figure A5.3 *Spreadsheet formulas for vertical balance sheet (Figure 11 7)*

	A	B	C/D/E	F	G
53		*RATIO ANALYSIS*		opening	closing
54					
55		Percentage owned		=B44/(B22+B10)*100	=G44/(H22+J10)*100
56		Gearing		=B35/B44*100	=J35/J44*100
57					
58		Liquidity		=SUM(B19:B21)/SUM(B25:B26)*100	=SUM(H19:H21)/SUM(+25:H26)*100
59		Current ratio (%)		=B22/B27*100	=H22/H27*100
60					
61		Fixed assets		=B10/(B10+B22)*100	=J10/(J10+H22)*100
62					
63		Return on net capital			=G39/G44*100
64					
65		Growth in net capital			=(G44-B44)/B44*100
66		Growth in assets			=(((J10+H22)-(B10+B22))/(B22+B10))*100
67		Growth in liabilities			=(((H27+J35)-(B35+B27))/(B27+B35))*100
68					
69					

Figure A5.4 *Spreadsheet formulas for balance sheet ratios (Figure 14.9*

	C	D	E	F
76	**FLOW OF FUNDS ANALYSIS**			£
77				
78	NET PROFIT (LOSS)			=G39
79	depreciation (+)		Depreciation is not shown on the balance sheet, and so has to be entered separately	12320
80	change in debtors (increase -, decrease +)			=-(H19-B19)
81	change in creditors (increase +, decrease -)			=H25-B25
82	valuations (increase -, decrease +)			=-(SUM(G14:G18)+H9)-(SUM(B14:B18)+B9))
83	benefits in kind (-)			=G43
84				=SUM(F78:F83)
85				
86	capital introduced			=G40
87	sale of land, property, investments			
88	increase in overdraft			=IF(H26-B26,H26-B26,0)
89	increase in loans			=IF(J35-B35>0,J35-B35,0)
90	reduction in cash balances			=IF((H20+H21)-(B20+B21)<0,-(H20+H21)-(B20+B21),0)
91				=SUM(F86:F90)
92			**TOTAL CASH AVAILABLE**	**=F91+F84**
93				
94				
95	**COMMITMENTS:**			
96	private drawings			=G41
97	tax payments			=G42
98	reduction in loans			=IF(J35-B35<0,-(J35-B35),0)
99				=SUM(F96:F98)
100				
101	purchase of land, property, investments		These figures cannot be derived directly from the balance sheet, and have to be entered separately	0
102	net purchase of orchard	15000		3000
103	purchase of machinery	-5000		=D104+D103
104	LESS sale of machinery			=IF(H26-B26<0,-(H26-B26),0)
105	repayment of overdraft			=IF((B20+B21)-(H20+H21)<0,-(B20+B21)-(H20+H21),0)
106	increase in cash balances			=SUM(F101:F106)
107				
108			**TOTAL CASH USED**	=F99+F107
109				

Figure A5.5   *Spreadsheet formulas for flow of funds analysis (Figure 14.10)*

	A	B	C	D	E	F
1						
2	*HOURS PER HECTARE/HEAD*					
3	*(from Nix, 1990)*					
4						
5	*ENTERPRISE*	*ha/hd*	*OCT*	*NOV*	*DEC*	
6						
7	*winter wheat*	*51.3*	*3.6*	*0.6*		
8	*winter barley*	*32.4*	*5.1*	*0.6*		
9	*spring barley*	*27.2*	*0.7*	*1.1*	*0.7*	
10	*grass - leys*	*46.9*				
11	*- perm. pasture*	*38.2*				
12	*silage*	*40*				
13	*dairy cows*	*115*	*2.5*	*2.5*	*2.5*	
14	*followers (repl. units)*	*15*	*3.7*	*3.7*	*3.7*	
15	*ewes*	*190*	*0.25*	*0.2*	*0.2*	
16						
17						
18	TOTAL HOURS					
20	ENTERPRISE	ha/hd	OCT	NOV	DEC	
21						
22	winter wheat	=B7	=C7*B22	=D7*B22	=E7*B22	
23	winter barley	=B8	=C8*B23	=D8*B23	=E8*B23	
24	spring barley	=B9	=C9*B24	=D9*B24	=E9*B24	
25	grass - leys	=B10	=C10*B25	=D10*B25	=E10*B25	
26	- perm. pasture	=B11	=C11*B26	=D11*B26	=E11*B26	
27	silage	=B12	=C12*B27	=D12*B27	=E12*B27	
28	dairy cows	=B13	=C13*B28	=D13*B28	=E13*B28	
29	followers (repl. units)	=B14	=C14*B29	=D14*B29	=E14*B29	
30	ewes	=B15	=C15*B30	=D15*B30	=E15*B30	
31						
32	TOTAL HOURS NEEDED		=SUM(C22:C30)	=SUM(D22:D30)	=SUM(E22:E30)	
33						
34						
35	hours available/man/month (from Nix		182	131	132	
36						
37	TOTAL AVAILABLE (3.5 men)		=C35*3.5	=D35*3.5	=E35*3.5	
38						

Figure A5.6 *Spreadsheet formulas for labour profile (Figure 18.2)* 'year 0' means the very beginning of the project

The ^ symbol means 'to the power of'

	A	B	C	D	E	F	G
1							
2		**Project 1**					
3							
4				'hurdle' rate (%):	15		
5				second rate (%):	18		
6							
7		year	annual net cash flow	factors for 'hurdle' discount rate	present values at 'hurdle' rate	factors for second discount rate	present values at second discount rate
8							
9							
10							
11		0	-1000	1	=D11*C11	1	=C11*F11
12		1	600	=1/(1+E4/100)^B12	=C12*D12	=1/(1+E5/100)^B12	=C12*F12
13		2	300	=1/(1+E4/100)^B13	=C13*D13	=1/(1+E5/100)^B13	=C13*F13
14		3	200	=1/(1+E4/100)^B14	=C14*D14	=1/(1+E5/100)^B14	=C14*F14
15		4	200	=1/(1+E4/100)^B15	=C15*D15	=1/(1+E5/100)^B15	=C15*F15
16		5	100	=1/(1+E4/100)^B16	=C16*D16	=1/(1+E5/100)^B16	=C16*F16
17							=SUM(G11:G17)
18				Net Present Value:	=SUM(E11:E17)		
19							
20				Internal Rate of Return:	=(E18/(E18-G18))*(E5-E4)+E4 %		
21							
22							
23							
24							
25							

Check this against the interpolation formula in Chapter 19

Figure A5.7 *Spreadsheet for NPV and IRR calculation (Figure 19.10)*

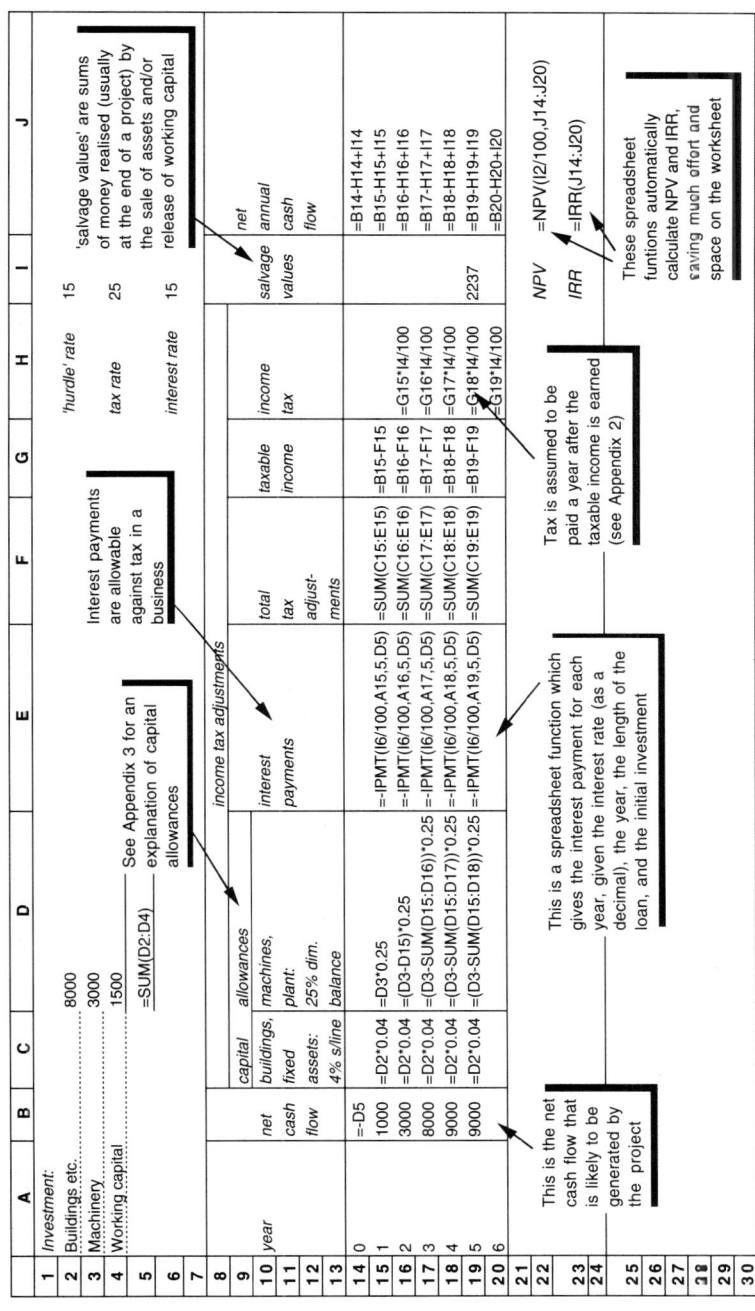

The spreadsheet (rotated 90°) contains the following content:

	A	B	C	D	E	F	G	H	I	J
1	*Investment:*									
2	Buildings, etc........	8000						'hurdle' rate	15	'salvage values' are sums of money realised (usually at the end of a project) by the sale of assets and/or release of working capital
3	Machinery...............	3000						tax rate	25	
4	Working capital.......	1500						interest rate	15	
5				=SUM(D2:D4)	See Appendix 3 for an explanation of capital allowances					
6										
7							income tax adjustments			
8										net
9			capital	allowances					salvage	annual
10	*year*	*net cash flow*	*buildings, fixed assets: 4% s/line*	*machines, plant: 25% dim. balance*	*interest payments*	*total tax adjust- ments*	*taxable income*	*income tax*	*values*	*cash flow*
11										
12										
13		=-D5								
14	0	1000	=D2*0.04	=D3*0.25	=-IPMT(I6/100,A15,5,D5)	=SUM(C15:E15)	=B15-F15	=G15*14/100		=B14-H14+I14
15	1	3000	=D2*0.04	=(D3-D15)*0.25	=-IPMT(I6/100,A16,5,D5)	=SUM(C16:E16)	=B16-F16	=G16*14/100		=B15-H15+I15
16	2	8000	=D2*0.04	=(D3-SUM(D15:D16))*0.25	=-IPMT(I6/100,A17,5,D5)	=SUM(C17:E17)	=B17-F17	=G17*14/100		=B16-H16+I16
17	3	9000	=D2*0.04	=(D3-SUM(D15:D17))*0.25	=-IPMT(I6/100,A18,5,D5)	=SUM(C18:E18)	=B18-F18	=G18*14/100		=B17-H17+I17
18	4	9000	=D2*0.04	=(D3-SUM(D15:D18))*0.25	=-IPMT(I6/100,A19,5,D5)	=SUM(C19:E19)	=B19-F19	=G19*14/100	2237	=B18-H18+I18
19	5									=B19-H19+I19
20	6									=B20-H20+I20
21										
22		This is the net cash flow that is likely to be generated by the project			This is a spreadsheet function which gives the interest payment for each year, given the interest rate (as a decimal), the year, the length of the loan, and the initial investment		Tax is assumed to be paid a year after the taxable income is earned (see Appendix 2)		NPV	=NPV(I2/100,J14:J20)
23									IRR	=IRR(J14:J20)
24										
25										These spreadsheet funtions automatically calculate NPV and IRR, saving much effort and space on the worksheet
26										
27										
28										
29										
30										

Interest payments are allowable against tax in a business

Figure A5.8 *Spreadsheet for more advanced DCF calculation (see Figure A5.9)*

Initial investment:

Buildings and fixtures	8000
Machinery	3000
Extra working capital	1500
	12500

'Hurdle'discount rate (%):	15
Marginal tax rate (%):	25
Loan interest rate (%):	15

Year	Net cash flow	Capital allowances — Buildings, fixed assets: 4% s/line	Capital allowances — Machines, plant: 25% dim. balance	Income tax adjustments — Interest payments	Income tax adjustments — Total tax adjustments	Income tax adjustments — Taxable income	Income tax adjustments — Income tax	Salvage values	Net annual cash flow
0	-12500								-12500
1	1000	320	750	1875	2945	-1945			1000
2	3000	320	563	1597	2479	521	-486		3486
3	8000	320	422	1277	2019	5981	130		7870
4	9000	320	316	909	1546	7454	1495		7505
5	9000	320	237	486	1044	7956	1864	2237	9373
6							1989		-1989

Net present value at hurdle rate	3714
Internal rate of return	26%

Figure A5.9 *More advanced DCF calculation, based on Figure A5.8*

	A	B	C	D	E	F	G	H	Q
1	Milk cash flow				Average yields:	cows?	5000		
2	calculation:					heifers?	4500		
3	September start				Basic milk price (p/l):		19.25		
4									
5		milk	calvings		litres of milk produced				
6		price(p/l)	cows	heifers	September	October	November		TOTAL
7	September	=G3+4.5			=(G1*C7+G2*D7)*0.136	=(G1*C7+G2*D7)*0.16	=(G1*C7+G2*D7)*0.144		=SUM(E7:P7)
8	October	=G3+3.7			=(G1*C8+G2*D8)*0	=(G1*C8+G2*D8)*0.136	=(G1*C8+G2*D8)*0.16		=SUM(E8:P8)
9	November	=G3+0.45			=(G1*C9+G2*D9)*0	=(G1*C9+G2*D9)*0	=(G1*C9+G2*D9)*0.136		=SUM(E9:P9)
10	December	=G3+0.45			=(G1*C10+G2*D10)*0.032	=(G1*C10+G2*D10)*0	=(G1*C10+G2*D10)*0		=SUM(E10:P10)
11	January	=G3+0.45			=(G1*C11+G2*D11)*0.048	=(G1*C11+G2*D11)*0.032	=(G1*C11+G2*D11)*0		=SUM(E11:P11)
12	February	=G3+0.45			=(G1*C12+G2*D12)*0.064	=(G1*C12+G2*D12)*0.048	=(G1*C12+G2*D12)*0.032		=SUM(E12:P12)
13	March	=G3+0.45			=(G1*C13+G2*D13)*0.08	=(G1*C13+G2*D13)*0.064	=(G1*C13+G2*D13)*0.048		=SUM(E13:P13)
14	April	=G3-0.5			=(G1*C14+G2*D14)*0.096	=(G1*C14+G2*D14)*0.08	=(G1*C14+G2*D14)*0.064		=SUM(E14:P14)
15	May	=G3-2.5			=(G1*C15+G2*D15)*0.112	=(G1*C15+G2*D15)*0.096	=(G1*C15+G2*D15)*0.08		=SUM(E15:P15)
16	June	=G3-2			=(G1*C16+G2*D16)*0.128	=(G1*C16+G2*D16)*0.112	=(G1*C16+G2*D16)*0.096		=SUM(E16:P16)
17	July	=G3+3.8			=(G1*C17+G2*D17)*0.144	=(G1*C17+G2*D17)*0.128	=(G1*C17+G2*D17)*0.112		=SUM(E17:P17)
18	August	=G3+5.3			=(G1*C18+G2*D18)*0.16	=(G1*C18+G2*D18)*0.144	=(G1*C18+G2*D18)*0.128		=SUM(E18:P18)
19	Litres		produced		=SUM(E7:E18)	=SUM(F7:F18)	=SUM(G7:G18)		=SUM(E19:P19)
20									
21	milk value				=E19*B7/100	=F19*B8/100	=G19*B9/100		=SUM(E21:P21)

You can find tables of seasonal milk price adjustments in Nix and various MMB publications

The factors in the formulae represent a crude version of the Russel lactation curve calculation described in Chapter 17. Reading across from the first month, the full sequence is 0.136, 0.16, 0.144, 0.128, 0.112, 0.096, 0.08, 0.064, 0.048, 0.032, 0, 0. The sequence is repeated for each of the succeeding months, staggered by one month each time.

Figure A5.10 *Spreadsheet formulas for milk production calculator (see Figure A5.11)*

Milk cash flow calculation: September start

Average yields: cows? 5000
heifers? 4500
Basic milk price (p/l): 19

	Milk price (p/l)	Calvings Cows	Calvings Heifers	Litres of milk produced Sep	Oct	Nov	Dec	Jan	Feb	Mar	Apr	May	Jun	July	Aug	TOTAL
September	23.75	26	8	22576	26560	23904	21248	18592	15936	13280	10624	7968	5312	0	0	166000
October	22.95	34	4	0	25568	30080	27072	24064	21056	18048	15040	12032	9024	6016	0	188000
November	19.7	22		0	0	14960	17600	15840	14080	12320	10560	8800	7040	5280	3520	106480
December	19.7	15		2400	0	0	10200	12000	10800	9600	8400	7200	6000	4800	3600	71400
January	19.7	8	2	2352	1568	0	0	6664	7840	7056	6272	5488	4704	3920	3136	45864
February	19.7	4		1280	960	640	0	0	2720	3200	2880	2560	2240	1920	1600	18400
March	19.7	7		2800	2240	1680	1120	0	0	4760	5600	5040	4480	3920	3360	31640
April	18.75	2		960	800	640	480	320	0	0	1360	1600	1440	1280	1120	8880
May	16.75	0		0	0	0	0	0	0	0	0	0	0	0	0	0
June	17.25	1		640	560	480	400	320	240	160	0	0	680	800	720	4280
July	23.05	5	16	13968	12416	10864	9312	7760	6208	4656	3104	0	0	13192	15520	81480
August	24.55	8	12	15040	13536	12032	10528	9024	7520	6016	4512	3008	0	0	12784	81216
Total milk produced (litres)				62016	84208	95280	97960	94584	86400	79096	68352	53696	40920	41128	45360	803640
Value of milk produced				14729	19326	18770	19298	18633	17021	15582	13465	10578	8061	8102	8936	172501

Figure A5.11 *Milk production calculator (based on Figure A5.10)*

Index

Note: A page number in bold type refers to that part of the text where the index item is defined or described. On the page concerned, the item is defined by the use of italics.